CONTENTS

INTRODUCTION

It's been a huge trend recently, that bigger and bigger number of manufacturers decided to start marketing convection toasting ovens as air fryers.

These air fryer ovens are claimed to produce crispier food, that's more evenly cooked. These ovens also accommodate several slices of toast, a standard 5-pound chicken, an 8-inch cake, or even a big size 13-inch pizza. These toaster ovens also come with more useful accessories than a traditional small air fryer, such as a baking tray, a pizza ceramic stone, and in some cases, with two oven racks. Therefore, you barely need to buy a special equipment to bake in the toaster ovens, as you do with many air fryers.

Overall, any branded toaster oven air fryer on the market outperforms the pod-shaped air fryers. The reason is very simple - the toaster oven fryers have more space to spread out the food out so it cooks evenly and browns better. Also, most of them do offer additional cooking features like toast, dehydrate, or bake. Some types also contain a rotisserie mechanism.

Though it's worth mentioning is that you can get similar air-fried experience when cooking the food in a full-size traditional oven with convection. But as you may guess, a full-size oven is so much larger than a small toaster oven air fryer or air fryer alone; it would take way longer to preheat and to cook the food. The toaster ovens preheat immediately, making it the optimal choice for speedy and effortless "air-fried" cooking.

In this book, I've prepared simple and delicious meals that are easy to make in any toaster oven air fryer as long as you are ready to throw in a few ingredients and turn the knob. Cooking becomes easier and easier thanks to new technologies and optimized cooking appliances, so why not eat healthy, yet crunchy comfort food. Let's begin!

APPETIZERS AND SIDE DISHES

1. Delicious Chicken Wings With Alfredo Sauce

Servings: 4
Cooking Time: 60 Minutes
Ingredients:
- 1 ½ pounds chicken wings
- Salt and black pepper to taste
- ½ cup Alfredo sauce

Directions:
1. Preheat on Air Fry function to 370 F. Season the wings with salt and pepper. Arrange them on the greased basket without touching. Fit in the baking tray and cook for 20 minutes until no longer pink in the center. Work in batches if needed. Increase the heat to 390 F and cook for 5 minutes more. Remove to a large bowl and drizzle with the Alfredo sauce. Serve.

2. Wonton Poppers

Servings: 10
Cooking Time: 10 Minutes
Ingredients:
- Nonstick cooking spray
- 1 package refrigerated square wonton wrappers
- 1 8-ounce package cream cheese, softened
- 3 jalapenos, seeds and ribs removed, finely chopped
- 1/2 cup shredded cheddar cheese

Directions:
1. Place baking pan in position 2 of the oven. Lightly spray fryer basket with cooking spray.
2. In a large bowl, combine all ingredients except the wrappers until combined.
3. Lay wrappers in a single layer on a baking sheet. Spoon a teaspoon of filling in the center. Moisten the edges with water and fold wrappers over filling, pinching edges to seal. Place in a single layer in the basket.
4. Place the basket in the oven and set to air fry on 375°F for 10 minutes. Cook until golden brown and crisp, turning over halfway through cooking time. Repeat with remaining ingredients. Serve immediately.
- **Nutrition Info:** Calories 287, Total Fat 11g, Saturated Fat 6g, Total Carbs 38g, Net Carbs 37g, Protein 9g, Sugar 1g, Fiber 1g, Sodium 485mg, Potassium 98mg, Phosphorus 104mg

3. Holiday Pumpkin Wedges

Servings: 3
Cooking Time: 30 Minutes
Ingredients:
- ½ pumpkin, washed and cut into wedges
- 1 tbsp paprika
- 1 whole lime, squeezed
- 1 cup paleo dressing
- 1 tbsp balsamic vinegar
- Salt and black pepper to taste
- 1 tsp turmeric

Directions:
1. Preheat on Air Fry function to 360 F. Place the pumpkin wedges in your Air Fryer baking tray and cook for 20 minutes. In a bowl, mix lime juice, vinegar, turmeric, salt, pepper and paprika to form a marinade. Pour the marinade over pumpkin and cook for 5 more minutes.

4. Cheddar Cheese Cauliflower Casserole

Servings: 8
Cooking Time: 35 Minutes
Ingredients:
- 4 cups cauliflower florets
- 1 1/2 cups cheddar cheese, shredded
- 1 cup sour cream
- 4 bacon slices, cooked and crumbled
- 3 green onions, chopped

Directions:
1. Fit the oven with the rack in position
2. Boil water in a large pot. Add cauliflower in boiling water and cook for 8-10 minutes or until tender. Drain well.
3. Transfer cauliflower in a large bowl.
4. Add half bacon, half green onion, 1 cup cheese, and sour cream in cauliflower bowl and mix well.
5. Transfer mixture into a greased baking dish and sprinkle with remaining cheese.
6. Set to bake at 350 F for 30 minutes. After 5 minutes place the baking dish in the preheated oven.
7. Garnish with remaining green onion and bacon.
8. Serve and enjoy.
- **Nutrition Info:** Calories 213 Fat 17.1 g Carbohydrates 4.7 g Sugar 1.5 g Protein 10.8 g Cholesterol 45 mg

5. Rice Flour Bites

Servings: 4
Cooking Time: 12 Minutes
Ingredients:
- 6 tablespoons milk
- ½ teaspoon vegetable oil
- ¾ cup rice flour
- 1 oz. Parmesan cheese, shredded

Directions:
1. In a bowl, add milk, flour, oil and cheese and mix until a smooth dough forms.
2. Make small equal-sized balls from the dough.

3. Press "Power Button" of Air Fry Oven and turn the dial to select the "Air Fry" mode.
4. Press the Time button and again turn the dial to set the cooking time to 12 minutes.
5. Now push the Temp button and rotate the dial to set the temperature at 300 degrees F.
6. Press "Start/Pause" button to start.
7. When the unit beeps to show that it is preheated, open the lid.
8. Arrange the balls in "Air Fry Basket" and insert in the oven.
9. Serve warm.
- **Nutrition Info:** Calories 148 Total Fat 3 g Saturated Fat 1.5 g Cholesterol 7 mg Sodium 77 mg Total Carbs 25.1 g Fiber 0.7 g Sugar 1.1 g Protein 4.8 g

6. Apple & Cinnamon Chips

Servings:2
Cooking Time: 25 Minutes
Ingredients:
- 1 tsp sugar
- 1 tsp salt
- 1 whole apple, sliced
- ½ tsp cinnamon
- Confectioners' sugar for serving

Directions:
1. Preheat your oven to 400 F on Bake function. In a bowl, mix cinnamon, salt, and sugar. Add in the apple slices and toss to coat. Transfer to a greased baking tray. Press Start and set the time to 10 minutes. When ready, dust with sugar and serve chilled.

7. Potato Chips With Creamy Lemon Dip

Servings:3
Cooking Time: 25 Minutes
Ingredients:
- 3 large potatoes
- 1 cup sour cream
- 2 scallions, white part minced
- 3 tbsp olive oil.
- ½ tsp lemon juice
- salt and black pepper

Directions:
1. Preheat on AirFry function to 350 F. Cut the potatoes into thin slices; do not peel them. Brush them with olive oil and season with salt and pepper. Arrange on the frying basket.
2. Press Start on the oven and cook for 20-25 minutes. Season with salt and pepper. To prepare the dip, mix together the sour cream, olive oil, scallions, lemon juice, salt, and pepper.

8. Brussels Sprouts With Garlic

Servings: 2

Cooking Time: 25 Minutes
Ingredients:
- 1 lb Brussels sprouts, trimmed
- ½ tsp garlic, chopped
- 2 tbsp olive oil
- Salt and black pepper to taste

Directions:
1. In a bowl, mix olive oil, garlic, salt, and pepper. Stir in the Brussels sprouts and let rest for 5 minutes. Place the coated sprouts in the Air Fryer basket and fit in the baking tray. Cook for 15 minutes at 380 F, shaking once. Serve warm.

9. Simple Roasted Asparagus

Servings: 4
Cooking Time: 10 Minutes
Ingredients:
- 1 bunch asparagus
- 4 tablespoons olive oil
- Salt and pepper to taste

Directions:
1. Start by preheating toaster oven to 425°F.
2. Wash the asparagus and cut off the bottom inch.
3. Toss the asparagus in olive oil and lay flat on a baking sheet.
4. Sprinkle salt and pepper over asparagus.
5. Roast in the oven for 10 minutes.
- **Nutrition Info:** Calories: 127, Sodium: 1 mg, Dietary Fiber: 0.7 g, Total Fat: 14.0 g, Total Carbs: 1.3 g, Protein: 0.7 g.

10. Asparagus Wrapped In Bacon

Servings:4
Cooking Time: 25 Minutes
Ingredients:
- 20 spears asparagus
- 4 bacon slices
- 1 tbsp olive oil
- 1 tbsp sesame oil
- 1 garlic clove, minced

Directions:
1. Preheat on AirFry function to 380 F. In a bowl, mix the oils, sugar, and garlic. Separate the asparagus into 4 bunches (5 spears in 1 bunch) and wrap each bunch with a bacon slice.
2. Drizzle the bunches with oil mix. Put them in the frying basket and place in the oven. Press Start and cook for 8 minutes. Serve warm.

11. Tasty Butternut Squash

Servings: 4
Cooking Time: 15 Minutes
Ingredients:
- 4 cups butternut squash, cut into 1-inch pieces

- 1 tbsp brown sugar
- 2 tbsp olive oil
- 1 tsp Chinese 5 spice powder

Directions:
1. Fit the oven with the rack in position 2.
2. Toss squash into the bowl with remaining ingredients.
3. Transfer squash in the air fryer basket then places the air fryer basket in the baking pan.
4. Place a baking pan on the oven rack. Set to air fry at 400 F for 15 minutes.
5. Serve and enjoy.
- **Nutrition Info:** Calories 132 Fat 7.1 g Carbohydrates 18.6 g Sugar 5.3 g Protein 1.4 g Cholesterol 0 mg

12. Air Fried Eggplant Cubes

Servings: 2
Cooking Time: 12 Minutes
Ingredients:
- 1 eggplant, cut into cubes
- 1/4 tsp oregano
- 1 tbsp olive oil
- 1/2 tsp garlic powder

Directions:
1. Fit the oven with the rack in position 2.
2. Add all ingredients into the large bowl and toss well.
3. Transfer eggplant into in air fryer basket then places the air fryer basket in the baking pan.
4. Place a baking pan on the oven rack. Set to air fry at 390 F for 12 minutes.
5. Serve and enjoy.
- **Nutrition Info:** Calories 120 Fat 7.4 g Carbohydrates 14.1 g Sugar 7.1 g Protein 2.4 g Cholesterol 0 mg

13. Paprika Potatoes

Servings: 4
Cooking Time: 30 Minutes
Ingredients:
- 1 lb baby potatoes, quartered
- 1/4 tsp rosemary, crushed
- 1/2 tsp thyme
- 2 tbsp paprika
- 2 tbsp coconut oil, melted
- 1 tbsp olive oil
- Pepper
- Salt

Directions:
1. Fit the oven with the rack in position
2. Place potatoes in a baking dish and sprinkle with paprika, rosemary, thyme, pepper, and salt.
3. Drizzle with oil and melted coconut oil.
4. Set to bake at 425 F for 35 minutes. After 5 minutes place the baking dish in the preheated oven.

5. Serve and enjoy.
- **Nutrition Info:** Calories 165 Fat 10.9 g Carbohydrates 16.2 g Sugar 0.4 g Protein 3.4 g Cholesterol 0 mg

14. Baked Potatoes Eggplant

Servings: 4
Cooking Time: 40 Minutes
Ingredients:
- 2 medium eggplants, cut into pieces
- 1 tbsp lemon juice
- 1 lb potatoes, cut into cubes
- 1/4 cup olive oil
- Pepper
- Salt

Directions:
1. Fit the oven with the rack in position
2. Add eggplant, potatoes, oil, pepper, and salt in a baking dish and toss well.
3. Set to bake at 400 F for 45 minutes. After 5 minutes place the baking dish in the preheated oven.
4. Drizzle with lemon juice and serve.
- **Nutrition Info:** Calories 244 Fat 13.2 g Carbohydrates 31.4 g Sugar 8.3 g Protein 4.2 g Cholesterol 0 mg

15. Crispy Eggplant Fries

Servings: 2
Cooking Time: 20 Minutes
Ingredients:
- 1 eggplant, sliced
- 1 tsp olive oil
- 1 tsp soy sauce
- Salt to taste

Directions:
1. Preheat on Air Fry function to 400 F. Make a marinade of 1 tsp oil, soy sauce, and salt. Mix well. Add in the eggplant slices and let stand for 5 minutes. Place the prepared eggplant slices in the cooking basket and fit in the baking tray. Cook for 8 minutes. Serve warm.

16. Bread Sticks

Servings: 6
Cooking Time: 6 Minutes
Ingredients:
- 1 egg 1/8 teaspoon ground cinnamon
- Pinch of ground nutmeg Pinch of ground cloves
- Salt, to taste
- 2 bread slices
- 1 tablespoon butter, softened
- Nonstick cooking spray
- 1 tablespoon icing sugar

Directions:
1. In a bowl, add the eggs, cinnamon, nutmeg, cloves and salt and beat until well combined.

2. Spread the butter over both sides of the slices evenly.
3. Cut each bread slice into strips.
4. Dip bread strips into egg mixture evenly.
5. Press "Power Button" of Air Fry Oven and turn the dial to select the "Air Fry" mode.
6. Press the Time button and again turn the dial to set the cooking time to 6 minutes.
7. Now push the Temp button and rotate the dial to set the temperature at 355 degrees F.
8. Press "Start/Pause" button to start.
9. When the unit beeps to show that it is preheated, open the lid.
10. Arrange the breadsticks in "Air Fry Basket" and insert in the oven.
11. After 2 minutes of cooking, spray the both sides of the bread strips with cooking spray.
12. Serve immediately with the topping of icing sugar.
- **Nutrition Info:** Calories 41 Total Fat 2.8 g Saturated Fat 1.5 g Cholesterol 32 mg Sodium 72 mg Total Carbs 3 g Fiber 0.1 g Sugar 1.5 g Protein 1.2 g

17. Baked Italian Vegetables

Servings: 6
Cooking Time: 30 Minutes
Ingredients:
- 1 eggplant, sliced
- 1 onion, sliced
- 1 potato, peel & cut into chunks
- 1 bell pepper, cut into strips
- 2 zucchini, sliced
- 2 tomatoes, quartered
- 5 fresh basil leaves, sliced
- 2 tsp Italian seasoning
- 2 tbsp olive oil
- Pepper
- Salt

Directions:
1. Fit the oven with the rack in position
2. Add all ingredients except basil leaves into the mixing bowl and toss well.
3. Transfer vegetable mixture on a prepared baking pan.
4. Set to bake at 400 F for 35 minutes. After 5 minutes place the baking dish in the preheated oven.
5. Garnish with basil leaves and serve.
- **Nutrition Info:** Calories 117 Fat 5.6 g Carbohydrates 16.6 g Sugar 6.6 g Protein 2.9 g Cholesterol 1 mg

18. Broccoli Olives Tomatoes

Servings: 4
Cooking Time: 10 Minutes
Ingredients:
- 4 cups broccoli florets
- 1/2 tsp lemon zest, grated

- 2 garlic cloves, minced
- 1 tbsp olive oil
- 1 tsp dried oregano
- 10 olives, pitted and sliced
- 1 tbsp fresh lemon juice
- 1 cup cherry tomatoes
- 1/4 tsp salt

Directions:
1. Fit the oven with the rack in position
2. Add broccoli, garlic, oil, tomatoes, and salt in a large bowl and toss well.
3. Spread broccoli mixture onto the baking pan.
4. Set to bake at 450 F for 15 minutes. After 5 minutes place the baking pan in the preheated oven.
5. Meanwhile, mix together oregano, olives, lemon juice, and lemon zest in a mixing bowl.
6. Add roasted vegetables to the bowl and toss well.
7. Serve and enjoy.
- **Nutrition Info:** Calories 86 Fat 5.1 g Carbohydrates 9.4 g Sugar 2.9 g Protein 3.2 g Cholesterol 0 mg

19. Cauliflower And Barley Risotto

Servings: 4
Cooking Time: 1 Hour
Ingredients:
- 1 cauliflower head, separated into florets
- 4 tablespoons extra virgin olive oil
- Salt and ground black pepper, to taste
- ½ cup Parmesan cheese, grated
- 2 garlic cloves, peeled and minced
- 1 cup pearled barley
- 2 tablespoons fresh parsley, chopped
- 1 tablespoon butter
- 1 yellow onion, peeled and chopped
- 3 cups chicken stock
- 2 thyme sprigs

Directions:
1. Spread the cauliflower florets in an upholstered pan, add 3 tablespoons of oil, salt and pepper, mix to coat, place in the oven at 425 degrees Fahrenheit and bake for 20 minutes, turning every 10 minutes.
2. Remove the cauliflower from the oven, sprinkle with ¼ cup of cheese and cook for 5 minutes. Put the Instant Pot in the sauté mode, add 1 tablespoon of oil and heat.
3. Add the onion, mix and cook for 5 minutes. Add the garlic, mix and cook for 1 minute. Add the broth, thyme and barley, mix, cover the Instant Pot and cook for 25 minutes in the Manual setting.
4. Release the pressure, uncover the Instant Pot, mix the barley, throw away the thyme, add the butter, the rest of the cheese, the

cauliflower, salt, pepper and parsley. Mix the risotto, divide it between the plates and serve.
- **Nutrition Info:** Calories: 350, Fat: 16, Fiber: 10, Carbohydrate: 25, Proteins: 14.6

20. Baked Artichoke Hearts

Servings: 6
Cooking Time: 25 Minutes
Ingredients:
- 15 oz frozen artichoke hearts, defrosted
- 1 tbsp olive oil
- Pepper
- Salt

Directions:
1. Fit the oven with the rack in position
2. Arrange artichoke hearts in baking pan and drizzle with olive oil. Season with pepper and salt.
3. Set to bake at 400 F for 30 minutes. After 5 minutes place the baking pan in the preheated oven.
4. Serve and enjoy.
- **Nutrition Info:** Calories 53 Fat 2.4 g Carbohydrates 7.5 g Sugar 0.7 g Protein 2.3 g Cholesterol 0 mg

21. Ham & Pineapple Tortilla Pizzas

Servings:2
Cooking Time: 15 Minutes
Ingredients:
- 2 tortillas
- 8 ham slices
- 8 mozzarella cheese slices
- 8 thin pineapple slices
- 2 tbsp tomato sauce
- 1 tsp dried parsley

Directions:
1. Preheat on Pizza function to 330 F. Spread the tomato sauce onto the tortillas. Arrange 4 ham slices on each tortilla. Top with pineapple and mozzarella slices and sprinkle with parsley. Place in the oven and press Start. Cook for 10 minutes and serve.

22. Butternut Squash Croquettes

Servings:4
Cooking Time: 17 Minutes
Ingredients:
- $1/3$ butternut squash, peeled and grated
- $1/3$ cup all-purpose flour
- 2 eggs, whisked
- 4 cloves garlic, minced
- 1½ tablespoons olive oil
- 1 teaspoon fine sea salt
- $1/3$ teaspoon freshly ground black pepper, or more to taste
- $1/3$ teaspoon dried sage
- A pinch of ground allspice

Directions:
1. Line the air fryer basket with parchment paper. Set aside.
2. In a mixing bowl, stir together all the ingredients until well combined.
3. Make the squash croquettes: Use a small cookie scoop to drop tablespoonfuls of the squash mixture onto a lightly floured surface and shape into balls with your hands. Transfer them to the basket.
4. Put the air fryer basket on the baking pan and slide into Rack Position 2, select Air Fry, set temperature to 345ºF (174ºC), and set time to 17 minutes.
5. When cooking is complete, the squash croquettes should be golden brown. Remove from the oven to a plate and serve warm.

23. Baked Vegetables

Servings: 6
Cooking Time: 30 Minutes
Ingredients:
- 2 zucchini, sliced
- 2 tomatoes, quartered
- 6 fresh basil leaves, sliced
- 2 tsp Italian seasoning
- 2 tbsp olive oil
- 1 eggplant, sliced
- 1 onion, sliced
- 1 bell pepper, cut into strips
- Pepper
- Salt

Directions:
1. Fit the oven with the rack in position
2. Add all ingredients except basil leaves into the bowl and toss well.
3. Transfer vegetable mixture in parchment-lined baking pan.
4. Set to bake at 400 F for 35 minutes. After 5 minutes place the baking pan in the preheated oven.
5. Garnish with basil and serve.
- **Nutrition Info:** Calories 96 Fat 5.5 g Carbohydrates 11.7 g Sugar 6.4 g Protein 2.3 g Cholesterol 1 mg

24. Mac & Cheese Quiche With Greek Yogurt

Servings:4
Cooking Time: 30 Minutes
Ingredients:
- 8 tbsp leftover macaroni with cheese
- Extra cheddar cheese for serving
- Pastry as much needed for forming 4 shells
- Salt and black pepper to taste
- 1 tsp garlic puree
- 2 tbsp Greek yogurt
- 2 whole eggs

- 1 cup milk

Directions:
1. Preheat on AirFry function to 360 F. Roll the pastry to form 4 shells. Place them in a greased baking pan. In a bowl, mix leftover macaroni with cheese, yogurt, eggs, milk, and garlic.
2. Divide the mixture between the pastry shells. Top with the cheese evenly. Press Start and cook for 20 minutes. Serve chilled.

25. Polenta Sticks

Servings: 4
Cooking Time: 6 Minutes
Ingredients:
- 1 tablespoon oil
- 2½ cups cooked polenta
- Salt, to taste
- ¼ cup Parmesan cheese

Directions:
1. Place the polenta in a lightly greased baking pan.
2. With a plastic wrap, cover and refrigerate for about 1 hour or until set.
3. Remove from the refrigerator and cut into desired sized slices.
4. Sprinkle with salt.
5. Press "Power Button" of Air Fry Oven and turn the dial to select the "Air Fry" mode.
6. Press the Time button and again turn the dial to set the cooking time to 6 minutes.
7. Now push the Temp button and rotate the dial to set the temperature at 350 degrees F.
8. Press "Start/Pause" button to start.
9. When the unit beeps to show that it is preheated, open the lid.
10. Arrange the pan over the "Wire Rack" and insert in the oven.
11. Top with cheese and serve.
- **Nutrition Info:** Calories 397 Total Fat 5.6g Saturated Fat 1.3 g Cholesterol 4mg Sodium 127 mg Total Carbs 76.2 g Fiber 2.5 g Sugar 1 g Protein 9.1 g

26. Buffalo Quesadillas

Servings: 8
Cooking Time: 5 Minutes
Ingredients:
- Nonstick cooking spray
- 2 cups chicken, cooked & chopped fine
- ½ cup Buffalo wing sauce
- 2 cups Monterey Jack cheese, grated
- ½ cup green onions, sliced thin
- 8 flour tortillas, 8-inch diameter
- ¼ cup blue cheese dressing

Directions:
1. Lightly spray the baking pan with cooking spray.

2. In a medium bowl, add chicken and wing sauce and toss to coat.
3. Place tortillas, one at a time on work surface. Spread ¼ of the chicken mixture over tortilla and sprinkle with cheese and onion. Top with a second tortilla and place on the baking pan.
4. Set oven to broil on 400°F for 8 minutes. After 5 minutes place baking pan in position 2. Cook quesadillas 2-3 minutes per side until toasted and cheese has melted. Repeat with remaining ingredients.
5. Cut quesadillas in wedges and serve with blue cheese dressing or other dipping sauce.
- **Nutrition Info:** Calories 376, Total Fat 20g, Saturated Fat 8g, Total Carbs 27g, Net Carbs 26g, Protein 22g, Sugar 2g, Fiber 2g, Sodium 685mg, Potassium 201mg, Phosphorus 301mg

27. Rosemary Chickpeas

Servings:4
Cooking Time: 20 Minutes
Ingredients:
- 2 (14.5-ounce) cans chickpeas, rinsed
- 2 tbsp olive oil
- 1 tsp dried rosemary
- ½ tsp dried thyme
- ¼ tsp dried sage
- ¼ tsp salt

Directions:
1. In a bowl, mix together chickpeas, oil, rosemary, thyme, sage, and salt. Transfer to a baking pan. Select Bake function, adjust the temperature to 380 F, and press Start. Cook for 15 minutes.

28. Crispy Sausage Bites

Servings: 12
Cooking Time: 15 Minutes
Ingredients:
- Nonstick cooking spray
- 2 lbs. spicy pork sausage
- 1 ½ cups Bisquick
- 4 cups sharp cheddar cheese, grated
- ½ cup onion, diced fine
- 2 tsp pepper
- 2 tsp garlic, diced fine

Directions:
1. Lightly spray baking pan with cooking spray.
2. In a large bowl, combine all ingredients. Form into 1-inch balls and place on baking pan, these will need to be cooked in batches.
3. Set oven to bake on 375°F for 20 minutes. After 5 minutes, place baking pan in position 2 and cook 12-15 minutes or until golden brown. Repeat with remaining sausage bites. Serve immediately.

- **Nutrition Info:** Calories 432, Total Fat 32g, Saturated Fat 13g, Total Carbs 14g, Net Carbs 14g, Protein 22g, Sugar 1g, Fiber 0g, Sodium 803mg, Potassium 286mg, Phosphorus 298mg

29. Avocado, Tomato, And Grape Salad With Crunchy Potato Croutons

Servings: 2
Cooking Time: 10 Minutes
Ingredients:
- Potato croutons:
- 1 medium-small russet potato
- 2 cloves garlic
- 1 tablespoon extra light olive oil
- 1 tablespoon nutritional yeast
- 1/2 teaspoon garlic powder
- 1/2 teaspoon onion powder
- 1/2 teaspoon dried thyme
- 1/2 teaspoon dried rosemary
- 1/2 teaspoon dried oregano
- 1/2 teaspoon chili powder
- 1/4 teaspoon Himalayan sea salt
- 1/3 teaspoon cayenne pepper
- Pinch red pepper flakes
- Black pepper to taste
- Salad:
- 1 cup grape tomatoes
- Small handful dried cranberries
- Small handful green grapes
- 2-3 sprigs cilantro
- 1 avocado
- 2 tablespoons extra-virgin olive oil
- 1 tablespoon nutritional yeast
- 1 tablespoon lemon juice
- 1/2 teaspoon pure maple syrup
- 1/4 teaspoon salt
- Few sprinkles ground pepper
- Small handful toasted pecans

Directions:
1. Peel and cut potatoes into 1-inch cubes.
2. Place potatoes in water with a pinch of salt for 1 hour.
3. When the hour has passed, preheat the toaster oven to 450°F.
4. Drain potatoes and dry them on multiple layers of paper towels, then return to bowl.
5. Peel and mince garlic, then add to bowl.
6. Add rest of crouton ingredients to the bowl and stir together.
7. Lay potatoes mixture across a greased baking sheet in a single layer and bake for 35 minutes, flipping halfway through.
8. Combine oil, yeast, syrup, lemon juice, salt and pepper together to create salad dressing.
9. Slice tomatoes in half and put in a bowl with cranberries and grapes.
10. Chop cilantro and add to bowl. Scoop out avocado and cut it into smaller pieces and add to bowl.
11. Drizzle dressing and mix well. Add potatoes and mix again, top with pecans and serve.
- **Nutrition Info:** Calories: 1032, Sodium: 560 mg, Dietary Fiber: 22.8 g, Total Fat: 84.9 g, Total Carbs: 64.2 g, Protein: 17.0 g.

30. Dill Pickles With Parmesan

Servings: 4
Cooking Time: 35 Minutes
Ingredients:
- 3 cups dill pickles, sliced, drained
- 2 eggs
- 2 tsp water
- 1 cup grated Parmesan cheese
- 1 ½ cups breadcrumbs, smooth
- Black pepper to taste

Directions:
1. Preheat on Air Fry function to 400 F. In a bowl, add the breadcrumbs and black pepper and mix well. In another bowl, crack the eggs and beat with the water. Add the Parmesan cheese to a separate bowl.
2. Pull out the fryer basket and spray it lightly with cooking spray. Dredge the pickle slices it in the egg mixture, then in breadcrumbs and then in cheese. Place them in the basket without overlapping and fit in the baking tray. Cook for 4 minutes. Turn them and cook for further for 5 minutes until crispy. Serve with cheese dip.

31. Baked Garlic Mushrooms

Servings: 2
Cooking Time: 10 Minutes
Ingredients:
- 1 lb button mushrooms, clean and stems removed
- 2 tbsp olive oil
- 2 tbsp fresh chives, sliced
- 3 garlic cloves, chopped
- 1/2 tsp salt

Directions:
1. Fit the oven with the rack in position
2. Add mushrooms, chives, garlic, olive oil, and salt into the zip-lock bag and shake well.
3. Place mushrooms in baking pan.
4. Set to bake at 400 F for 15 minutes. After 5 minutes place the baking pan in the preheated oven.
5. Serve and enjoy.
- **Nutrition Info:** Calories 176 Fat 14.7 g Carbohydrates 9.1 g Sugar 4 g Protein 7.5 g Cholesterol 0 mg

32. Kale And Walnuts(1)

Servings: 4

Cooking Time: 8 Minutes

Ingredients:
- 3 garlic cloves
- 10 cups kale; roughly chopped.
- 1/3 cup parmesan; grated
- ½ cup almond milk
- ¼ cup walnuts; chopped.
- 1 tbsp. butter; melted
- ¼ tsp. nutmeg, ground
- Salt and black pepper to taste.

Directions:
1. In a pan that fits the air fryer, combine all the ingredients, toss, introduce the pan in the machine and cook at 360°F for 15 minutes
2. Divide between plates and serve.
- **Nutrition Info:** Calories: 160; Fat: 7g; Fiber: 2g; Carbs: 4g; Protein: 5g

33. Easy Parsnip Fries

Servings: 3
Cooking Time: 15 Minutes

Ingredients:
- 4 parsnips, sliced
- ¼ cup flour
- ¼ cup olive oil
- ¼ cup water
- A pinch of salt

Directions:
1. Preheat on Air Fry function to 390 F. In a bowl, add the flour, olive oil, water, and parsnips; mix to coat. Line the fries in the greased Air Fryer basket and fit in the baking tray. Cook for 15 minutes. Serve with yogurt and garlic dip.

34. Sunday Calamari Rings

Servings:4
Cooking Time: 20 Minutes

Ingredients:
- 1 lb calamari (squid), cut in rings
- ¼ cup flour
- 2 large beaten eggs
- 1 cup breadcrumbs

Directions:
1. Coat the calamari rings with the flour and dip them in the eggs. Then, roll in the breadcrumbs. Refrigerate for 2 hours. Line them in the frying basket and spray with cooking spray.
2. Select AirFry function, adjust the temperature to 380 F, and press Start. Cook for 14 minutes. Serve with garlic mayo and lemon wedges.

35. Healthy Parsnip Fries

Servings:3
Cooking Time: 20 Minutes

Ingredients:
- 4 large parsnips, sliced
- ¼ cup flour
- ¼ cup olive oil
- ¼ cup water
- A pinch of salt

Directions:
1. Preheat on AirFry function to 390 F. In a bowl, mix the flour, olive oil, water, and parsnip slices. Mix well and toss to coat.
2. Arrange the fries on the frying basket and place in the oven. Press Start and cook for 15 minutes. Serve with yogurt and garlic paste.

36. Green Bean Casserole(1)

Servings: 4
Cooking Time: 20 Minutes

Ingredients:
- 1 lb. fresh green beans, edges trimmed
- ½ oz. pork rinds, finely ground
- 1 oz. full-fat cream cheese
- ½ cup heavy whipping cream.
- ¼ cup diced yellow onion
- ½ cup chopped white mushrooms
- ½ cup chicken broth
- 4 tbsp. unsalted butter.
- ¼ tsp. xanthan gum

Directions:
1. In a medium skillet over medium heat, melt the butter. Sauté the onion and mushrooms until they become soft and fragrant, about 3–5 minutes.
2. Add the heavy whipping cream, cream cheese and broth to the pan. Whisk until smooth. Bring to a boil and then reduce to a simmer. Sprinkle the xanthan gum into the pan and remove from heat
3. Chop the green beans into 2-inch pieces and place into a 4-cup round baking dish. Pour the sauce mixture over them and stir until coated. Top the dish with ground pork rinds. Place into the air fryer basket
4. Adjust the temperature to 320 Degrees F and set the timer for 15 minutes. Top will be golden and green beans fork tender when fully cooked. Serve warm.
- **Nutrition Info:** Calories: 267; Protein: 3.6g; Fiber: 3.2g; Fat: 23.4g; Carbs: 9.7g

37. Roasted Garlic(3)

Servings: 12 Cloves
Cooking Time: 20 Minutes

Ingredients:
- 1 medium head garlic
- 2 tsp. avocado oil

Directions:
1. Remove any hanging excess peel from the garlic but leave the cloves covered. Cut off

¼ of the head of garlic, exposing the tips of the cloves

2. Drizzle with avocado oil. Place the garlic head into a small sheet of aluminum foil, completely enclosing it. Place it into the air fryer basket. Adjust the temperature to 400 Degrees F and set the timer for 20 minutes. If your garlic head is a bit smaller, check it after 15 minutes
3. When done, garlic should be golden brown and very soft
4. To serve, cloves should pop out and easily be spread or sliced. Store in an airtight container in the refrigerator up to 5 days.
5. You may also freeze individual cloves on a baking sheet, then store together in a freezer-safe storage bag once frozen.
- **Nutrition Info:** Calories: 11; Protein: 2g; Fiber: 1g; Fat: 7g; Carbs: 0g

38. Baked Potatoes With Yogurt And Chives

Servings:4
Cooking Time: 35 Minutes
Ingredients:
- 4 (7-ounce / 198-g) russet potatoes, rinsed
- Olive oil spray
- ½ teaspoon kosher salt, divided
- ½ cup 2% plain Greek yogurt
- ¼ cup minced fresh chives
- Freshly ground black pepper, to taste

Directions:
1. Pat the potatoes dry and pierce them all over with a fork. Spritz the potatoes with olive oil spray. Sprinkle with ¼ teaspoon of the salt.
2. Transfer the potatoes to the baking pan.
3. Slide the baking pan into Rack Position 1, select Convection Bake, set temperature to 400ºF (205ºC), and set time to 35 minutes.
4. When cooking is complete, the potatoes should be fork-tender. Remove from the oven and split open the potatoes. Top with the yogurt, chives, the remaining ¼ teaspoon of salt, and finish with the black pepper. Serve immediately.

39. Homemade Prosciutto Wrapped Cheese Sticks

Servings: 6
Cooking Time: 50 Minutes
Ingredients:
- 1 lb cheddar cheese
- 12 slices of prosciutto
- 1 cup flour
- 2 eggs, beaten
- 4 tbsp olive oil
- 1 cup breadcrumbs

Directions:

1. Cut the cheese into 6 equal sticks. Wrap each piece with 2 prosciutto slices. Place them in the freezer just enough to set. Preheat on Air Fry function to 390 F. Dip the croquettes into flour first, then in eggs, and coat with breadcrumbs. Drizzle the basket with oil and fit in the baking tray. Cook for 10 minutes or until golden. Serve.

40. Baked Potatoes & Carrots

Servings: 2
Cooking Time: 40 Minutes
Ingredients:
- 1/2 lb potatoes, cut into 1-inch cubes
- 1/2 onion, diced
- 1/2 tsp Italian seasoning
- 1/4 tsp garlic powder
- 1/2 lb carrots, peeled & cut into chunks
- 1 tbsp olive oil
- Pepper
- Salt

Directions:
1. Fit the oven with the rack in position
2. In a large bowl, toss carrots, potatoes, garlic powder, Italian seasoning, oil, onion, pepper, and salt.
3. Transfer carrot potato in baking pan.
4. Set to bake at 400 F for 45 minutes. After 5 minutes place the baking pan in the preheated oven.
5. Serve and enjoy.
- **Nutrition Info:** Calories 201 Fat 7.5 g Carbohydrates 32 g Sugar 8.2 g Protein 3.2 g Cholesterol 1 mg

41. Garlicky Roasted Chicken With Lemon

Servings:4
Cooking Time: 60 Minutes
Ingredients:
- 1 whole chicken (around 3.5 lb)
- 1 tbsp olive oil
- Salt and black pepper to taste
- 1 lemon, cut into quarters
- 5 garlic cloves

Directions:
1. Rub the chicken with olive oil and season with salt and pepper. Stuff the cavity with lemon and garlic. Place chicken, breast-side down on a baking tray. Tuck the legs and wings tips under.
2. Select Bake function, adjust the temperature to 360 F, and press Start. Bake for 30 minutes, turn breast-side up, and bake it for another 15 minutes. Let rest for 5-6 minutes then carve.

42. Baked Eggplant Pepper & Mushrooms

Servings: 4
Cooking Time: 20 Minutes

Ingredients:
- 2 eggplants
- 2 cups mushrooms
- 1/4 tsp black pepper
- 4 bell peppers
- 2 tbsp olive oil
- 1 tsp salt

Directions:
1. Fit the oven with the rack in position
2. Cut all vegetables into the small bite-sized pieces and place in a baking dish.
3. Drizzle vegetables with olive oil and season with pepper and salt.
4. Set to bake at 390 F for 25 minutes. After 5 minutes place the baking dish in the preheated oven.
5. Serve and enjoy.
- **Nutrition Info:** Calories 87 Fat 4 g Carbohydrates 13.2 g Sugar 7.4 g Protein 2.5 g Cholesterol 0 mg

43. Balsamic Keto Vegetables

Servings: 3
Cooking Time: 20 Minutes
Ingredients:
- 1/2-pound cauliflower florets
- 1/2-pound button mushrooms, whole
- 1 cup pearl onions, whole
- Pink Himalayan salt and ground black pepper, to taste
- 1/4 teaspoon smoked paprika
- 1 teaspoon garlic powder
- 1/2 teaspoon dried thyme
- 1/2 teaspoon dried marjoram
- 3 tablespoons olive oil
- 2 tablespoons balsamic vinegar

Directions:
1. Toss all ingredients in a large mixing dish.
2. Roast in the preheated Air Fryer at 400 degrees F for 5 minutes. Shake the basket and cook for 7 minutes more.
3. Serve with some extra fresh herbs if desired.
- **Nutrition Info:** 170 Calories; 14g Fat; 7g Carbs; 2g Protein; 5g Sugars; 9g Fiber

44. Jicama Fries(2)

Servings: 4
Cooking Time: 20 Minutes
Ingredients:
- 1 small jicama; peeled.
- ¼ tsp. onion powder.
- ¾tsp. chili powder.
- ¼ tsp. ground black pepper.
- ¼ tsp. garlic powder.

Directions:
1. Cut jicama into matchstick-sized pieces.
2. Place pieces into a small bowl and sprinkle with remaining ingredients. Place the fries into the air fryer basket

3. Adjust the temperature to 350 Degrees F and set the timer for 20 minutes. Toss the basket two or three times during cooking. Serve warm.
- **Nutrition Info:** Calories: 37; Protein: 0.8g; Fiber: 4.7g; Fat: 0.1g; Carbs: 8.7g

45. Cheesy Crisps

Servings: 3
Cooking Time: 25 Minutes
Ingredients:
- 4 tbsp grated cheddar cheese + extra for rolling
- 1 cup flour + extra for kneading
- ¼ tsp chili powder
- ½ tsp baking powder
- 3 tsp butter
- A pinch of salt

Directions:
1. In a bowl, add the cheddar cheese, flour, baking powder, chili powder, butter, and salt and mix until the mixture becomes crusty. Add some drops of water and mix well to get a dough. Remove the dough on a flat surface.
2. Rub some extra flour in your palms and on the surface and knead the dough for a while. Using a rolling pin, roll the dough out into a thin sheet. With a pastry cutter, cut the dough into your desired lings' shape. Add the cheese lings to the greased baking tray and cook for 8 minutes at 350 F on Air Fry function, flipping once halfway through. Serve.

46. Roasted Vegetable And Kale Salad

Servings: 4
Cooking Time: 40 Minutes
Ingredients:
- 1 bunch kale, stems removed and chopped into ribbons
- 4 small or 2 large beets, peeled and cut roughly into 1-inch pieces
- 1/2 small butternut squash, peeled and cubed into 1-inch pieces
- 1 small red onion, sliced into 8 wedges
- 1 medium fennel bulb, sliced into 8 wedges
- 1 red pepper
- 3 tablespoons olive oil
- 1/2 cup coarsely chopped walnuts
- 3/4 teaspoon salt
- Pepper to taste
- 2 ounces goat cheese

Directions:
1. Cut the beets and pepper into one-inch pieces.
2. Remove the stems from the kale and chop into thin pieces.
3. Cut fennel and red onion into wedges.

4. Preheat the toaster oven to 425°F.
5. Toss together all vegetables, except kale, in a large bowl with oil, salt, and pepper.
6. Spread over a baking sheet and roast for 40 minutes turning halfway through.
7. At the 30-minute mark, remove tray from oven and sprinkle walnuts over and around vegetables.
8. Toss kale with dressing of choice and top with vegetables. Crumble goat cheese over salad and serve.
- **Nutrition Info:** Calories: 321, Sodium: 569 mg, Dietary Fiber: 5.5 g, Total Fat: 25.1 g, Total Carbs: 17.5 g, Protein: 11.1 g.

47. Mashed Squash

Servings: 4
Cooking Time: 20 Minutes
Ingredients:
- 2 acorn squashes, cut into halves and seeded
- ½ cup water
- ¼ teaspoon baking soda
- 2 tablespoons butter
- Salt and ground black pepper, to taste
- ½ teaspoon fresh nutmeg, grated
- 2 tablespoons brown sugar

Directions:
1. Sprinkle the pumpkin halves with salt, pepper and baking soda and place them in the steam basket of the Instant Pot.
2. Add water to the Instant Pot, cover and cook for 20 minutes in manual configuration. Relieve the pressure, take the pumpkin and set it on a plate to cool. Scrape the flesh of the pumpkin and place it in a bowl.
3. Add salt, pepper, butter, sugar and nutmeg and mash with a potato masher. Mix well and serve.
- **Nutrition Info:** Calories: 140, Fat: 1, Fiber: 0.5, Carbohydrate: 10.5, Proteins: 1.7

48. Maple Shrimp With Coconut

Servings: 3
Cooking Time: 30 Minutes
Ingredients:
- 1 lb jumbo shrimp, peeled and deveined
- ¾ cup shredded coconut
- 1 tbsp maple syrup
- ½ cup breadcrumbs
- ⅓ cup cornstarch
- ½ cup milk

Directions:
1. Pour the cornstarch in a zipper bag, add shrimp, zip the bag up and shake vigorously to coat with the cornstarch. Mix the syrup and milk in a bowl and set aside.

2. In a separate bowl, mix the breadcrumbs and shredded coconut. Open the zipper bag and remove each shrimp while shaking off excess starch. Dip shrimp in the milk mixture and then in the crumb mixture while pressing loosely to trap enough crumbs and coconut.
3. Place in the basket without overcrowding and fit in the baking tray. Cook for 12 minutes at 350 F on Air Fry function, flipping once halfway through until golden brown. Serve warm.

49. Molasses Cashew Delight

Servings: 4
Cooking Time: 20 Minutes
Ingredients:
- 3 cups cashews
- 3 tbsp liquid smoke
- 2 tsp salt
- 2 tbsp molasses

Directions:
1. Preheat on Air Fry function to 360 F. In a bowl, add salt, liquid, molasses, and cashews; toss to coat thoroughly. Place the cashews in the frying baking tray and cook for 10 minutes, shaking every 5 minutes. Serve.

50. Crispy Cinnamon Apple Chips

Servings: 4
Cooking Time: 10 Minutes
Ingredients:
- 2 apples, cored and cut into thin slices
- 2 heaped teaspoons ground cinnamon
- Cooking spray

Directions:
1. Spritz the air fryer basket with cooking spray.
2. In a medium bowl, sprinkle the apple slices with the cinnamon. Toss until evenly coated. Spread the coated apple slices on the pan in a single layer.
3. Put the air fryer basket on the baking pan and slide into Rack Position 2, select Air Fry, set temperature to 350ºF (180ºC) and set time to 10 minutes.
4. After 5 minutes, remove from the oven. Stir the apple slices and return to the oven to continue cooking.
5. When cooking is complete, the slices should be until crispy. Remove from the oven and let rest for 5 minutes before serving.

51. Buttery Garlic Croutons

Servings:4
Cooking Time: 20 Minutes
Ingredients:
- 2 cups bread, cubed
- 2 tbsp butter, melted

- Garlic salt and black pepper to taste

Directions:
1. In a bowl, toss the bread cubes with butter, garlic salt, and pepper until well-coated. Place them in a baking tray. Select AirFry function, adjust the temperature to 400 F, and press Start. Cook for 12 minutes until golden brown and crispy. Serve in salads or soups.

52. Jalapeños Peppers With Chicken & Bacon

Servings:4
Cooking Time: 40 Minutes
Ingredients:
- 8 jalapeño peppers, halved lengthwise
- 4 chicken breasts, butterflied and halved
- 6 oz cream cheese
- 6 oz Cheddar cheese
- 16 slices bacon
- 1 cup breadcrumbs
- Salt and black pepper to taste
- 2 eggs

Directions:
1. Season the chicken with salt and pepper. In a bowl, add cream cheese and cheddar cheese and mix well. Take each jalapeño and spoon in the cheese mixture to the brim. On a working board, flatten each piece of chicken and lay 2 bacon slices each on them. Place a stuffed jalapeno on each laid out chicken and bacon set, and wrap the jalapeños in them.
2. Preheat on AirFry function to 350 F. Add the eggs to a bowl and pour the breadcrumbs in another bowl. Also, set a flat plate aside. Take each wrapped jalapeño and dip it into the eggs and then in the breadcrumbs. Place them on the flat plate. Lightly grease the fryer basket with cooking spray. Arrange 4-5 breaded jalapeños on the basket and press Start.
3. AirFry for 7 minutes, turn the jalapeños and cook for 4 minutes. Once ready, remove them onto a paper towel-lined plate. Serve with a sweet dip for an enhanced taste.

53. Flavored Mashed Sweet Potatoes

Servings: 8
Cooking Time: 9 Minutes
Ingredients:
- 3 pounds sweet potatoes, peeled and chopped
- Salt and ground black pepper, to taste
- 2 garlic cloves
- ½ teaspoon dried parsley
- ½ teaspoon dried rosemary
- ¼ teaspoon dried sage
- ½ teaspoon dried thyme

- 1½ cups water
- ½ cup Parmesan cheese, grated
- 2 tablespoon butter
- ¼ cup milk

Directions:
1. Place the potatoes and garlic in the Instant Pot, add 1 ½ cups of water to the Instant Pot, cover and cook for 10 minutes in the manual setting.
2. Relieve the pressure, drain the water, transfer the potatoes and garlic to a bowl and mix them using a hand mixer.
3. Add butter, cheese, milk, salt, pepper, parsley, sage, rosemary and thyme and mix well. Divide between plates and serve.
- **Nutrition Info:** Calories: 240, Fat: 1, Fiber: 8.2, Carbohydrate: 34, Proteins: 4.5

54. Cod Nuggets

Servings: 5
Cooking Time: 8 Minutes
Ingredients:
- 1 cup all-purpose flour
- 2 eggs
- ¾ cup breadcrumbs
- Pinch of salt
- 2 tablespoons olive oil
- 1 lb. cod, cut into 1x2½-inch strips

Directions:
1. In a shallow dish, place the flour.
2. Crack the eggs in a second dish and beat well.
3. In a third dish, mix together the breadcrumbs, salt, and oil.
4. Coat the nuggets with flour, then dip into beaten eggs and finally, coat with the breadcrumbs.
5. Press "Power Button" of Air Fry Oven and turn the dial to select the "Air Fry" mode.
6. Press the Time button and again turn the dial to set the cooking time to 8 minutes.
7. Now push the Temp button and rotate the dial to set the temperature at 390 degrees F.
8. Press "Start/Pause" button to start.
9. When the unit beeps to show that it is preheated, open the lid.
10. Arrange the nuggets in "Air Fry Basket" and insert in the oven.
11. Serve warm.
- **Nutrition Info:** Calories 323 Total Fat 9.2 g Saturated Fat 1.7 g Cholesterol 115 mg Sodium 245 mg Total Carbs 30.9 g Fiber 1.4 g Sugar 1.2 g Protein 27.7 g

55. Sweet Carrot Puree

Servings: 4
Cooking Time: 5 Minutes
Ingredients:
- Salt, to taste

- 1 cup water
- 1 teaspoon brown sugar
- 1½ pounds carrots, peeled and chopped
- 1 tablespoon butter, softened
- 1 tablespoon honey

Directions:
1. Place the carrots in the Instant Pot, add the water, cover and cook for 4 minutes in the Manual setting.
2. Release the pressure naturally, drain the carrots and place them in a bowl.
3. Mix with an immersion blender, add the butter, salt and honey. Mix again, add the sugar on top and serve.
- **Nutrition Info:** Calories: 50, Fat: 1, Fiber: 3, Carbohydrate: 11, Proteins: 1

56. Traditional Indian Kofta

Servings: 4
Cooking Time: 20 Minutes
Ingredients:
- Veggie Balls:
- 3/4-pound zucchini, grated and well drained
- 1/4-pound kohlrabi, grated and well drained
- 2 cloves garlic, minced
- 1 tablespoon Garam masala
- 1 cup paneer, crumbled
- 1/4 cup coconut flour
- 1/2 teaspoon chili powder
- Himalayan pink salt and ground black pepper, to taste
- Sauce:
- 1 tablespoon sesame oil
- 1/2 teaspoon cumin seeds
- 2 cloves garlic, roughly chopped
- 1 onion, chopped
- 1 Kashmiri chili pepper, seeded and minced
- 1 (1-inchpiece ginger, chopped
- 1 teaspoon paprika
- 1 teaspoon turmeric powder
- 2 ripe tomatoes, pureed
- 1/2 cup vegetable broth
- 1/4 full fat coconut milk

Directions:
1. Start by preheating your Air Fryer to 360 degrees F. Thoroughly combine the zucchini, kohlrabi, garlic, Garam masala, paneer, coconut flour, chili powder, salt and ground black pepper.
2. Shape the vegetable mixture into small balls and arrange them in the lightly greased cooking basket.
3. Cook in the preheated Air Fryer at 360 degrees F for 15 minutes or until thoroughly cooked and crispy. Repeat the process until you run out of ingredients.

4. Heat the sesame oil in a saucepan over medium heat and add the cumin seeds. Once the cumin seeds turn brown, add the garlic, onions, chili pepper, and ginger. Sauté for 2 to 3 minutes.
5. Add the paprika, turmeric powder, tomatoes, and broth; let it simmer, covered, for 4 to 5 minutes, stirring occasionally.
6. Add the coconut milk. Heat off; add the veggie balls and gently stir to combine.
- **Nutrition Info:** 259 Calories; 11g Fat; 1g Carbs; 19g Protein; 3g Sugars; 4g Fiber

57. Air Fryer Corn

Servings: 2
Cooking Time: 10 Minutes
Ingredients:
- 2 fresh ears of corn, remove husks, wash, and pat dry
- 1 tbsp fresh lemon juice
- 2 tsp oil
- Pepper
- Salt

Directions:
1. Fit the oven with the rack in position 2.
2. Cut the corn to fit in the air fryer basket.
3. Drizzle oil over the corn. Season with pepper and salt.
4. Place corn in the air fryer basket then places an air fryer basket in the baking pan.
5. Place a baking pan on the oven rack. Set to air fry at 400 F for 10 minutes.
6. Serve and enjoy.
7. Drizzle lemon juice over corn and serve.
- **Nutrition Info:** Calories 122 Fat 5.6 g Carbohydrates 18.2 g Sugar 4.2 g Protein 3.1 g Cholesterol 0 mg

58. Sausage Mushroom Caps(2)

Servings: 2
Cooking Time: 20 Minutes
Ingredients:
- ½ lb. Italian sausage
- 6 large Portobello mushroom caps
- ¼ cup grated Parmesan cheese.
- ¼ cup chopped onion
- 2 tbsp. blanched finely ground almond flour
- 1 tsp. minced fresh garlic

Directions:
1. Use a spoon to hollow out each mushroom cap, reserving scrapings.
2. In a medium skillet over medium heat, brown the sausage about 10 minutes or until fully cooked and no pink remains. Drain and then add reserved mushroom scrapings, onion, almond flour, Parmesan and garlic.

3. Gently fold ingredients together and continue cooking an additional minute, then remove from heat
4. Evenly spoon the mixture into mushroom caps and place the caps into a 6-inch round pan. Place pan into the air fryer basket
5. Adjust the temperature to 375 Degrees F and set the timer for 8 minutes. When finished cooking, the tops will be browned and bubbling. Serve warm.
- **Nutrition Info:** Calories: 404; Protein: 24.3g; Fiber: 4.5g; Fat: 25.8g; Carbs: 18.2g

59. Bbq Chicken Wings

Servings: 4
Cooking Time: 19 Minutes
Ingredients:
- 2 lbs. chicken wings
- 1 teaspoon olive oil
- 1 teaspoon smoked paprika
- 1 teaspoon garlic powder
- Salt and ground black pepper, as required
- ¼ cup BBQ sauce

Directions:
1. In a large bowl combine chicken wings, smoked paprika, garlic powder, oil, salt, and pepper and mix well.
2. Press "Power Button" of Air Fry Oven and turn the dial to select the "Air Fry" mode.
3. Press the Time button and again turn the dial to set the cooking time to 19 minutes.
4. Now push the Temp button and rotate the dial to set the temperature at 360 degrees F.
5. Press "Start/Pause" button to start.
6. When the unit beeps to show that it is preheated, open the lid.
7. Arrange the chicken wings in "Air Fry Basket" and insert in the oven.
8. After 12 minutes of cooking, flip the wings and coat with barbecue sauce evenly.
9. Serve immediately.
- **Nutrition Info:** Calories 468 Total Fat 18.1 g Saturated Fat 4.8 g Cholesterol 202mg Sodium 409 mg Total Carbs 6.5 g Fiber 0.4 g Sugar 4.3 g Protein 65.8 g

60. Garlic Herb Tomatoes

Servings: 4
Cooking Time: 45 Minutes
Ingredients:
- 10 medium-sized tomatoes
- 10 garlic cloves
- Bread crumbs
- Thyme
- Sage
- Oregano

Directions:
1. Start by finely chopping garlic and herbs.

2. Cut tomatoes in half and place cut-side up on a baking sheet lined with parchment paper.
3. Pour garlic and herb mixture over tomatoes.
4. Roast at 350°F for 30 minutes in toaster oven.
5. Top with bread crumbs and roast another 15 minutes.
- **Nutrition Info:** Calories: 103, Sodium: 68 mg, Dietary Fiber: 5.4 g, Total Fat: 1.3 g, Total Carbs: 21.4 g, Protein: 4.4 g.

61. Potato Croquettes

Servings: 4
Cooking Time: 8 Minutes
Ingredients:
- 2 medium Russet potatoes, peeled and cubed
- 2 tablespoons all-purpose flour
- ½ cup Parmesan cheese, grated
- 1 egg yolk
- 2 tablespoons chives, minced
- Pinch of ground nutmeg Salt and freshly ground black pepper, as needed
- 2 eggs
- ½ cup breadcrumbs
- 2 tablespoons vegetable oil

Directions:
1. In a pan of a boiling water, add the potatoes and cook for about 15 minutes.
2. Drain the potatoes well and transfer into a large bowl.
3. With a potato masher, mash the potatoes and set aside to cool completely.
4. In the bowl of mashed potatoes, add the flour, Parmesan cheese, egg yolk, chives, nutmeg, salt, and black pepper and mix until well combined.
5. Make small equal-sized balls from the mixture.
6. Now, roll each ball into a cylinder shape.
7. In a shallow dish, crack the eggs and beat well.
8. In another dish, mix together the breadcrumbs, and oil.
9. Dip the croquettes in egg mixture and then coat with the breadcrumbs mixture.
10. Press "Power Button" of Air Fry Oven and turn the dial to select the "Air Fry" mode.
11. Press the Time button and again turn the dial to set the cooking time to 8 minutes.
12. Now push the Temp button and rotate the dial to set the temperature at 390 degrees F.
13. Press "Start/Pause" button to start.
14. When the unit beeps to show that it is preheated, open the lid.
15. Arrange the croquettes in "Air Fry Basket" and insert in the oven.
16. Serve warm.

- **Nutrition Info:** Calories 283 Total Fat 13.4 g Saturated Fat 3.8 g Cholesterol 142 mg Sodium 263mg Total Carbs 29.9 g Fiber 3.3 g Sugar 2.3 g Protein 11.5 g

62. Pineapple Pork Ribs

Servings: 4
Cooking Time: 30 Minutes
Ingredients:
- 2 lb cut spareribs
- 7 oz salad dressing
- 1 (5-oz) can pineapple juice
- 2 cups water
- Salt and black pepper to taste

Directions:
1. Preheat your to 390 F on Bake function. Sprinkle the ribs with salt and pepper and place them in a greased baking dish. Cook for 15 minutes. Prepare the sauce by combining the salad dressing and the pineapple juice. Serve the ribs drizzled with the sauce.

63. Beans And Pork Mix

Servings: 4
Cooking Time: 20 Minutes
Ingredients:
- 1-pound pork stew meat, ground
- 1 red onion, chopped
- 1 tablespoon olive oil
- 1 cup canned kidney beans, drained and rinsed
- 1 teaspoon chili powder
- Salt and black pepper to the taste
- ¼ teaspoon cumin, ground

Directions:
1. Heat up your air fryer at 360 degrees F, add the meat and the onion and cook for 5 minutes.
2. Add the beans and the rest of the ingredients, toss and cook for 15 minutes more.
3. Divide everything into bowls and serve for breakfast.
- **Nutrition Info:** calories 203, fat 4, fiber 6, carbs 12, protein 4

64. Crunchy Asparagus With Cheese

Servings: 4
Cooking Time: 15 Minutes
Ingredients:
- 1 lb asparagus spears
- ¼ cup flour
- 1 cup breadcrumbs
- ½ cup Parmesan cheese, grated
- 2 eggs, beaten
- Salt and black pepper to taste

Directions:
1. Preheat on Air Fry function to 370 F. Combine the breadcrumbs and Parmesan cheese in a bowl. Season with salt and pepper.
2. Line a baking sheet with parchment paper. Dip the asparagus spears into the flour first, then into the eggs, and finally coat with crumbs.
3. Arrange them on the AirFryer Basket, fit in the baking sheet, and cook for about 8 to 10 minutes. Serve with melted butter, hollandaise sauce, or freshly squeezed lemon.

65. Bulgogi Burgers

Servings:4
Cooking Time: 10 Minutes
Ingredients:
- Burgers:
- 1 pound (454 g) 85% lean ground beef
- 2 tablespoons gochujang
- ¼ cup chopped scallions
- 2 teaspoons minced garlic
- 2 teaspoons minced fresh ginger
- 1 tablespoon soy sauce
- 1 tablespoon toasted sesame oil
- 2 teaspoons sugar
- ½ teaspoon kosher salt
- 4 hamburger buns
- Cooking spray
- Korean Mayo:
- 1 tablespoon gochujang
- ¼ cup mayonnaise
- 2 teaspoons sesame seeds
- ¼ cup chopped scallions
- 1 tablespoon toasted sesame oil

Directions:
1. Combine the ingredients for the burgers, except for the buns, in a large bowl. Stir to mix well, then wrap the bowl in plastic and refrigerate to marinate for at least an hour.
2. Spritz the air fryer basket with cooking spray.
3. Divide the meat mixture into four portions and form into four balls. Bash the balls into patties.
4. Arrange the patties in the pan and spritz with cooking spray.
5. Put the air fryer basket on the baking pan and slide into Rack Position 2, select Air Fry, set temperature to 350ºF (180ºC) and set time to 10 minutes.
6. Flip the patties halfway through the cooking time.
7. Meanwhile, combine the ingredients for the Korean mayo in a small bowl. Stir to mix well.
8. When cooking is complete, the patties should be golden brown.
9. Remove the patties from the oven and assemble with the buns, then spread the Korean mayo over the patties to make the burgers. Serve immediately.

66. Grilled Cheese Sandwich

Servings: 1 Person
Cooking Time: 12 Minutes
Ingredients:
- 2 slices of bread
- 2 pieces of bacon
- ½ tsp of olive oil side
- Tomatoes
- Jack cheese
- Peach preserves

Directions:
1. If you have left over bacon from air fried bacon recipe you can get two pieces. However, if you do not have any leftover bacon you can get two pieces and fry them at 200 degree Celsius.

2. Place olive oil on the side of the bread slices. Layer the rest of the ingredients on the non-oiled side following the following steps, peach preserves, tomatoes, jack cheese and cooked bacon.
3. Press down the bread to allow it to cook a little bit and peach side down too to allow the bread and the peel to spread evenly.
4. Place the sandwich in an air fryer and cook it for 12 minutes
5. at 393 degrees Fahrenheit.
6. Serve once you are done.
- **Nutrition Info:** Calories 282 Fats 18g, Carbs 18g, Proteins 12g, Sodium: 830 Mg, Potassium: 250mg

67. Giant Strawberry Pancake

Servings: 3
Cooking Time: 30 Minutes
Ingredients:
- 3 eggs, beaten
- 2 tbsp butter, melted
- ½ cup flour
- 2 tbsp sugar, powdered
- ½ cup milk
- 1 ½ cups fresh strawberries, sliced

Directions:
1. Preheat on Bake function to 350 F. In a bowl, mix flour, milk, eggs, and vanilla until fully incorporated. Add the mixture a greased with melted butter pan.
2. Place the pan in your toaster oven and cook for 12-16 minutes until the pancake is fluffy and golden brown. Drizzle powdered sugar and toss sliced strawberries on top.

68. Sweet Pineapple Oatmeal

Servings: 6
Cooking Time: 45 Minutes
Ingredients:
- 2 cups old-fashioned oats
- 1/2 cup coconut flakes
- 1 cup pineapple, crushed
- 2 eggs, lightly beaten
- 1/3 cup yogurt
- 1/3 cup butter, melted
- 1/2 tsp baking powder
- 1/3 cup brown sugar
- 1/2 tsp vanilla
- 2/3 cup milk
- 1/2 tsp salt

Directions:
1. Fit the oven with the rack in position
2. In a mixing bowl, mix together oats, baking powder, brown sugar, and salt.
3. In a separate bowl, beat eggs with vanilla, milk, yogurt, and butter.
4. Add egg mixture into the oat mixture and stir to combine.

5. Add coconut and pineapple and stir to combine.
6. Pour oat mixture into the greased 8-inch baking dish.
7. Set to bake at 350 F for 50 minutes, after 5 minutes, place the baking dish in the oven.
8. Serve and enjoy.
- **Nutrition Info:** Calories 304 Fat 16.4 g Carbohydrates 33.2 g Sugar 13.6 g Protein 7.5 g Cholesterol 85 mg

69. Breakfast Egg Tomato

Servings: 2
Cooking Time: 24 Minutes
Ingredients:
- 2 eggs
- 2 large fresh tomatoes 1 tsp fresh parsley Pepper
- Salt

Directions:
1. Preheat the air fryer to 325 F.
2. Cut off the top of a tomato and spoon out the tomato innards.
3. Break the egg in each tomato and place in air fryer basket and cook for 24 minutes.
4. Season with parsley, pepper, and salt.
5. Serve and enjoy.
- **Nutrition Info:** Calories 95 Fat 5 g Carbohydrates 7.5 g Sugar 5.1 g Protein 7 g Cholesterol 164 mg

70. Corned Beef Hash With Eggs

Servings:4
Cooking Time: 25 Minutes
Ingredients:
- 2 medium Yukon Gold potatoes, peeled and cut into ¼-inch cubes
- 1 medium onion, chopped
- $^1/_3$ cup diced red bell pepper
- 3 tablespoons vegetable oil
- ½ teaspoon dried thyme
- ½ teaspoon kosher salt, divided
- ½ teaspoon freshly ground black pepper, divided
- ¾ pound (340 g) corned beef, cut into ¼-inch pieces
- 4 large eggs

Directions:
1. In a large bowl, stir together the potatoes, onion, red pepper, vegetable oil, thyme, ¼ teaspoon of the salt and ¼ teaspoon of the pepper. Spread the vegetable mixture into the baking pan in an even layer.
2. Slide the baking pan into Rack Position 2, select Roast, set temperature to 375ºF (190ºC) and set time to 25 minutes.
3. After 15 minutes, remove the pan from the oven and add the corned beef. Stir the mixture to incorporate the corned beef.

Return the pan to the oven and continue cooking.

4. After 5 minutes, remove the pan from the oven. Using a large spoon, create 4 circles in the hash to hold the eggs. Gently crack an egg into each circle. Season the eggs with the remaining ¼ teaspoon of the salt and ¼ teaspoon of the pepper. Return the pan to the oven. Continue cooking for 3 to 5 minutes, depending on how you like your eggs.
5. When cooking is complete, remove the pan from the oven. Serve immediately.

71. Cashew Granola With Cranberries

Servings: 6
Cooking Time: 12 Minutes
Ingredients:
- 3 cups old-fashioned rolled oats
- 2 cups raw cashews
- 1 cup unsweetened coconut chips
- ½ cup honey
- ¼ cup vegetable oil
- $1/3$ cup packed light brown sugar
- ¼ teaspoon kosher salt
- 1 cup dried cranberries

Directions:
1. In a large bowl, stir together all the ingredients, except for the cranberries. Spread the mixture in the baking pan in an even layer.
2. Slide the baking pan into Rack Position 1, select Convection Bake, set temperature to 325ºF (163ºC) and set time to 12 minutes.
3. After 5 to 6 minutes, remove the pan and stir the granola. Return the pan to the oven and continue cooking.
4. When cooking is complete, remove the pan. Let the granola cool to room temperature. Stir in the cranberries before serving.

72. Baked Breakfast Quiche

Servings: 6
Cooking Time: 45 Minutes
Ingredients:
- 6 eggs
- 1 cup milk
- 1 cup cheddar cheese, grated
- 1 cup tomatoes, chopped
- Pepper
- Salt

Directions:
1. Fit the oven with the rack in position
2. In a bowl, whisk eggs with cheese, milk, pepper, and salt. Stir in tomatoes.
3. Pour egg mixture into the greased pie dish.
4. Set to bake at 350 F for 50 minutes, after 5 minutes, place the pie dish in the oven.
5. Serve and enjoy.

- **Nutrition Info:** Calories 165 Fat 11.5 g Carbohydrates 3.8 g Sugar 3.1 g Protein 11.8 g Cholesterol 187 mg

73. Omelet Egg Muffins

Servings: 12
Cooking Time: 20 Minutes
Ingredients:
- 12 eggs, lightly beaten
- 1 cup tomatoes, chopped
- 4 tbsp water
- 1 tsp Italian seasoning
- 1 cup fresh spinach, chopped
- 1/2 tsp pepper
- 1/4 tsp salt

Directions:
1. Fit the oven with the rack in position
2. Spray 12-cups muffin tin with cooking spray and set aside.
3. Whisk eggs in a bowl with water, Italian seasoning, pepper, and salt.
4. Add spinach and tomatoes to the egg mixture and whisk well.
5. Pour egg mixture into the greased muffin tin.
6. Set to bake at 350 F for 25 minutes, after 5 minutes, place muffin tin in the oven.
7. Serve and enjoy.
- **Nutrition Info:** Calories 68 Fat 4.5 g Carbohydrates 1.1 g Sugar 0.8 g Protein 5.8 g Cholesterol 164 mg

74. Glazed Strawberry Toast

Servings: 4 Toasts
Cooking Time: 8 Minutes
Ingredients:
- 4 slices bread, ½-inch thick
- 1 cup sliced strawberries
- 1 teaspoon sugar
- Cooking spray

Directions:
1. On a clean work surface, lay the bread slices and spritz one side of each slice of bread with cooking spray.
2. Place the bread slices in the air fryer basket, sprayed side down. Top with the strawberries and a sprinkle of sugar.
3. Put the air fryer basket on the baking pan and slide into Rack Position 2, select Air Fry, set temperature to 375ºF (190ºC), and set time to 8 minutes.
4. When cooking is complete, the toast should be well browned on each side. Remove from the oven to a plate and serve.

75. Fresh Kale & Cottage Omelet

Servings: 1
Cooking Time: 15 Minutes
Ingredients:

- 3 eggs
- 3 tbsp cottage cheese
- 3 tbsp chopped kale
- ½ tbsp chopped basil
- ½ tbsp chopped parsley
- Salt and black pepper to taste
- 1 tsp olive oil

Directions:
1. Beat the eggs with salt and pepper in a bowl. Stir in the rest of the ingredients. Drizzle a baking pan with olive oil. Pour in the mixture and place it into the oven. Cook for 10-12 minutes on Bake function at 360 F until slightly golden and set. Serve.

76. Ham And Cheese Toast

Servings: 1
Cooking Time: 6 Minutes
Ingredients:
- 1 slice bread
- 1 teaspoon butter, at room temperature
- 1 egg
- Salt and freshly ground black pepper, to taste
- 2 teaspoons diced ham
- 1 tablespoon grated Cheddar cheese

Directions:
1. On a clean work surface, use a 2½-inch biscuit cutter to make a hole in the center of the bread slice with about ½-inch of bread remaining.
2. Spread the butter on both sides of the bread slice. Crack the egg into the hole and season with salt and pepper to taste. Transfer the bread to the air fryer basket.
3. Put the air fryer basket on the baking pan and slide into Rack Position 2, select Air Fry, set temperature to 325ºF (163ºC), and set time to 6 minutes.
4. After 5 minutes, remove the pan from the oven. Scatter the cheese and diced ham on top and continue cooking for an additional 1 minute.
5. When cooking is complete, the egg should be set and the cheese should be melted. Remove the toast from the oven to a plate and let cool for 5 minutes before serving.

77. Cabbage And Pork Gyoza

Servings: 48 Gyozas
Cooking Time: 10 Minutes
Ingredients:
- 1 pound (454 g) ground pork
- 1 head Napa cabbage (about 1 pound / 454 g), sliced thinly and minced
- ½ cup minced scallions
- 1 teaspoon minced fresh chives
- 1 teaspoon soy sauce
- 1 teaspoon minced fresh ginger

- 1 tablespoon minced garlic
- 1 teaspoon granulated sugar
- 2 teaspoons kosher salt
- 48 to 50 wonton or dumpling wrappers
- Cooking spray

Directions:
1. Spritz the air fryer basket with cooking spray. Set aside.
2. Make the filling: Combine all the ingredients, except for the wrappers in a large bowl. Stir to mix well.
3. Unfold a wrapper on a clean work surface, then dab the edges with a little water. Scoop up 2 teaspoons of the filling mixture in the center.
4. Make the gyoza: Fold the wrapper over to filling and press the edges to seal. Pleat the edges if desired. Repeat with remaining wrappers and fillings.
5. Arrange the gyozas in the pan and spritz with cooking spray.
6. Put the air fryer basket on the baking pan and slide into Rack Position 2, select Air Fry, set temperature to 360ºF (182ºC) and set time to 10 minutes.
7. Flip the gyozas halfway through the cooking time.
8. When cooked, the gyozas will be golden brown.
9. Serve immediately.

78. Amazing Strawberry Pancake

Servings:4
Cooking Time: 30 Minutes
Ingredients:
- 3 eggs, beaten
- 2 tbsp unsalted butter
- ½ cup flour
- 2 tbsp sugar, powdered
- ½ cup milk
- 1 ½ cups fresh strawberries, sliced

Directions:
1. Preheat to 330 F on Bake function. Add butter to a pan and melt over low heat. In a bowl, mix flour, milk, eggs, and vanilla. Add the mixture to the pan with melted butter.
2. Place the pan in the oven and press Start. Cook for 14-16 minutes until the pancake is fluffy and golden brown. Drizzle powdered sugar and toss sliced strawberries on top.

79. Ham Shirred Eggs With Parmesan

Servings:2
Cooking Time: 20 Minutes
Ingredients:
- 4 eggs
- 2 tbsp heavy cream
- 4 ham slices
- 3 tbsp Parmesan cheese, shredded

- ¼ tsp paprika
- Salt and black pepper to taste
- 2 tsp chives, chopped

Directions:
1. Preheat on AirFry function to 320 F. Arrange the ham slices on the bottom of a greased pan to cover it completely. Whisk 1 egg along with the heavy cream, salt, and pepper in a bowl.
2. Pour the mixture over the ham slices. Crack the other eggs on top. Sprinkle with Parmesan cheese and press Start. Cook for 14 minutes. Sprinkle with paprika and chives and serve.

80. Zucchini Squash Pita Sandwiches Recipe

Servings:x
Cooking Time:x
Ingredients:
- 1 small Zucchini Squash, (5-6 ounces)
- Salt and Pepper, to taste
- 2 Whole Wheat Pitas
- 1/2 cup Hummus
- 1 1/2 cups Fresh Spinach, (2 handfuls)
- 1/2 cup Diced Red Bell Pepper, (about half a large pepper)
- 1/2 cup Chopped Red Onion, (about 1/4 a large onion)
- 2 teaspoons Olive Oil
- 1/4 teaspoon Dried Oregano
- 1/4 teaspoon Dried Thyme
- 1/4 teaspoon Garlic Powder
- 2 tablespoons Crumbled Feta Cheese, (about 1 ounce)

Directions:
1. Adjust the cooking rack to the lowest placement and preheat toaster oven to 425°F on the BAKE setting.
2. While the oven preheats, quarter the zucchini lengthwise and then cut into 1/2-inch thick pieces. Cut the bell pepper and onion into 1-inch thick pieces.
3. Add the vegetables to a roasting pan. Drizzle with oil and sprinkle over the oregano, garlic powder, and salt and pepper, to taste. Toss to combine.
4. Roast vegetables for 10 minutes. Carefully remove the pan and stir. Return pan to oven and continue cooking until the vegetables have softened and started to brown, about 5 minutes more. Remove from the toaster oven and set aside.
5. Reduce the temperature to 375°F and warm the pitas by placing them directly on the cooking rack for 1 to 2 minutes.
6. Spread warm pitas with hummus. Layer with spinach, roasted vegetables, and crumbled feta.

81. Easy Egg Bites

Servings: 6
Cooking Time: 30 Minutes
Ingredients:
- 5 eggs
- 3 bacon slices, cooked & chopped
- 4 tbsp cottage cheese
- 1/2 cup cheddar cheese, shredded
- 1/4 tsp pepper
- 1/4 tsp salt

Directions:
1. Fit the oven with the rack in position
2. Spray 6-cups muffin tin with cooking spray and set aside.
3. Add all ingredients except bacon into the blender and blend for 30 seconds.
4. Pour egg mixture into the prepared muffin tin then divide cooked bacon evenly in all egg cups.
5. Set to bake at 325 F for 35 minutes. After 5 minutes place muffin tin in the preheated oven.
6. Serve and enjoy.
- **Nutrition Info:** Calories 151 Fat 10.9 g Carbohydrates 0.9 g Sugar 0.4 g Protein 11.8 g Cholesterol 158 mg

82. Spinach Zucchini Egg Muffins

Servings: 12
Cooking Time: 20 Minutes
Ingredients:
- 8 eggs
- 1 cup baby spinach, chopped
- 1 red bell pepper, diced
- 1/4 cup green onion, chopped
- 12 bacon slices, cooked and crumbled
- 2 small zucchini, sliced
- 1/4 cup almond milk
- 2 tbsp parsley, chopped
- 1 tbsp olive oil
- Pepper
- Salt

Directions:
1. Fit the oven with the rack in position
2. Spray 12-cups muffin tin with cooking spray and set aside.
3. Heat olive oil in a pan over medium heat.
4. Add parsley, spinach, green onion, red bell pepper to the pan and sauté until spinach is wilted.
5. In a bowl, whisk eggs with almond milk, pepper, and salt.
6. Add sautéed vegetables, bacon, and zucchini to the egg mixture and stir well.
7. Pour egg mixture into the greased muffin tin.
8. Set to bake at 350 F for 25 minutes, after 5 minutes, place muffin tin in the oven.
9. Serve and enjoy.

- **Nutrition Info:** Calories 174 Fat 13.3 g Carbohydrates 2.5 g Sugar 1.3 g Protein 11.3 g Cholesterol 130 mg

83. Healthy Squash

Servings: 4
Cooking Time: 25 Minutes
Ingredients:
- 2 lbs yellow squash, cut into half-moons
- 1 tsp Italian seasoning
- ¼ tsp pepper
- 1 tbsp olive oil
- ¼ tsp salt

Directions:
1. Add all ingredients into the large bowl and toss well.
2. Preheat the air fryer to 400 F.
3. Add squash mixture into the air fryer basket and cook for 10 minutes.
4. Shake basket and cook for another 10 minutes.
5. Shake once again and cook for 5 minutes more.
- **Nutrition Info:** Calories 70, Fat 4 g, Carbohydrates 7 g, Sugar 4 g, Protein 2 g, Cholesterol 1 mg

84. Smart Oven Baked Oatmeal Recipe

Servings:x
Cooking Time:x
Ingredients:
- 1 small Ripe Banana, (6 inches long, abut 1/4 cup mashed)
- 1 tablespoon Flax Meal
- 1/2 cup Non-Dairy Milk, plus 2 tablespoons (like Almond Milk or Soy Milk)
- 1 cup Old Fashioned Rolled Oats
- 2 teaspoons Pure Maple Syrup
- 2 teaspoons Olive Oil
- 1/2 teaspoon Ground Cinnamon
- 1/2 teaspoon Pure Vanilla Extract
- 1/4 teaspoon Baking Powder
- 1/8 teaspoon Fine Sea Salt
- 1/4 cup Pecan Pieces, (1 ounce)

Directions:
1. Adjust the cooking rack to the bottom position and preheat toaster oven to 350°F on the BAKE setting. Grease a 7 x 5-inch toaster oven-safe baking dish.
2. In a large bowl, add the banana and mash well. Stir in the flaxseed meal, maple syrup, olive oil, cinnamon, vanilla, baking powder, salt, milk, oats, and pecan pieces. Pour mixture into prepared baking dish.
3. Bake oatmeal until the middle is set and browned on the edges, about 25 to 35 minutes. (For softer scoop able oatmeal bake 25 to 30 minutes, for firm oatmeal bake 30 to 35 minutes.)

4. Let sit at least 10 minutes before slicing and serving.

85. Pea And Potato Samosas With Chutney

Servings: 16 Samosas
Cooking Time: 22 Minutes
Ingredients:
- Dough:
- 4 cups all-purpose flour, plus more for flouring the work surface
- ¼ cup plain yogurt
- ½ cup cold unsalted butter, cut into cubes
- 2 teaspoons kosher salt
- 1 cup ice water
- Filling:
- 2 tablespoons vegetable oil
- 1 onion, diced
- 1½ teaspoons coriander
- 1½ teaspoons cumin
- 1 clove garlic, minced
- 1 teaspoon turmeric
- 1 teaspoon kosher salt
- ½ cup peas, thawed if frozen
- 2 cups mashed potatoes
- 2 tablespoons yogurt
- Cooking spray
- Chutney:
- 1 cup mint leaves, lightly packed
- 2 cups cilantro leaves, lightly packed
- 1 green chile pepper, deseeded and minced
- ½ cup minced onion
- Juice of 1 lime
- 1 teaspoon granulated sugar
- 1 teaspoon kosher salt
- 2 tablespoons vegetable oil

Directions:
1. Put the flour, yogurt, butter, and salt in a food processor. Pulse to combine until grainy. Pour in the water and pulse until a smooth and firm dough forms.
2. Transfer the dough on a clean and lightly floured working surface. Knead the dough and shape it into a ball. Cut in half and flatten the halves into 2 discs. Wrap them in plastic and let sit in refrigerator until ready to use.
3. Meanwhile, make the filling: Heat the vegetable oil in a saucepan over medium heat.
4. Add the onion and sauté for 5 minutes or until lightly browned.
5. Add the coriander, cumin, garlic, turmeric, and salt and sauté for 2 minutes or until fragrant.
6. Add the peas, potatoes, and yogurt and stir to combine well. Turn off the heat and allow to cool.

7. Meanwhile, combine the ingredients for the chutney in a food processor. Pulse to mix well until glossy. Pour the chutney in a bowl and refrigerate until ready to use.
8. Make the samosas: Remove the dough discs from the refrigerator and cut each disc into 8 parts. Shape each part into a ball, then roll the ball into a 6-inch circle. Cut the circle in half and roll each half into a cone.
9. Scoop up 2 tablespoons of the filling into the cone, press the edges of the cone to seal and form into a triangle. Repeat with remaining dough and filling.
10. Spritz the air fryer basket with cooking spray. Arrange the samosas in the pan and spritz with cooking spray.
11. Put the air fryer basket on the baking pan and slide into Rack Position 2, select Air Fry, set temperature to 360ºF (182ºC) and set time to 15 minutes.
12. Flip the samosas halfway through the cooking time.
13. When cooked, the samosas will be golden brown and crispy.
14. Serve the samosas with the chutney.

86. Thai Pork Sliders

Servings: 6 Sliders
Cooking Time: 14 Minutes
Ingredients:
- 1 pound (454 g) ground pork
- 1 tablespoon Thai curry paste
- 1½ tablespoons fish sauce
- ¼ cup thinly sliced scallions, white and green parts
- 2 tablespoons minced peeled fresh ginger
- 1 tablespoon light brown sugar
- 1 teaspoon ground black pepper
- 6 slider buns, split open lengthwise, warmed
- Cooking spray

Directions:
1. Spritz the air fryer basket with cooking spray.
2. Combine all the ingredients, except for the buns in a large bowl. Stir to mix well.
3. Divide and shape the mixture into six balls, then bash the balls into six 3-inch-diameter patties.
4. Arrange the patties in the basket and spritz with cooking spray.
5. Put the air fryer basket on the baking pan and slide into Rack Position 2, select Air Fry, set temperature to 375ºF (190ºC) and set time to 14 minutes.
6. Flip the patties halfway through the cooking time.
7. When cooked, the patties should be well browned.

8. Assemble the buns with patties to make the sliders and serve immediately.

87. Crispy Crab And Cream Cheese Wontons

Servings:6 To 8
Cooking Time: 10 Minutes
Ingredients:
- 24 wonton wrappers, thawed if frozen
- Cooking spray
- Filling:
- 5 ounces (142 g) lump crabmeat, drained and patted dry
- 4 ounces (113 g) cream cheese, at room temperature
- 2 scallions, sliced
- 1½ teaspoons toasted sesame oil
- 1 teaspoon Worcestershire sauce
- Kosher salt and ground black pepper, to taste

Directions:
1. Spritz the air fryer basket with cooking spray.
2. In a medium-size bowl, place all the ingredients for the filling and stir until well mixed. Prepare a small bowl of water alongside.
3. On a clean work surface, lay the wonton wrappers. Scoop 1 teaspoon of the filling in the center of each wrapper. Wet the edges with a touch of water. Fold each wonton wrapper diagonally in half over the filling to form a triangle.
4. Arrange the wontons in the pan. Spritz the wontons with cooking spray.
5. Put the air fryer basket on the baking pan and slide into Rack Position 2, select Air Fry, set temperature to 350ºF (180ºC) and set time to 10 minutes.
6. Flip the wontons halfway through the cooking time.
7. When cooking is complete, the wontons will be crispy and golden brown.
8. Serve immediately.

88. Cheesy Hash Brown Casserole

Servings: 8
Cooking Time: 45 Minutes
Ingredients:
- 32 oz hash browns
- 1 stick butter, melted
- 1/3 tsp black pepper
- 16 oz sour cream
- 2 cups cheddar cheese, grated
- 1 small onion, diced
- 10 oz can chicken soup

Directions:
1. Fit the oven with the rack in position

2. Spray 9*13-inch casserole dish with cooking spray and set aside.
3. In a large bowl, add hash browns, 1 1/2 cups cheddar cheese, onion, sour cream, soup, butter, and black pepper and mix until well combined.
4. Transfer hash brown mixture into the prepared casserole dish and spread well.
5. Top with remaining cheese.
6. Set to bake at 350 F for 50 minutes. After 5 minutes place the casserole dish in the preheated oven.
7. Serve and enjoy.
- **Nutrition Info:** Calories 673 Fat 49 g Carbohydrates 46 g Sugar 2.5 g Protein 13.3 g Cholesterol 88 mg

89. Peanut Butter & Honey Porridge

Servings:4
Cooking Time: 5 Minutes
Ingredients:
- 2 cups steel-cut oats
- 1 cup flax seeds
- 1 tbsp peanut butter
- 1 tbsp butter
- 4 cups milk
- 4 tbsp honey

Directions:
1. Preheat on Bake function to 390 F. Combine all of the ingredients in an ovenproof bowl. Place in the oven and press Start. Cook for 7 minutes. Stir and serve.

90. Vanilla Brownies With White Chocolate & Walnuts

Servings: 4
Cooking Time: 35 Minutes
Ingredients:
- 6 oz dark chocolate, chopped
- 6 oz butter
- ¾ cup white sugar
- 3 eggs, beaten
- 2 tsp vanilla extract
- ¾ cup flour
- ¼ cup cocoa powder
- 1 cup chopped walnuts
- 1 cup white chocolate chips

Directions:
1. Line a baking pan with parchment paper. In a saucepan, melt chocolate and butter over low heat. Do not stop stirring until you obtain a smooth mixture. Let cool slightly and whisk in eggs and vanilla. Sift flour and cocoa and stir to mix well.
2. Sprinkle the walnuts over and add the white chocolate into the batter. Pour the batter into the pan and cook for 20 minutes in the

oven at 350 F on Bake function. Serve chilled with raspberry syrup and ice cream.

91. Eggs In Avocado Cups

Servings: 2
Cooking Time: 10 Minutes
Ingredients:
- 1 avocado, halved and pitted
- 2 large eggs
- Salt and ground black pepper, as required
- 2 cooked bacon slices, crumbled

Directions:
1. Carefully, scoop out about 2 teaspoons of flesh from each avocado half.
2. Crack 1 egg in each avocado half and sprinkle with salt and black pepper.
3. Press "Power Button" of Air Fry Oven and turn the dial to select the "Air Roast" mode.
4. Press the Time button and again turn the dial to set the cooking time to 10 minutes.
5. Now push the Temp button and rotate the dial to set the temperature at 375 degrees F.
6. Press "Start/Pause" button to start.
7. When the unit beeps to show that it is preheated, open the lid and line the "Sheet Pan" with a lightly, grease piece of foil Arrange avocado halves into the "Sheet Pan" and insert in the oven.
8. Top each avocado half with bacon pieces and serve.
- **Nutrition Info:** Calories: 300 Cal Total Fat: 26.6 g Saturated Fat: 6.4 g Cholesterol: 190 mg Sodium: 229 mg Total Carbs: 9 g Fiber: 6.7 g Sugar: 0.9 g Protein: 9.7 g

92. Maple Walnut Pancake

Servings:4
Cooking Time: 20 Minutes
Ingredients:
- 3 tablespoons melted butter, divided
- 1 cup flour
- 2 tablespoons sugar
- 1½ teaspoons baking powder
- ¼ teaspoon salt
- 1 egg, beaten
- ¾ cup milk
- 1 teaspoon pure vanilla extract
- ½ cup roughly chopped walnuts
- Maple syrup or fresh sliced fruit, for serving

Directions:
1. Grease the baking pan with 1 tablespoon of melted butter.
2. Mix together the flour, sugar, baking powder, and salt in a medium bowl. Add the beaten egg, milk, the remaining 2 tablespoons of melted butter, and vanilla and stir until the batter is sticky but slightly lumpy.

3. Slowly pour the batter into the greased baking pan and scatter with the walnuts.
4. Slide the baking pan into Rack Position 1, select Convection Bake, set temperature to 330ºF (166ºC) and set time to 20 minutes.
5. When cooked, the pancake should be golden brown and cooked through.
6. Let the pancake rest for 5 minutes and serve topped with the maple syrup or fresh fruit, if desired.

93. Eggs In A Hole

Servings: 1
Cooking Time: 7 Minutes
Ingredients:
- 2 eggs
- 2 slices of bread
- 2 tsp butter
- Pepper and salt to taste

Directions:
1. Using a jar punch two holes in the middle of your bread slices. This is the area where you will place your eggs.
2. Preheat your fryer to 330-degree Fahrenheit for about 5 minutes. Spread a tablespoon of butter into the pan and then add bread from the slices.
3. Crack the eggs and place them at the center of the bread slices and lightly season them with salt and pepper.
4. Take out your slices and rebutter the pan with the remaining butter and fry the other part for 3 minutes.
5. Serve while hot.
- **Nutrition Info:** Calories 787 Fat 51g, Carbohydrates 60g, Proteins 22g.

94. Sweet Potato Chickpeas Hash

Servings: 4
Cooking Time: 30 Minutes
Ingredients:
- 14.5 oz can chickpeas, drained
- 1 tsp paprika
- 1 tsp garlic powder
- 1 sweet potato, peeled and cubed
- 1 tbsp olive oil
- 1 bell pepper, chopped
- 1 onion, diced
- 1/2 tsp ground black pepper
- 1 tsp salt

Directions:
1. Fit the oven with the rack in position
2. Spread sweet potato, chickpeas, bell pepper, and onion in a baking pan.
3. Drizzle with oil and season with paprika, garlic powder, pepper, and salt. Stir well.
4. Set to bake at 390 F for 35 minutes, after 5 minutes, place the baking pan in the oven.

- **Nutrition Info:** Calories 203 Fat 4.9 g Carbohydrates 34.9 g Sugar 4.7 g Protein 6.5 g Cholesterol 0 mg

95. Cheesy Artichoke-mushroom Frittata

Servings:6
Cooking Time: 15 Minutes
Ingredients:
- 8 eggs
- ½ teaspoon kosher salt
- ¼ cup whole milk
- ¾ cup shredded Mozzarella cheese, divided
- 2 tablespoons unsalted butter, melted
- 1 cup coarsely chopped artichoke hearts
- ¼ cup chopped onion
- ½ cup mushrooms
- ¼ cup grated Parmesan cheese
- ¼ teaspoon freshly ground black pepper

Directions:
1. In a medium bowl, whisk together the eggs and salt. Let rest for a minute or two, then pour in the milk and whisk again. Stir in ½ cup of the Mozzarella cheese.
2. Grease the baking pan with the butter. Stir in the artichoke hearts and onion and toss to coat with the butter.
3. Slide the baking pan into Rack Position 2, select Roast, set temperature to 375ºF (190ºC) and set time to 12 minutes.
4. After 5 minutes, remove from the oven. Spread the mushrooms over the vegetables. Pour the egg mixture on top. Stir gently just to distribute the vegetables evenly. Return the pan to the oven and continue cooking for 5 to 7 minutes, or until the edges are set. The center will still be quite liquid.
5. Select Convection Broil, set temperature to Low and set time to 3 minutes. After 1 minute, remove the pan and sprinkle the remaining ¼ cup of the Mozzarella and Parmesan cheese over the frittata. Return the pan to the oven and continue cooking for 2 minutes.
6. When cooking is complete, the cheese should be melted with the top completely set but not browned. Sprinkle the black pepper on top and serve.

96. Olives And Kale

Servings: 4
Cooking Time: 30 Minutes
Ingredients:
- 4 eggs; whisked
- 1 cup kale; chopped.
- ½ cup black olives, pitted and sliced
- 2 tbsp. cheddar; grated
- Cooking spray
- A pinch of salt and black pepper

Directions:

1. Take a bowl and mix the eggs with the rest of the ingredients except the cooking spray and whisk well.
2. Now, take a pan that fits in your air fryer and grease it with the cooking spray, pour the olives mixture inside, spread
3. Put the pan into the machine and cook at 360°F for 20 minutes. Serve for breakfast hot.
- **Nutrition Info:** Calories: 220; Fat: 13g; Fiber: 4g; Carbs: 6g; Protein: 12g

97. Apple-cinnamon Empanadas

Servings: 2-4
Cooking Time: 30 Minutes
Ingredients:
- 2-3 baking apples, peeled & diced
- 2 tsp.s of cinnamon
- 1/4 cup white sugar
- 1 tablespoon brown sugar
- 1 tablespoon of water
- 1/2 tablespoon cornstarch
- ¼ tsp. of vanilla extract
- 2 tablespoons of margarine or margarine
- 4 pre-made empanada dough shells (Goya)

Directions:
1. In a bowl, add together white sugar, brown sugar, cornstarch and cinnamon; set aside. Put the diced apples in a pot and place on a stovetop.
2. Add the combined dry ingredients to the apples, then add the water, vanilla extract, and margarine; stirring well to mix.
3. Cover pot and cook on high heat. Once it starts boiling, lower heat and simmer, until the apples are soft. Remove from the heat and cool.
4. Lay the empanada shells on a clean counter. Ladle the apple mixture into each of the shells, being careful to prevent spillage over the edges. Fold shells to fully cover apple mixture, seal edges with water, pressing down to secure with a fork.
5. Cover the air fryer basket with tin foil but leave the edges uncovered so that air can circulate through the basket. Place the empanadas shells in the foil lined air fryer basket, set temperature at 350°F and timer for 15 minutes.
6. Halfway through, slide the frying basket out and flip the empanadas using a spatula. Remove when golden, and serve directly from the basket onto plates.
- **Nutrition Info:** Calories 113 Fat 8.2 g Carbohydrates 0.3 g Sugar 0.2 g Protein 5.4 g Cholesterol 18 mg

98. Parsley Onion & Feta Tart

Servings: 4

Cooking Time: 30 Minutes
Ingredients:
- 3 ½ pounds Feta cheese
- Black pepper to taste
- 1 whole onion, chopped
- 2 tbsp parsley, chopped
- 1 egg yolk
- 5 sheets frozen filo pastry

Directions:
1. Cut each of the 5 filo sheets into three equal-sized strips. Cover the strips with oil. In a bowl, mix onion, pepper, feta, salt, egg yolk, and parsley.
2. Make triangles using the cut strips and add a little bit of the feta mixture on top of each triangle. Place the triangles in a greased baking sheet and cook for 5 minutes at 400 F on Bake function. Serve sprinkled with green onions.

99. Broccoli Asparagus Frittata

Servings: 6
Cooking Time: 20 Minutes
Ingredients:
- 6 eggs
- 1/2 cup onion, diced & sautéed
- 1 cup asparagus, chopped & sautéed
- 1 cup broccoli, chopped & sautéed
- 3 bacon slices, cooked & chopped
- 1/3 cup parmesan cheese, grated
- 1/2 cup milk
- 1/2 tsp pepper
- 1 tsp salt

Directions:
1. Fit the oven with the rack in position
2. In a mixing bowl, whisk eggs with milk, cheese, pepper, and salt.
3. Add onion, asparagus, broccoli, and bacon and stir well.
4. Pour egg mixture into the greased baking dish.
5. Set to bake at 350 F for 25 minutes. After 5 minutes place the baking dish in the preheated oven.
6. Serve and enjoy.
- **Nutrition Info:** Calories 154 Fat 9.9 g Carbohydrates 4.6 g Sugar 2.4 g Protein 12.4 g Cholesterol 179 mg

100. Cauliflower Hash Brown

Servings: 4
Cooking Time: 10 Minutes
Ingredients:
- 2 cups cauliflower, finely grated, soaked and drained
- 2 tablespoons xanthan gum
- Salt, to taste
- Pepper powder, to taste
- 2 teaspoons chili flakes

- 1 teaspoon garlic
- 1 teaspoon onion powder
- 2 teaspoons vegetable oil

Directions:
1. Preheat the Air fryer to 300-degree F and grease an Air fryer basket with oil.
2. Heat vegetable oil in a nonstick pan and add cauliflower.
3. Sauté for about 4 minutes and dish out the cauliflower in a plate.
4. Mix the cauliflower with xanthum gum, salt, chili flakes, garlic and onion powder.
5. Mix well and refrigerate the hash for about 20 minutes.
6. Place the hash in the Air fryer basket and cook for about 10 minutes.
7. Flip the hash after cooking halfway through and dish out to serve warm.
- **Nutrition Info:** Calories: 291, Fat: 2.8g, Carbs: 6.5g, Sugar: 4.5g, Protein: 6.6g, Sodium: 62mg

101.Air Fried Crispy Spring Rolls

Servings:4
Cooking Time: 18 Minutes
Ingredients:
- 4 spring roll wrappers
- ½ cup cooked vermicelli noodles
- 1 teaspoon sesame oil
- 1 tablespoon freshly minced ginger
- 1 tablespoon soy sauce
- 1 clove garlic, minced
- ½ red bell pepper, deseeded and chopped
- ½ cup chopped carrot
- ½ cup chopped mushrooms
- ¼ cup chopped scallions
- Cooking spray

Directions:
1. Spritz the air fryer basket with cooking spray and set aside.
2. Heat the sesame oil in a saucepan on medium heat. Sauté the ginger and garlic in the sesame oil for 1 minute, or until fragrant. Add soy sauce, red bell pepper, carrot, mushrooms and scallions. Sauté for 5 minutes or until the vegetables become tender. Mix in vermicelli noodles. Turn off the heat and remove them from the saucepan. Allow to cool for 10 minutes.
3. Lay out one spring roll wrapper with a corner pointed toward you. Scoop the noodle mixture on spring roll wrapper and fold corner up over the mixture. Fold left and right corners toward the center and continue to roll to make firmly sealed rolls.
4. Arrange the spring rolls in the pan and spritz with cooking spray.
5. Put the air fryer basket on the baking pan and slide into Rack Position 2, select Air Fry,

set temperature to 340ºF (171ºC) and set time to 12 minutes.
6. Flip the spring rolls halfway through the cooking time.
7. When done, the spring rolls will be golden brown and crispy.
8. Serve warm.

102.Cheesy Breakfast Casserole

Servings:4
Cooking Time: 16 Minutes
Ingredients:
- 6 slices bacon
- 6 eggs
- Salt and pepper, to taste
- Cooking spray
- ½ cup chopped green bell pepper
- ½ cup chopped onion
- ¾ cup shredded Cheddar cheese

Directions:
1. Place the bacon in a skillet over medium-high heat and cook each side for about 4 minutes until evenly crisp. Remove from the heat to a paper towel-lined plate to drain. Crumble it into small pieces and set aside.
2. Whisk the eggs with the salt and pepper in a medium bowl.
3. Spritz the baking pan with cooking spray.
4. Place the whisked eggs, crumbled bacon, green bell pepper, and onion in the prepared pan.
5. Slide the baking pan into Rack Position 1, select Convection Bake, set temperature to 400ºF (205ºC) and set time to 8 minutes.
6. After 6 minutes, remove the pan from the oven. Scatter the Cheddar cheese all over. Return the pan to the oven and continue to cook for another 2 minutes.
7. When cooking is complete, let sit for 5 minutes and serve on plates.

103.Apple Fritter Loaf

Servings: 10
Cooking Time: 1 Hour
Ingredients:
- Butter flavored cooking spray
- 1/3 cup brown sugar, packed
- 1 tsp. cinnamon, divided
- 1 ½ cups apples, chopped
- 2/3 cup + 1 tsp. sugar, divided
- ½ cup + ½ tbsp. butter, soft, divided
- 2 eggs
- 2 ¼ tsp. vanilla, divided
- 1 ½ cups flour
- 2 tsp baking powder
- ¼ tsp salt
- ½ cup + 2 tbsp. milk
- 1/2 cup powdered sugar

Directions:

1. Place rack in position 1 of the oven. Spray an 8-inch loaf pan with cooking spray.
2. In a small bowl, combine brown sugar and ½ teaspoon cinnamon.
3. Place apples in a medium bowl and sprinkle with remaining cinnamon and 1 teaspoon sugar, toss to coat.
4. In a large bowl, beat remaining sugar and butter until smooth.
5. Beat in eggs and 2 teaspoons vanilla until combined. Stir in flour, baking powder, and salt until combined.
6. Add ½ cup milk and beat until smooth. Pour half the batter in the prepared pan. Add half the apples then remaining batter. Add the remaining apples over the top, pressing lightly. Sprinkle brown sugar mixture over the apples.
7. Set oven to convection bake at 325°F for 5 minutes. Once timer goes, off place bread on the rack and set timer to 1 hour. Bread is done when it passes the toothpick test.
8. Let cool in pan 10 minutes, then invert onto wire rack to cool.
9. In a small bowl, whisk together powdered sugar and butter until smooth. Whisk in remaining milk and vanilla and drizzle over cooled bread.
- **Nutrition Info:** Calories 418, Total Fat 14g, Saturated Fat 8g, Total Carbs 44g, Net Carbs 43g, Protein 4g, Sugar 28g, Fiber 1g, Sodium 85mg, Potassium 190mg, Phosphorus 128mg

104. Creamy Bacon & Egg Wraps With Spicy Salsa

Servings: 3
Cooking Time: 15 Minutes
Ingredients:
- 3 tortillas
- 2 previously scrambled eggs
- 3 slices bacon, cut into strips
- 3 tbsp salsa
- 3 tbsp cream cheese, divided
- 1 cup grated pepper Jack cheese

Directions:
1. Preheat on Air Fry to 390 F. Spread cream cheese onto tortillas. Divide the eggs and bacon between the tortillas. Top with salsa. Sprinkle with cheese. Roll up the tortillas. Place in a greased baking pan and cook for 10 minutes. Serve.

105. Creamy Mushroom And Spinach Omelet

Servings: 2
Cooking Time: 10 Minutes
Ingredients:
- 4 eggs, lightly beaten
- 2 tbsp heavy cream
- 2 cups spinach, chopped
- 1 cup mushrooms, chopped
- 3 oz feta cheese, crumbled
- 1 tbsp fresh parsley, chopped
- Salt and black pepper to taste

Directions:
1. Spray a baking pan with cooking spray. In a bowl, whisk eggs and heavy cream until combined. Stir in spinach, mushrooms, feta, salt, and pepper.
2. Pour into the basket tray and cook in your for 6-10 minutes at 350 F on Bake function until golden and set. Sprinkle with parsley, cut into wedges, and serve.

106. Creamy Potato Gratin With Nutmeg

Servings: 4
Cooking Time: 30 Minutes
Ingredients:
- 1 lb potatoes, peeled and sliced
- ½ cup sour cream
- ½ cup mozzarella cheese, grated
- ½ cup milk
- ½ tsp nutmeg
- Salt and black pepper to taste

Directions:
1. Preheat on Bake function to 390 F. In a bowl, combine sour cream, milk, pepper, salt, and nutmeg. Place the potato slices in the bowl with the milk mixture and stir to coat well.
2. Transfer the mixture to a baking dish and press Start. Cook for 20 minutes, then sprinkle grated cheese on top and cook for 5 more minutes. Serve warm.

107. Green Cottage Omelet

Servings: 1
Cooking Time: 20 Minutes
Ingredients:
- 3 eggs
- 3 tbsp cottage cheese
- 3 tbsp kale, chopped
- ½ tbsp fresh parsley, chopped
- Salt and black pepper to taste
- 1 tsp olive oil

Directions:
1. Beat the eggs with a pinch of salt and black pepper in a bowl. Stir in the rest of the ingredients. Drizzle a baking pan with olive oil. Pour the pan into the oven and press Start. Cook for 15 minutes on Bake function at 360 F until slightly golden and set. Serve warm.

108. Easy Cheese Egg Casserole

Servings: 10
Cooking Time: 40 Minutes

Ingredients:
- 12 eggs
- 8 oz cheddar cheese, shredded
- 1/3 cup milk
- 1/4 tsp pepper
- 1 tsp salt

Directions:
1. Fit the oven with the rack in position
2. Spray 9*13-inch casserole dish with cooking spray and set aside.
3. In a bowl, whisk eggs with milk, pepper, and salt.
4. Add shredded cheese and stir well.
5. Pour egg mixture into the prepared casserole dish.
6. Set to bake at 350 F for 45 minutes. After 5 minutes place the casserole dish in the preheated oven.
7. Serve and enjoy.
- **Nutrition Info:** Calories 171 Fat 12.9 g Carbohydrates 1.1 g Sugar 0.9 g Protein 12.6 g Cholesterol 221 mg

109.Avocado Cauliflower Toast

Servings: 2
Cooking Time: 30 Minutes
Ingredients:
- 1: 12-oz.steamer bag cauliflower
- ½ cup shredded mozzarella cheese
- 1 large egg.
- 1 ripe medium avocado
- ½ tsp. garlic powder.
- ¼ tsp. ground black pepper

Directions:
1. Cook cauliflower according to package instructions. Remove from bag and place into cheesecloth or clean towel to remove excess moisture.
2. Place cauliflower into a large bowl and mix in egg and mozzarella. Cut a piece of parchment to fit your air fryer basket
3. Separate the cauliflower mixture into two and place it on the parchment in two mounds. Press out the cauliflower mounds into a ¼-inch-thick rectangle. Place the parchment into the air fryer basket.
4. Adjust the temperature to 400 Degrees F and set the timer for 8 minutes
5. Flip the cauliflower halfway through the cooking time
6. When the timer beeps, remove the parchment and allow the cauliflower to cool 5 minutes.
7. Cut open the avocado and remove the pit. Scoop out the inside, place it in a medium bowl and mash it with garlic powder and pepper. Spread onto the cauliflower.
- **Nutrition Info:** Calories: 278; Protein: 14.1g; Fiber: 8.2g; Fat: 15.6g; Carbs: 15.9g

110.Cinnamon French Toasts

Servings: 2
Cooking Time: 5 Minutes
Ingredients:
- 2 eggs
- ¼ cup whole milk
- 3 tablespoons sugar
- 2 teaspoons olive oil
- 1/8 teaspoon vanilla extract
- 1/8 teaspoon ground cinnamon
- 4 bread slices

Directions:
1. In a large bowl, mix together all the ingredients except bread slices.
2. Coat the bread slices with egg mixture evenly.
3. Press "Power Button" of Air Fry Oven and turn the dial to select the "Air Fry" mode.
4. Press the Time button and again turn the dial to set the cooking time to 6 minutes.
5. Now push the Temp button and rotate the dial to set the temperature at 390 degrees F.
6. Press "Start/Pause" button to start.
7. When the unit beeps to show that it is preheated, open the lid and lightly, grease the sheet pan.
8. Arrange the bread slices into "Air Fry Basket" and insert in the oven.
9. Flip the bread slices once halfway through.
10. Serve warm.
- **Nutrition Info:** Calories: 238 Cal Total Fat: 10.6 g Saturated Fat: 2.7 g Cholesterol: 167 mg Sodium: 122 mg Total Carbs: 20.8 g Fiber: 0.5 g Sugar: 0.9 g Protein: 7.9 g

111.Moist Orange Bread Loaf

Servings: 10
Cooking Time: 50 Minutes
Ingredients:
- 4 eggs
- 4 oz butter, softened
- 1 cup of orange juice
- 1 orange zest, grated
- 1 cup of sugar
- 2 tsp baking powder
- 2 cups all-purpose flour
- 1 tsp vanilla

Directions:
1. Fit the oven with the rack in position
2. In a large bowl, whisk eggs and sugar until creamy.
3. Whisk in vanilla, butter, orange juice, and orange zest.
4. Add flour and baking powder and mix until combined.
5. Pour batter into the greased 9*5-inch loaf pan.
6. Set to bake at 350 F for 55 minutes, after 5 minutes, place the loaf pan in the oven.

7. Slice and serve.
- **Nutrition Info:** Calories 286 Fat 11.3 g Carbohydrates 42.5 g Sugar 22.4 g Protein 5.1 gCholesterol 90 mg

112.Middle Eastern Shakshuka With Smoked Paprika

Servings:x
Cooking Time:x
Ingredients:
- 2 Tbsp olive oil
- ½ yellow onion, diced
- 1 small serrano or jalapeno chili, seeds removed, diced
- 1 tsp cumin
- 1 tsp paprika
- ½ tsp smoked paprika
- ¼ tsp coriander
- 2 eggs
- 1 can chopped tomatoes
- ½ green pepper, diced
- Salt and pepper, to taste
- Chopped parsley or cilantro

Directions:
1. Preheat oven over medium heat.
2. Heat olive oil and saute onion until softened.
3. Add tomatoes, green pepper and chili. Cook for 4-5 minutes.
4. Add seasonings and cook for several minutes until liquid slightly reduces.
5. Make two indentations in mixture and crack eggs into them. Cover and
6. cook until eggs are done.
7. Sprinkle with salt, pepper, parsley and cilantro and serve while bubbly and hot.

113.Breakfast Tater Tot Casserole

Servings:4
Cooking Time: 17 To 18 Minutes
Ingredients:
- 4 eggs
- 1 cup milk
- Salt and pepper, to taste
- 12 ounces (340 g) ground chicken sausage
- 1 pound (454 g) frozen tater tots, thawed
- ¾ cup grated Cheddar cheese
- Cooking spray

Directions:
1. Whisk together the eggs and milk in a medium bowl. Season with salt and pepper to taste and stir until mixed. Set aside.
2. Place a skillet over medium-high heat and spritz with cooking spray. Place the ground sausage in the skillet and break it into smaller pieces with a spatula or spoon. Cook for 3 to 4 minutes until the sausage starts to brown, stirring occasionally. Remove from heat and set aside.
3. Coat the baking pan with cooking spray. Arrange the tater tots in the baking pan.
4. Slide the baking pan into Rack Position 1, select Convection Bake, set temperature to 400ºF (205ºC) and set time to 14 minutes.
5. After 6 minutes, remove the pan from the oven. Stir the tater tots and add the egg mixture and cooked sausage. Return the pan to the oven and continue cooking.
6. After 6 minutes, remove the pan from the oven. Scatter the cheese on top of the tater tots. Return the pan to the oven and continue to cook for another 2 minutes.
7. When done, the cheese should be bubbly and melted.
8. Let the mixture cool for 5 minutes and serve warm.

114.Apple Butter Pancake

Servings:x
Cooking Time:x
Ingredients:
- 1 tsp cinnamon
- ½ tsp ginger
- 3 large eggs, room temperature
- ¾ cup whole milk
- ¾ cup all-purpose flour
- 1 tsp almond extract
- ¼ tsp salt
- 2 Granny Smith apples, peeled, cored and sliced
- 1 Tbsp sugar
- 4 Tbsp butter, divided
- 2 tsp light brown sugar

Directions:
1. Preheat oven to 400°F.
2. Whisk together eggs, milk, flour, extract and salt.
3. Place sliced apples in a bowl with sugar, cinnamon and ginger.
4. Melt 2 Tbsp butter in heated oven.
5. Sprinkle brown sugar inside pot.
6. Add apples and cook until apples have softened. Transfer to plate.
7. Wipe out oven and melt remaining 2 Tbsp butter.
8. When pot is very hot, add apples and pour batter. Bake for about 13-15 minutes.

115.Lamb And Feta Hamburgers

Servings: 4 Burgers
Cooking Time: 16 Minutes
Ingredients:
- 1½ pounds (680 g) ground lamb
- ¼ cup crumbled feta
- 1½ teaspoons tomato paste
- 1½ teaspoons minced garlic
- 1 teaspoon ground dried ginger
- 1 teaspoon ground coriander

- ¼ teaspoon salt
- ¼ teaspoon cayenne pepper
- 4 kaiser rolls or hamburger buns, split open lengthwise, warmed
- Cooking spray

Directions:
1. Spritz the air fryer basket with cooking spray.
2. Combine all the ingredients, except for the buns, in a large bowl. Coarsely stir to mix well.
3. Shape the mixture into four balls, then pound the balls into four 5-inch diameter patties.
4. Arrange the patties in the pan and spritz with cooking spray.
5. Put the air fryer basket on the baking pan and slide into Rack Position 2, select Air Fry, set temperature to 375ºF (190ºC) and set time to 16 minutes.
6. Flip the patties halfway through the cooking time.
7. When cooking is complete, the patties should be well browned.
8. Assemble the buns with patties to make the burgers and serve immediately.

116.Whole-wheat Blueberry Scones

Servings:14
Cooking Time: 20 Minutes
Ingredients:
- ½ cup low-fat buttermilk
- ¾ cup orange juice
- Zest of 1 orange
- 2¼ cups whole-wheat pastry flour
- $^1/_3$ cup agave nectar
- ¼ cup canola oil
- 1 teaspoon baking soda
- 1 teaspoon cream of tartar
- 1 cup fresh blueberries

Directions:
1. In a small bowl, stir together the buttermilk, orange juice and orange zest.
2. In a large bowl, whisk together the flour, agave nectar, canola oil, baking soda and cream of tartar.
3. Add the buttermilk mixture and blueberries to the bowl with the flour mixture. Mix gently by hand until well combined.
4. Transfer the batter onto a lightly floured baking pan. Pat into a circle about ¾ inch thick and 8 inches across. Use a knife to cut the circle into 14 wedges, cutting almost all the way through.
5. Slide the baking pan into Rack Position 1, select Convection Bake, set temperature to 375ºF (190ºC) and set time to 20 minutes.

6. When cooking is complete, remove the pan and check the scones. They should be lightly browned.
7. Let rest for 5 minutes and cut completely through the wedges before serving.

117.Fluffy Frittata With Bell Pepper

Servings:x
Cooking Time:x
Ingredients:
- 8 eggs
- 2 Tbsp whole milk
- 1 Tbsp butter
- Coarse salt, freshly ground pepper, to taste
- ½ zucchini diced
- 1 bell Pepper seeded and diced

Directions:
1. Preheat oven to 400°F.
2. Heat oven over medium heat. Add butter.
3. In a bowl, add remaining ingredients. Pour mixture into oven.
4. When eggs are half set and edges begin to pull away, place frittata in
5. the oven and bake for about 10 minutes, or until center is no longer jiggly.
6. Cut into wedges or slide out onto serving plate.

118.Chocolate Banana Bread

Servings:4
Cooking Time: 30 Minutes
Ingredients:
- ¼ cup cocoa powder
- 6 tablespoons plus 2 teaspoons all-purpose flour, divided
- ½ teaspoon kosher salt
- ¼ teaspoon baking soda
- 1½ ripe bananas
- 1 large egg, whisked
- ¼ cup vegetable oil
- ½ cup sugar
- 3 tablespoons buttermilk or plain yogurt (not Greek)
- ½ teaspoon vanilla extract
- 6 tablespoons chopped white chocolate
- 6 tablespoons chopped walnuts

Directions:
1. Mix together the cocoa powder, 6 tablespoons of the flour, salt, and baking soda in a medium bowl.
2. Mash the bananas with a fork in another medium bowl until smooth. Fold in the egg, oil, sugar, buttermilk, and vanilla, and whisk until thoroughly combined. Add the wet mixture to the dry mixture and stir until well incorporated.
3. Combine the white chocolate, walnuts, and the remaining 2 tablespoons of flour in a third bowl and toss to coat. Add this

mixture to the batter and stir until well incorporated. Pour the batter into the baking pan and smooth the top with a spatula.
4. Slide the baking pan into Rack Position 1, select Convection Bake, set temperature to 310ºF (154ºC) and set time to 30 minutes.
5. When done, a toothpick inserted into the center of the bread should come out clean.
6. Remove from the oven and allow to cool on a wire rack for 10 minutes before serving.

119.Perfect Chicken Casserole

Servings: 8
Cooking Time: 30 Minutes
Ingredients:
- 8 eggs
- 1 cup mozzarella cheese, shredded
- 8 oz can crescent rolls
- 1 1/2 cups basil pesto
- 3/4 lb chicken breasts, cooked & shredded
- Pepper
- Salt

Directions:
1. Fit the oven with the rack in position
2. Spray a 9*13-inch baking dish with cooking spray and set aside.
3. In a bowl, mix shredded chicken and pesto and set aside.
4. In a separate bowl, eggs, pepper, and salt.
5. Roll out the crescent roll into the prepared baking dish. Top with shredded chicken.
6. Pour egg mixture over chicken and top with shredded mozzarella cheese.
7. Set to bake at 350 F for 35 minutes. After 5 minutes place the baking dish in the preheated oven.
8. Serve and enjoy.
- **Nutrition Info:** Calories 266 Fat 14.3 g Carbohydrates 11.7 g Sugar 2.4 g Protein 21 g Cholesterol 203 mg

120.Smart Oven Breakfast Sandwich

Servings:x
Cooking Time:x
Ingredients:
- 1 large egg
- 1 slice cheese
- Salt and pepper, to taste
- 1 English muffin, split

Directions:
1. Coat a small 4-inch round metal pan with cooking oil.
2. Crack egg into prepared pan, poke yolk with a fork or toothpick, and season with salt and pepper.
3. Place pan and split English muffin in the center of the cooking rack in your toaster oven.

4. Select the TOAST setting on DARK and toast for one cycle.
5. Check the egg and muffin and remove if ready. If further cooking is needed, set for another cycle of toasting until desired level of doneness is achieved.
6. Layer egg and cheese inside English muffin and enjoy.

121.Pumpkin And Yogurt Bread

Servings: 4
Cooking Time: 15 Minutes
Ingredients:
- 2 large eggs
- 8 tablespoons pumpkin puree
- 6 tablespoons banana flour
- 4 tablespoons plain Greek yogurt
- 6 tablespoons oats
- 4 tablespoons honey
- 2 tablespoons vanilla essence
- Pinch of ground nutmeg

Directions:
1. Preheat the Air fryer to 360 ºF and grease a loaf pan.
2. Mix together all the ingredients except oats in a bowl and beat with the hand mixer until smooth.
3. Add oats and mix until well combined.
4. Transfer the mixture into the prepared loaf pan and place in the Air fryer.
5. Cook for about 15 minutes and remove from the Air fryer.
6. Place onto a wire rack to cool and cut the bread into desired size slices to serve.
- **Nutrition Info:** Calories: 212 Cal Total Fat: 3.4 g Saturated Fat: 0 g Cholesterol: 0 mg Sodium: 49 mg Total Carbs: 36 g Fiber: 0 g Sugar: 20.5 g Protein: 6.6 g

122.Zucchini And Carrot Pudding

Servings: 4
Cooking Time: 15 Minutes
Ingredients:
- 1 cup carrots, shredded
- 1 cup zucchinis, grated
- 1 cup heavy cream
- 1 cup wild rice
- 2 cups coconut milk
- 1 teaspoon cardamom, ground
- 2 teaspoons sugar
- Cooking spray

Directions:
1. Spray your air fryer with cooking spray, add the carrots, zucchinis and the other ingredients, toss, cover and cook at 365 degrees F for 15 minutes.
2. Divide the pudding into bowls and serve for breakfast.

- **Nutrition Info:** calories 172, fat 7, fiber 4, carbs 14, protein 5

123.Avocado And Zucchini Mix

Servings: 4
Cooking Time: 15 Minutes
Ingredients:
- 2 avocados, peeled, pitted and roughly cubed
- 2 zucchinis, roughly cubed
- 1 tablespoon olive oil
- 2 spring onions, chopped
- 8 eggs, whisked
- 1 teaspoon sweet paprika
- A pinch of salt and black pepper
- 1 tablespoon dill, chopped

Directions:
1. Heat up the air fryer with the oil at 350 degrees F, add the zucchinis and the spring onions and cook for 2 minutes.
2. Add the avocados and the other ingredients, cook the mix for 13 minutes more, divide into bowls and serve.

- **Nutrition Info:** calories 232, fat 12, fiber 2, carbs 10, protein 5

124.Easy Cheesy Breakfast Casserole

Servings: 8
Cooking Time: 30 Minutes
Ingredients:
- 6 eggs, lightly beaten
- 8 oz can crescent rolls
- 2 cups cheddar cheese, shredded
- 1 lb breakfast sausage, cooked

Directions:
1. Fit the oven with the rack in position
2. Spray a 9*13-inch baking dish with cooking spray and set aside.
3. Spread crescent rolls in the bottom of the prepared baking dish and top with sausage, egg, and cheese.
4. Set to bake at 350 F for 35 minutes. After 5 minutes place the baking dish in the preheated oven.
5. Serve and enjoy.
- **Nutrition Info:** Calories 465 Fat 34.6 g Carbohydrates 11.8 g Sugar 2.4 g Protein 24.2 g Cholesterol 200 mg

LUNCH RECIPES

125. Chicken And Celery Stew

Servings: 6
Cooking Time: 12 Minutes
Ingredients:
- 1 lb. chicken breasts, skinless; boneless and cubed
- 4 celery stalks; chopped.
- ½ cup coconut cream
- 2 red bell peppers; chopped.
- 2 tsp. garlic; minced
- 1 tbsp. butter, soft
- Salt and black pepper to taste.

Directions:
1. Grease a baking dish that fits your air fryer with the butter, add all the ingredients in the pan and toss them.
2. Introduce the dish in the fryer, cook at 360°F for 30 minutes, divide into bowls and serve
- **Nutrition Info:** Calories: 246; Fat: 12g; Fiber: 2g; Carbs: 6g; Protein: 12g

126. Barbecue Air Fried Chicken

Servings: 10
Cooking Time: 26 Minutes
Ingredients:
- 1 teaspoon Liquid Smoke
- 2 cloves Fresh Garlic smashed
- 1/2 cup Apple Cider Vinegar
- 3 pounds Chuck Roast well-marbled with intramuscular fat
- 1 Tablespoon Kosher Salt
- 1 Tablespoon Freshly Ground Black Pepper
- 2 teaspoons Garlic Powder
- 1.5 cups Barbecue Sauce
- 1/4 cup Light Brown Sugar + more for sprinkling
- 2 Tablespoons Honey optional and in place of 2 TBL sugar

Directions:
1. Add meat to the Instant Pot Duo Crisp Air Fryer Basket, spreading out the meat.
2. Select the option Air Fry.
3. Close the Air Fryer lid and cook at 300 degrees F for 8 minutes. Pause the Air Fryer and flip meat over after 4 minutes.
4. Remove the lid and baste with more barbecue sauce and sprinkle with a little brown sugar.
5. Again Close the Air Fryer lid and set the temperature at 400°F for 9 minutes. Watch meat though the lid and flip it over after 5 minutes.
- **Nutrition Info:** Calories 360, Total Fat 16g, Total Carbs 27g, Protein 27g

127. Ricotta Toasts With Salmon

Servings: 2
Cooking Time: 4 Minutes
Ingredients:
- 4 bread slices
- 1 garlic clove, minced
- 8 oz. ricotta cheese
- 1 teaspoon lemon zest
- Freshly ground black pepper, to taste
- 4 oz. smoked salmon

Directions:
1. In a food processor, add the garlic, ricotta, lemon zest and black pepper and pulse until smooth.
2. Spread ricotta mixture over each bread slices evenly.
3. Press "Power Button" of Air Fry Oven and turn the dial to select the "Air Fry" mode.
4. Press the Time button and again turn the dial to set the cooking time to 4 minutes.
5. Now push the Temp button and rotate the dial to set the temperature at 355 degrees F.
6. Press "Start/Pause" button to start.
7. When the unit beeps to show that it is preheated, open the lid and lightly, grease the sheet pan.
8. Arrange the bread slices into "Air Fry Basket" and insert in the oven.
9. Top with salmon and serve.
- **Nutrition Info:** Calories: 274 Cal Total Fat: 12 g Saturated Fat: 6.3 g Cholesterol: 48 mg Sodium: 1300 mg Total Carbs: 15.7 g Fiber: 0.5 g Sugar: 1.2 g Protein: 24.8 g

128. Delightful Turkey Wings

Servings: 4
Cooking Time: 26 Minutes
Ingredients:
- 2 pounds turkey wings
- 4 tablespoons chicken rub
- 3 tablespoons olive oil

Directions:
1. Preheat the Air fryer to 380 degree F and grease an Air fryer basket.
2. Mix the turkey wings, chicken rub, and olive oil in a bowl until well combined.
3. Arrange the turkey wings into the Air fryer basket and cook for about 26 minutes, flipping once in between.
4. Dish out the turkey wings in a platter and serve hot.
- **Nutrition Info:** Calories: 204, Fat: 15.5g, Carbohydrates: 3g, Sugar: 0g, Protein: 12g, Sodium: 465mg

129.Parmigiano Reggiano And Prosciutto Toasts With Balsamic Glaze

Servings: 8
Cooking Time: 15 Minutes
Ingredients:
- 3 ounces thinly sliced prosciutto, cut crosswise into 1/4-inch-wide strips
- 1 (3-ounce) piece Parmigiano Reggiano cheese
- 1/2 cup balsamic vinegar
- 1 medium red onion, thinly sliced
- 1 loaf ciabatta, cut into 3/4-inch-thick slices
- 1 tablespoon extra-virgin olive oil
- 1 clove garlic
- Black pepper to taste

Directions:
1. Preheat toaster oven to 350°F.
2. Place onion in a bowl of cold water and let sit for 10 minutes.
3. Bring vinegar to a boil, then reduce heat and simmer for 5 minutes.
4. Remove from heat completely and set aside to allow the vinegar to thicken.
5. Drain the onion.
6. Brush the tops of each bun with oil, rub with garlic, and sprinkle with pepper.
7. Use a vegetable peeler to make large curls of Parmigiano Reggiano cheese and place them on the bun.
8. Bake for 15 minutes or until the bread just starts to crisp.
9. Sprinkle prosciutto and onions on top, then drizzle vinegar and serve.
- **Nutrition Info:** Calories: 154, Sodium: 432 mg, Dietary Fiber: 1.0 g, Total Fat: 5.6 g, Total Carbs: 17.3 g, Protein: 8.1 g.

130.Orange Chicken Rice

Servings: 4
Cooking Time: 55 Minutes
Ingredients:
- 3 tablespoons olive oil
- 1 medium onion, chopped
- 1 3/4 cups chicken broth
- 1 cup brown basmati rice
- Zest and juice of 2 oranges
- Salt to taste
- 4 (6-oz.) boneless, skinless chicken thighs
- Black pepper, to taste
- 2 tablespoons fresh mint, chopped
- 2 tablespoons pine nuts, toasted

Directions:
1. Spread the rice in a casserole dish and place the chicken on top.
2. Toss the rest of the Ingredients: in a bowl and liberally pour over the chicken.
3. Press "Power Button" of Air Fry Oven and turn the dial to select the "Bake" mode.

4. Press the Time button and again turn the dial to set the cooking time to 55 minutes.
5. Now push the Temp button and rotate the dial to set the temperature at 350 degrees F.
6. Once preheated, place the casserole dish inside and close its lid.
7. Serve warm.
- **Nutrition Info:** Calories 231 Total Fat 20.1 g Saturated Fat 2.4 g Cholesterol 110 mg Sodium 941 mg Total Carbs 30.1 g Fiber 0.9 g Sugar 1.4 g Protein 14.6 g

131.Chicken Caprese Sandwich

Servings: 2
Cooking Time: 3 Minutes
Ingredients:
- 2 leftover chicken breasts, or pre-cooked breaded chicken
- 1 large ripe tomato
- 4 ounces mozzarella cheese slices
- 4 slices of whole grain bread
- 1/4 cup olive oil
- 1/3 cup fresh basil leaves
- Salt and pepper to taste

Directions:
1. Start by slicing tomatoes into thin slices.
2. Layer tomatoes then cheese over two slices of bread and place on a greased baking sheet.
3. Toast in the toaster oven for about 2 minutes or until the cheese is melted.
4. Heat chicken while the cheese melts.
5. Remove from oven, sprinkle with basil, and add chicken.
6. Drizzle with oil and add salt and pepper.
7. Top with other slice of bread and serve.
- **Nutrition Info:** Calories: 808, Sodium: 847 mg, Dietary Fiber: 5.2 g, Total Fat: 43.6 g, Total Carbs: 30.7 g, Protein: 78.4 g.

132.Chicken Legs With Dilled Brussels Sprouts

Servings: 2
Cooking Time: 10 Minutes
Ingredients:
- 2 chicken legs
- 1/2 teaspoon paprika
- 1/2 teaspoon kosher salt
- 1/2 teaspoon black pepper
- 1/2 pound Brussels sprouts
- 1 teaspoon dill, fresh or dried

Directions:
1. Start by preheating your Air Fryer to 370 degrees F.
2. Now, season your chicken with paprika, salt, and pepper. Transfer the chicken legs to the cooking basket. Cook for 10 minutes.
3. Flip the chicken legs and cook an additional 10 minutes. Reserve.

4. Add the Brussels sprouts to the cooking basket; sprinkle with dill. Cook at 380 degrees F for 15 minutes, shaking the basket halfway through.
5. Serve with the reserved chicken legs.
- **Nutrition Info:** 365 Calories; 21g Fat; 3g Carbs; 36g Protein; 2g Sugars; 3g Fiber

133.Squash And Zucchini Mini Pizza

Servings: 4
Cooking Time: 15 Minutes
Ingredients:
- 1 pizza crust
- 1/2 cup parmesan cheese
- 4 tablespoons oregano
- 1 zucchini
- 1 yellow summer squash
- Olive oil
- Salt and pepper

Directions:
1. Start by preheating toaster oven to 350°F.
2. If you are using homemade crust, roll out 8 mini portions; if crust is store-bought, use a cookie cutter to cut out the portions.
3. Sprinkle parmesan and oregano equally on each piece. Layer the zucchini and squash in a circle – one on top of the other – around the entire circle.
4. Brush with olive oil and sprinkle salt and pepper to taste.
5. Bake for 15 minutes and serve.
- **Nutrition Info:** Calories: 151, Sodium: 327 mg, Dietary Fiber: 3.1 g, Total Fat: 8.6 g, Total Carbs: 10.3 g, Protein: 11.4 g.

134.Spicy Egg And Ground Turkey Bake

Servings: 6
Cooking Time: 10 Minutes
Ingredients:
- 1½ pounds ground turkey
- 6 whole eggs, well beaten
- 1/3 teaspoon smoked paprika
- 2 egg whites, beaten
- Tabasco sauce, for drizzling
- 2 tablespoons sesame oil
- 2 leeks, chopped
- 3 cloves garlic, finely minced
- 1 teaspoon ground black pepper
- 1/2 teaspoon sea salt

Directions:
1. Warm the oil in a pan over moderate heat; then, sweat the leeks and garlic until tender; stir periodically.
2. Next, grease 6 oven safe ramekins with pan spray. Divide the sautéed mixture among six ramekins.
3. In a bowl, beat the eggs and egg whites using a wire whisk. Stir in the smoked paprika, salt and black pepper; whisk until

everything is thoroughly combined. Divide the egg mixture among the ramekins.
4. Air-fry approximately 22 minutes at 345 degrees F. Drizzle Tabasco sauce over each portion and serve.
- **Nutrition Info:** 298 Calories; 16g Fat; 4g Carbs; 16g Protein; 9g Sugars; 7g Fiber

135.Lobster Tails

Servings: 2
Cooking Time: 8 Minutes
Ingredients:
- 2 6oz lobster tails
- 1 tsp salt
- 1 tsp chopped chives
- 2 Tbsp unsalted butter melted
- 1 Tbsp minced garlic
- 1 tsp lemon juice

Directions:
1. Combine butter, garlic, salt, chives, and lemon juice to prepare butter mixture.
2. Butterfly lobster tails by cutting through shell followed by removing the meat and resting it on top of the shell.
3. Place them on the tray in the Instant Pot Duo Crisp Air Fryer basket and spread butter over the top of lobster meat. Close the Air Fryer lid, select the Air Fry option and cook on 380°F for 4 minutes.
4. Open the Air Fryer lid and spread more butter on top, cook for extra 2-4 minutes until done.
- **Nutrition Info:** Calories 120, Total Fat 12g, Total Carbs 2g, Protein 1g

136.Simple Turkey Breast

Servings: 10
Cooking Time: 40 Minutes
Ingredients:
- 1: 8-poundsbone-in turkey breast
- Salt and black pepper, as required
- 2 tablespoons olive oil

Directions:
1. Preheat the Air fryer to 360 degree F and grease an Air fryer basket.
2. Season the turkey breast with salt and black pepper and drizzle with oil.
3. Arrange the turkey breast into the Air Fryer basket, skin side down and cook for about 20 minutes.
4. Flip the side and cook for another 20 minutes.
5. Dish out in a platter and cut into desired size slices to serve.
- **Nutrition Info:** Calories: 719, Fat: 35.9g, Carbohydrates: 0g, Sugar: 0g, Protein: 97.2g, Sodium: 386mg

137.Boneless Air Fryer Turkey Breasts

Servings: 4
Cooking Time: 50 Minutes
Ingredients:
- 3 lb boneless breast
- ¼ cup mayonnaise
- 2 tsp poultry seasoning
- 1 tsp salt
- ½ tsp garlic powder
- ¼ tsp black pepper

Directions:
1. Choose the Air Fry option on the Instant Pot Duo Crisp Air fryer. Set the temperature to 360°F and push start. The preheating will start.
2. Season your boneless turkey breast with mayonnaise, poultry seasoning, salt, garlic powder, and black pepper.
3. Once preheated, Air Fry the turkey breasts on 360°F for 1 hour, turning every 15 minutes or until internal temperature has reached a temperature of 165°F.
- **Nutrition Info:** Calories 558, Total Fat 18g, Total Carbs 1g, Protein 98g

138.Zucchini And Cauliflower Stew

Servings: 4
Cooking Time: 12 Minutes
Ingredients:
- 1 cauliflower head, florets separated
- 1 ½ cups zucchinis; sliced
- 1 handful parsley leaves; chopped.
- ½ cup tomato puree
- 2 green onions; chopped.
- 1 tbsp. balsamic vinegar
- 1 tbsp. olive oil
- Salt and black pepper to taste.

Directions:
1. In a pan that fits your air fryer, mix the zucchinis with the rest of the ingredients except the parsley, toss, introduce the pan in the air fryer and cook at 380°F for 20 minutes
2. Divide into bowls and serve for lunch with parsley sprinkled on top.
- **Nutrition Info:** Calories: 193; Fat: 5g; Fiber: 2g; Carbs: 4g; Protein: 7g

139.Spanish Chicken Bake

Servings: 4
Cooking Time: 25 Minutes
Ingredients:
- ½ onion, quartered
- ½ red onion, quartered
- ½ lb. potatoes, quartered
- 4 garlic cloves
- 4 tomatoes, quartered
- 1/8 cup chorizo

- ¼ teaspoon paprika powder
- 4 chicken thighs, boneless
- ¼ teaspoon dried oregano
- ½ green bell pepper, julienned
- Salt
- Black pepper

Directions:
1. Toss chicken, veggies, and all the Ingredients: in a baking tray.
2. Press "Power Button" of Air Fry Oven and turn the dial to select the "Bake" mode.
3. Press the Time button and again turn the dial to set the cooking time to 25 minutes.
4. Now push the Temp button and rotate the dial to set the temperature at 425 degrees F.
5. Once preheated, place the baking pan inside and close its lid.
6. Serve warm.
- **Nutrition Info:** Calories 301 Total Fat 8.9 g Saturated Fat 4.5 g Cholesterol 57 mg Sodium 340 mg Total Carbs 24.7 g Fiber 1.2 g Sugar 1.3 g Protein 15.3 g

140.Seven-layer Tostadas

Servings: 6
Cooking Time: 5 Minutes
Ingredients:
- 1 (16-ounce) can refried pinto beans
- 1-1/2 cups guacamole
- 1 cup light sour cream
- 1/2 teaspoon taco seasoning
- 1 cup shredded Mexican cheese blend
- 1 cup chopped tomatoes
- 1/2 cup thinly sliced green onions
- 1/2 cup sliced black olives
- 6-8 whole wheat flour tortillas small enough to fit in your oven
- Olive oil

Directions:
1. Start by placing baking sheet into toaster oven while preheating it to 450°F. Remove pan and drizzle with olive oil.
2. Place tortillas on pan and cook in oven until they are crisp, turn at least once, this should take about 5 minutes or less.
3. In a medium bowl, mash refried beans to break apart any chunks, then microwave for 2 1/2 minutes.
4. Stir taco seasoning into the sour cream. Chop vegetables and halve olives.
5. Top tortillas with ingredients in this order: refried beans, guacamole, sour cream, shredded cheese, tomatoes, onions, and olives.
- **Nutrition Info:** Calories: 657, Sodium: 581 mg, Dietary Fiber: 16.8 g, Total Fat: 31.7 g, Total Carbs: 71.3 g, Protein: 28.9 g.

141.Lemon Chicken Breasts

Servings: 4
Cooking Time: 30 Minutes
Ingredients:
- 1/4 cup olive oil
- 3 tablespoons garlic, minced
- 1/3 cup dry white wine
- 1 tablespoon lemon zest, grated
- 2 tablespoons lemon juice
- 1 1/2 teaspoons dried oregano, crushed
- 1 teaspoon thyme leaves, minced
- Salt and black pepper
- 4 skin-on boneless chicken breasts
- 1 lemon, sliced

Directions:
1. Whisk everything in a baking pan to coat the chicken breasts well.
2. Place the lemon slices on top of the chicken breasts.
3. Spread the mustard mixture over the toasted bread slices.
4. Press "Power Button" of Air Fry Oven and turn the dial to select the "Bake" mode.
5. Press the Time button and again turn the dial to set the cooking time to 30 minutes.
6. Now push the Temp button and rotate the dial to set the temperature at 370 degrees F.
7. Once preheated, place the baking pan inside and close its lid.
8. Serve warm.
- **Nutrition Info:** Calories 388 Total Fat 8 g Saturated Fat 1 g Cholesterol 153mg sodium 339 mg Total Carbs 8 g Fiber 1 g Sugar 2 g Protein 13 g

142.Easy Prosciutto Grilled Cheese

Servings: 1
Cooking Time: 5 Minutes
Ingredients:
- 2 slices muenster cheese
- 2 slices white bread
- Four thinly-shaved pieces of prosciutto
- 1 tablespoon sweet and spicy pickles

Directions:
1. Set toaster oven to the Toast setting.
2. Place one slice of cheese on each piece of bread.
3. Put prosciutto on one slice and pickles on the other.
4. Transfer to a baking sheet and toast for 4 minutes or until the cheese is melted.
5. Combine the sides, cut, and serve.
- **Nutrition Info:** Calories: 460, Sodium: 2180 mg, Dietary Fiber: 0 g, Total Fat: 25.2 g, Total Carbs: 11.9 g, Protein: 44.2 g.

143.Kale And Pine Nuts

Servings: 4
Cooking Time: 12 Minutes
Ingredients:
- 10 cups kale; torn
- 1/3 cup pine nuts
- 2 tbsp. lemon zest; grated
- 1 tbsp. lemon juice
- 2 tbsp. olive oil
- Salt and black pepper to taste.

Directions:
1. In a pan that fits the air fryer, combine all the ingredients, toss, introduce the pan in the machine and cook at 380°F for 15 minutes
2. Divide between plates and serve as a side dish.
- **Nutrition Info:** Calories: 121; Fat: 9g; Fiber: 2g; Carbs: 4g; Protein: 5g

144.Glazed Lamb Chops

Servings: 4
Cooking Time: 15 Minutes
Ingredients:
- 1 tablespoon Dijon mustard
- ½ tablespoon fresh lime juice
- 1 teaspoon honey
- ½ teaspoon olive oil
- Salt and ground black pepper, as required
- 4 (4-ounce) lamb loin chops

Directions:
1. In a black pepper large bowl, mix together the mustard, lemon juice, oil, honey, salt, and black pepper.
2. Add the chops and coat with the mixture generously.
3. Place the chops onto the greased "Sheet Pan".
4. Press "Power Button" of Ninja Foodi Digital Air Fry Oven and turn the dial to select the "Air Bake" mode.
5. Press the Time button and again turn the dial to set the cooking time to 15 minutes.
6. Now push the Temp button and rotate the dial to set the temperature at 390 degrees F.
7. Press "Start/Pause" button to start.
8. When the unit beeps to show that it is preheated, open the lid.
9. Insert the "Sheet Pan" in oven.
10. Flip the chops once halfway through.
11. Serve hot.
- **Nutrition Info:** Calories: 224 kcal Total Fat: 9.1 g Saturated Fat: 3.1 g Cholesterol: 102 mg Sodium: 169 mg Total Carbs: 1.7 g Fiber: 0.1 g Sugar: 1.5 g Protein: 32 g

145.Turkey And Broccoli Stew

Servings: 4
Cooking Time: 12 Minutes
Ingredients:
- 1 broccoli head, florets separated

- 1 turkey breast, skinless; boneless and cubed
- 1 cup tomato sauce
- 1 tbsp. parsley; chopped.
- 1 tbsp. olive oil
- Salt and black pepper to taste.

Directions:
1. In a baking dish that fits your air fryer, mix the turkey with the rest of the ingredients except the parsley, toss, introduce the dish in the fryer, bake at 380°F for 25 minutes
2. Divide into bowls, sprinkle the parsley on top and serve.
- **Nutrition Info:** Calories: 250; Fat: 11g; Fiber: 2g; Carbs: 6g; Protein: 12g

146.Garlic Chicken Potatoes

Servings: 4
Cooking Time: 30 Minutes
Ingredients:
- 2 lbs. red potatoes, quartered
- 3 tablespoons olive oil
- 1/2 teaspoon cumin seeds
- Salt and black pepper, to taste
- 4 garlic cloves, chopped
- 2 tablespoons brown sugar
- 1 lemon (1/2 juiced and 1/2 cut into wedges)
- Pinch of red pepper flakes
- 4 skinless, boneless chicken breasts
- 2 tablespoons cilantro, chopped

Directions:
1. Place the chicken, lemon, garlic, and potatoes in a baking pan.
2. Toss the spices, herbs, oil, and sugar in a bowl.
3. Add this mixture to the chicken and veggies then toss well to coat.
4. Press "Power Button" of Air Fry Oven and turn the dial to select the "Bake" mode.
5. Press the Time button and again turn the dial to set the cooking time to 30 minutes.
6. Now push the Temp button and rotate the dial to set the temperature at 400 degrees F.
7. Once preheated, place the baking pan inside and close its lid.
8. Serve warm.
- **Nutrition Info:** Calories 545 Total Fat 36.4 g Saturated Fat 10.1 g Cholesterol 200 mg Sodium 272 mg Total Carbs 40.7 g Fiber 0.2 g Sugar 0.1 g Protein 42.5 g

147.Sweet & Sour Pork

Servings: 4
Cooking Time: 27 Minutes
Ingredients:
- 2 pounds Pork cut into chunks
- 2 large Eggs
- 1 teaspoon Pure Sesame Oil (optional)

- 1 cup Potato Starch (or cornstarch)
- 1/2 teaspoon Sea Salt
- 1/4 teaspoon Freshly Ground Black Pepper
- 1/16 teaspoon Chinese Five Spice
- 3 Tablespoons Canola Oil
- Oil Mister

Directions:
1. In a mixing bowl, combine salt, potato starch, Chinese Five Spice, and peppers.
2. In another bowl, beat the eggs & add sesame oil.
3. Then dredge the pieces of Pork into the Potato Starch and remove the excess. Then dip each piece into the egg mixture, shake off excess, and then back into the Potato Starch mixture.
4. Place pork pieces into the Instant Pot Duo Crisp Air Fryer Basket after spray the pork with oil.
5. Close the Air Fryer lid and cook at 340°F for approximately 8 to12 minutes (or until pork is cooked), shaking the basket a couple of times for evenly distribution.
- **Nutrition Info:** Calories 521, Total Fat 21g, Total Carbs 23g, Protein 60g

148.Chicken Breasts With Chimichurri

Servings: 1
Cooking Time: 35 Minutes
Ingredients:
- 1 chicken breast, bone-in, skin-on
- Chimichurri
- ½ bunch fresh cilantro
- 1/4 bunch fresh parsley
- ½ shallot, peeled, cut in quarters
- ½ tablespoon paprika ground
- ½ tablespoon chili powder
- ½ tablespoon fennel ground
- ½ teaspoon black pepper, ground
- ½ teaspoon onion powder
- 1 teaspoon salt
- ½ teaspoon garlic powder
- ½ teaspoon cumin ground
- ½ tablespoon canola oil
- Chimichurri
- 2 tablespoons olive oil
- 4 garlic cloves, peeled
- Zest and juice of 1 lemon
- 1 teaspoon kosher salt

Directions:
1. Preheat the Air fryer to 300 degree F and grease an Air fryer basket.
2. Combine all the spices in a suitable bowl and season the chicken with it.
3. Sprinkle with canola oil and arrange the chicken in the Air fryer basket.
4. Cook for about 35 minutes and dish out in a platter.

5. Put all the ingredients in the blender and blend until smooth.
6. Serve the chicken with chimichurri sauce.
- **Nutrition Info:** Calories: 140, Fats: 7.9g, Carbohydrates: 1.8g, Sugar: 7.1g, Proteins: 7.2g, Sodium: 581mg

149.Roasted Fennel, Ditalini, And Shrimp

Servings: 4
Cooking Time: 30 Minutes
Ingredients:
- 1 pound extra large, thawed, tail-on shrimp
- 1 teaspoon fennel seeds
- 1 teaspoon salt
- 1 fennel bulb, halved and sliced crosswise
- 4 garlic cloves, chopped
- 2 tablespoons olive oil
- 1/2 teaspoon freshly ground black pepper
- Grated zest of 1 lemon
- 1/2 pound whole wheat ditalini

Directions:
1. Start by preheating toaster oven to 450°F.
2. Toast the seeds in a medium pan over medium heat for about 5 minutes, then toss with shrimp.
3. Add water and 1/2 teaspoon salt to the pan and bring the mixture to a boil.
4. Reduce heat and simmer for 30 minutes.
5. Combine fennel, garlic, oil, pepper, and remaining salt in a roasting pan.
6. Roast for 20 minutes, then add shrimp mixture and roast for another 5 minutes or until shrimp are cooked.
7. While the fennel is roasting, cook pasta per the directions on the package, drain, and set aside.
8. Remove the shrimp mixture and mix in pasta, roast for another 5 minutes.
- **Nutrition Info:** Calories: 420, Sodium: 890 mg, Dietary Fiber: 4.2 g, Total Fat: 10.2 g, Total Carbs: 49.5 g, Protein: 33.9 g.

150.Sweet Potato And Parsnip Spiralized Latkes

Servings: 12
Cooking Time: 20 Minutes
Ingredients:
- 1 medium sweet potato
- 1 large parsnip
- 4 cups water
- 1 egg + 1 egg white
- 2 scallions
- 1/2 teaspoon garlic powder
- 1/2 teaspoon sea salt
- 1/2 teaspoon ground pepper

Directions:
1. Start by spiralizing the sweet potato and parsnip and chopping the scallions, reserving only the green parts.

2. Preheat toaster oven to 425°F.
3. Bring 4 cups of water to a boil. Place all of your noodles in a colander and pour the boiling water over the top, draining well.
4. Let the noodles cool, then grab handfuls and place them in a paper towel; squeeze to remove as much liquid as possible.
5. In a large bowl, beat egg and egg white together. Add noodles, scallions, garlic powder, salt, and pepper, mix well.
6. Prepare a baking sheet; scoop out 1/4 cup of mixture at a time and place on sheet.
7. Slightly press down each scoop with your hands, then bake for 20 minutes, flipping halfway through.
- **Nutrition Info:** Calories: 24, Sodium: 91 mg, Dietary Fiber: 1.0 g, Total Fat: 0.4 g, Total Carbs: 4.3 g, Protein: 0.9 g.

151.Turkey Meatloaf

Servings: 4
Cooking Time: 20 Minutes
Ingredients:
- 1 pound ground turkey
- 1 cup kale leaves, trimmed and finely chopped
- 1 cup onion, chopped
- ½ cup fresh breadcrumbs
- 1 cup Monterey Jack cheese, grated
- 2 garlic cloves, minced
- ¼ cup salsa verde
- 1 teaspoon red chili powder
- ½ teaspoon ground cumin
- ½ teaspoon dried oregano, crushed
- Salt and ground black pepper, as required

Directions:
1. Preheat the Air fryer to 400 degree F and grease an Air fryer basket.
2. Mix all the ingredients in a bowl and divide the turkey mixture into 4 equal-sized portions.
3. Shape each into a mini loaf and arrange the loaves into the Air fryer basket.
4. Cook for about 20 minutes and dish out to serve warm.
- **Nutrition Info:** Calories: 435, Fat: 23.1g, Carbohydrates: 18.1g, Sugar: 3.6g, Protein: 42.2g, Sodium: 641mg

152.Simple Lamb Bbq With Herbed Salt

Servings: 8
Cooking Time: 1 Hour 20 Minutes
Ingredients:
- 2 ½ tablespoons herb salt
- 2 tablespoons olive oil
- 4 pounds boneless leg of lamb, cut into 2-inch chunks

Directions:
1. Preheat the air fryer to 390 ºF.

2. Place the grill pan accessory in the air fryer.
3. Season the meat with the herb salt and brush with olive oil.
4. Grill the meat for 20 minutes per batch.
5. Make sure to flip the meat every 10 minutes for even cooking.
- **Nutrition Info:** Calories: 347 kcal Total Fat: 17.8 g Saturated Fat: 0 g Cholesterol: 0 mg Sodium: 0 mg Total Carbs: 0 g Fiber: 0 g Sugar: 0 g Protein: 46.6 g

153.Crisp Chicken Casserole

Servings: 4
Cooking Time: 15 Minutes
Ingredients:
- 3 cup chicken, shredded
- 12 oz bag egg noodles
- 1/2 large onion
- 1/2 cup chopped carrots
- 1/4 cup frozen peas
- 1/4 cup frozen broccoli pieces
- 2 stalks celery chopped
- 5 cup chicken broth
- 1 tsp garlic powder
- salt and pepper to taste
- 1 cup cheddar cheese, shredded
- 1 package French's onions
- 1/4 cup sour cream
- 1 can cream of chicken and mushroom soup

Directions:
1. Place the chicken, vegetables, garlic powder, salt and pepper, and broth and stir. Then place it into the Instant Pot Duo Crisp Air Fryer Basket.
2. Press or lightly stir the egg noodles into the mix until damp/wet.
3. Select the option Air Fryer and cook for 4 minutes.
4. Stir in the sour cream, can of soup, cheese, and 1/3 of the French's onions.
5. Top with the remaining French's onions and close the Air Fryer lid and cook for about 10 more minutes.
- **Nutrition Info:** Calories 301, Total Fat 17g, Total Carbs 17g, Protein 20g

154.Vegetarian Philly Sandwich

Servings: 2
Cooking Time: 20 Minutes
Ingredients:
- 2 tablespoons olive oil
- 8 ounces sliced portabello mushrooms
- 1 vidalia onion, thinly sliced
- 1 green bell pepper, thinly sliced
- 1 red bell pepper, thinly sliced
- Salt and pepper
- 4 slices 2% provolone cheese
- 4 rolls

Directions:

1. Preheat toaster oven to 475°F.
2. Heat the oil in a medium sauce pan over medium heat.
3. Sauté mushrooms about 5 minutes, then add the onions and peppers and sauté another 10 minutes.
4. Slice rolls lengthwise and divide the vegetables into each roll.
5. Add the cheese and toast until the rolls start to brown and the cheese melts.
- **Nutrition Info:** Calories: 645, Sodium: 916 mg, Dietary Fiber: 7.2 g, Total Fat: 33.3 g, Total Carbs: 61.8 g, Protein: 27.1 g.

155.Rolled Salmon Sandwich

Servings: 1
Cooking Time: 5 Minutes
Ingredients:
- 1 piece of flatbread
- 1 salmon filet
- Pinch of salt
- 1 tablespoon green onion, chopped
- 1/4 teaspoon dried sumac
- 1/2 teaspoon thyme
- 1/2 teaspoon sesame seeds
- 1/4 English cucumber
- 1 tablespoon yogurt

Directions:
1. Start by peeling and chopping the cucumber. Cut the salmon at a 45-degree angle into 4 slices and lay them flat on the flatbread.
2. Sprinkle salmon with salt to taste. Sprinkle onions, thyme, sumac, and sesame seeds evenly over the salmon.
3. Broil the salmon for at least 3 minutes, but longer if you want a more well-done fish.
4. While you broil your salmon, mix together the yogurt and cucumber. Remove your flatbread from the toaster oven and put it on a plate, then spoon the yogurt mix over the salmon.
5. Fold the sides of the flatbread in and roll it up for a gourmet lunch that you can take on the go.
- **Nutrition Info:** Calories: 347, Sodium: 397 mg, Dietary Fiber: 1.6 g, Total Fat: 12.4 g, Total Carbs: 20.6 g, Protein: 38.9 g.

156.Turkey And Almonds

Servings: 2
Cooking Time: 10 Minutes
Ingredients:
- 1 big turkey breast, skinless; boneless and halved
- 2 shallots; chopped
- 1/3 cup almonds; chopped
- 1 tbsp. sweet paprika
- 2 tbsp. olive oil
- Salt and black pepper to taste.

Directions:

1. In a pan that fits the air fryer, combine the turkey with all the other ingredients, toss.
2. Put the pan in the machine and cook at 370°F for 25 minutes
3. Divide everything between plates and serve.
- **Nutrition Info:** Calories: 274; Fat: 12g; Fiber: 3g; Carbs: 5g; Protein: 14g

157.Jicama Fries(1)

Servings: 4
Cooking Time: 12 Minutes
Ingredients:
- 1 small jicama; peeled.
- ¼ tsp. onion powder.
- ¾tsp. chili powder
- ¼ tsp. ground black pepper
- ¼ tsp. garlic powder.

Directions:

1. Cut jicama into matchstick-sized pieces.
2. Place pieces into a small bowl and sprinkle with remaining ingredients. Place the fries into the air fryer basket
3. Adjust the temperature to 350 Degrees F and set the timer for 20 minutes. Toss the basket two or three times during cooking. Serve warm.
- **Nutrition Info:** Calories: 37; Protein: 8g; Fiber: 7g; Fat: 1g; Carbs: 7g

158.Greek Lamb Meatballs

Servings: 12
Cooking Time: 12 Minutes
Ingredients:
- 1 pound ground lamb
- ½ cup breadcrumbs
- ¼ cup milk
- 2 egg yolks
- 1 teaspoon ground coriander
- 1 teaspoon ground cumin
- 3 garlic cloves, minced
- 1 teaspoon dried oregano
- ½ teaspoon salt
- ½ teaspoon black pepper
- 1 lemon, juiced and zested
- ¼ cup fresh parsley, chopped
- ½ cup crumbled feta cheese
- Olive oil, for shaping
- Tzatziki, for dipping

Directions:

1. Combine all ingredients except olive oil in a large mixing bowl and mix until fully incorporated.
2. Form 12 meatballs, about 2 ounces each. Use olive oil on your hands so they don't stick to the meatballs. Set aside.
3. Select the Broil function on the COSORI Air Fryer Toaster Oven, set time to 12 minutes, then press Start/Cancel to preheat.

4. Place the meatballs on the food tray, then insert the tray at top position in the preheated air fryer toaster oven. Press Start/Cancel.
5. Take out the meatballs when done and serve with a side of tzatziki.
- **Nutrition Info:** Calories: 129 kcal Total Fat: 6.4 g Saturated Fat: 0 g Cholesterol: 0 mg Sodium: 0 mg Total Carbs: 4.9 g Fiber: 0 g Sugar: 0 g Protein: 12.9 g

159.Beer Coated Duck Breast

Servings: 2
Cooking Time: 20 Minutes
Ingredients:
- 1 tablespoon fresh thyme, chopped
- 1 cup beer
- 1: 10½-ouncesduck breast
- 6 cherry tomatoes
- 1 tablespoon olive oil
- 1 teaspoon mustard
- Salt and ground black pepper, as required
- 1 tablespoon balsamic vinegar

Directions:

1. Preheat the Air fryer to 390 degree F and grease an Air fryer basket.
2. Mix the olive oil, mustard, thyme, beer, salt, and black pepper in a bowl.
3. Coat the duck breasts generously with marinade and refrigerate, covered for about 4 hours.
4. Cover the duck breasts and arrange into the Air fryer basket.
5. Cook for about 15 minutes and remove the foil from breast.
6. Set the Air fryer to 355 degree F and place the duck breast and tomatoes into the Air Fryer basket.
7. Cook for about 5 minutes and dish out the duck breasts and cherry tomatoes.
8. Drizzle with vinegar and serve immediately.
- **Nutrition Info:** Calories: 332, Fat: 13.7g, Carbohydrates: 9.2g, Sugar: 2.5g, Protein: 34.6g, Sodium: 88mg

160.Parmesan Chicken Meatballs

Servings: 4
Cooking Time: 12 Minutes
Ingredients:
- 1-lb. ground chicken
- 1 large egg, beaten
- ½ cup Parmesan cheese, grated
- ½ cup pork rinds, ground
- 1 teaspoon garlic powder
- 1 teaspoon paprika
- 1 teaspoon kosher salt
- ½ teaspoon pepper
- Crust:
- ½ cup pork rinds, ground

Directions:

1. Toss all the meatball Ingredients: in a bowl and mix well.
2. Make small meatballs out this mixture and roll them in the pork rinds.
3. Place the coated meatballs in the air fryer basket.
4. Press "Power Button" of Air Fry Oven and turn the dial to select the "Bake" mode.
5. Press the Time button and again turn the dial to set the cooking time to 12 minutes.
6. Now push the Temp button and rotate the dial to set the temperature at 400 degrees F.
7. Once preheated, place the air fryer basket inside and close its lid.
8. Serve warm.
- **Nutrition Info:** Calories 529 Total Fat 17 g Saturated Fat 3 g Cholesterol 65 mg Sodium 391 mg Total Carbs 55 g Fiber 6 g Sugar 8 g Protein 41g

161. Ground Chicken Meatballs

Servings: 4
Cooking Time: 10 Minutes
Ingredients:
- 1-lb. ground chicken
- 1/3 cup panko
- 1 teaspoon salt
- 2 teaspoons chives
- 1/2 teaspoon garlic powder
- 1 teaspoon thyme
- 1 egg

Directions:

1. Toss all the meatball Ingredients: in a bowl and mix well.
2. Make small meatballs out this mixture and place them in the air fryer basket.
3. Press "Power Button" of Air Fry Oven and turn the dial to select the "Air Fry" mode.
4. Press the Time button and again turn the dial to set the cooking time to 10 minutes.
5. Now push the Temp button and rotate the dial to set the temperature at 350 degrees F.
6. Once preheated, place the air fryer basket inside and close its lid.
7. Serve warm.
- **Nutrition Info:** Calories 453 Total Fat 2.4 g Saturated Fat 3 g Cholesterol 21 mg Sodium 216 mg Total Carbs 18 g Fiber 2.3 g Sugar 1.2 g Protein 23.2 g

162. Roasted Stuffed Peppers

Servings: 4
Cooking Time: 20 Minutes
Ingredients:
- 4 ounces shredded cheddar cheese
- ½ tsp. Pepper
- ½ tsp. Salt
- 1 tsp. Worcestershire sauce
- ½ c. Tomato sauce
- 8 ounces lean ground beef
- 1 tsp. Olive oil
- 1 minced garlic clove
- ½ chopped onion
- 2 green peppers

Directions:

1. Preparing the ingredients. Ensure your instant crisp air fryer is preheated to 390 degrees. Spray with olive oil.
2. Cut stems off bell peppers and remove seeds. Cook in boiling salted water for 3 minutes.
3. Sauté garlic and onion together in a skillet until golden in color.
4. Take skillet off the heat. Mix pepper, salt, Worcestershire sauce, ¼ cup of tomato sauce, half of cheese and beef together.
5. Divide meat mixture into pepper halves. Top filled peppers with remaining cheese and tomato sauce.
6. Place filled peppers in the instant crisp air fryer.
7. Air frying. Close air fryer lid. Set temperature to 390°f, and set time to 20 minutes, bake 15-20 minutes.
- **Nutrition Info:** Calories: 295; Fat: 8g; Protein:23g; Sugar:2g

163. Tomato And Avocado

Servings: 4
Cooking Time: 12 Minutes
Ingredients:
- ½ lb. cherry tomatoes; halved
- 2 avocados, pitted; peeled and cubed
- 1 ¼ cup lettuce; torn
- 1/3 cup coconut cream
- A pinch of salt and black pepper
- Cooking spray

Directions:

1. Grease the air fryer with cooking spray, combine the tomatoes with avocados, salt, pepper and the cream and cook at 350°F for 5 minutes shaking once
2. In a salad bowl, mix the lettuce with the tomatoes and avocado mix, toss and serve.
- **Nutrition Info:** Calories: 226; Fat: 12g; Fiber: 2g; Carbs: 4g; Protein: 8g

164. Nutmeg Chicken Thighs

Servings: 4
Cooking Time: 10 Minutes
Ingredients:
- 2 lb. chicken thighs
- 2 tbsp. olive oil
- ½ tsp. nutmeg, ground
- A pinch of salt and black pepper

Directions:

1. Season the chicken thighs with salt and pepper and rub with the rest of the ingredients
2. Put the chicken thighs in air fryer's basket, cook at 360°F for 15 minutes on each side, divide between plates and serve.
- **Nutrition Info:** Calories: 271; Fat: 12g; Fiber: 4g; Carbs: 6g; Protein: 13g

165.Chicken With Veggies And Rice

Servings: 3
Cooking Time: 20 Minutes
Ingredients:
- 3 cups cold boiled white rice
- 1 cup cooked chicken, diced
- ½ cup frozen carrots
- ½ cup frozen peas
- ½ cup onion, chopped
- 6 tablespoons soy sauce
- 1 tablespoon vegetable oil

Directions:
1. Preheat the Air fryer to 360 degree F and grease a 7" nonstick pan.
2. Mix the rice, soy sauce, and vegetable oil in a bowl.
3. Stir in the remaining ingredients and mix until well combined.
4. Transfer the rice mixture into the pan and place in the Air fryer.
5. Cook for about 20 minutes and dish out to serve immediately.
- **Nutrition Info:** Calories: 405, Fat: 6.4g, Carbohydrates: 63g, Sugar: 3.5g, Protein: 21.7g, Sodium: 1500mg

166.Maple Chicken Thighs

Servings: 4
Cooking Time: 30 Minutes
Ingredients:
- 4 large chicken thighs, bone-in
- 2 tablespoons French mustard
- 2 tablespoons Dijon mustard
- 1 clove minced garlic
- 1/2 teaspoon dried marjoram
- 2 tablespoons maple syrup

Directions:
1. Mix chicken with everything in a bowl and coat it well.
2. Place the chicken along with its marinade in the baking pan.
3. Press "Power Button" of Air Fry Oven and turn the dial to select the "Bake" mode.
4. Press the Time button and again turn the dial to set the cooking time to 30 minutes.
5. Now push the Temp button and rotate the dial to set the temperature at 370 degrees F.
6. Once preheated, place the baking pan inside and close its lid.
7. Serve warm.

- **Nutrition Info:** Calories 301 Total Fat 15.8 g Saturated Fat 2.7 g Cholesterol 75 mg Sodium 189 mg Total Carbs 31.7 g Fiber 0.3 g Sugar 0.1 g Protein 28.2 g

167.Perfect Size French Fries

Servings: 1
Cooking Time: 30 Minutes
Ingredients:
- 1 medium potato
- 1 tablespoon olive oil
- Salt and pepper to taste

Directions:
1. Start by preheating your oven to 425°F.
2. Clean the potato and cut it into fries or wedges.
3. Place fries in a bowl of cold water to rinse.
4. Lay the fries on a thick sheet of paper towels and pat dry.
5. Toss in a bowl with oil, salt, and pepper.
6. Bake for 30 minutes.
- **Nutrition Info:** Calories: 284, Sodium: 13 mg, Dietary Fiber: 4.7 g, Total Fat: 14.2 g, Total Carbs: 37.3 g, Protein: 4.3 g.

168.Chicken Breast With Rosemary

Servings: 4
Cooking Time: 60 Minutes
Ingredients:
- 4 bone-in chicken breast halves
- 3 tablespoons softened butter
- 1/2 teaspoon salt
- 1/4 teaspoon pepper
- 1 tablespoon rosemary
- 1 tablespoon extra-virgin olive oil

Directions:
1. Start by preheating toaster oven to 400°F.
2. Mix butter, salt, pepper, and rosemary in a bowl.
3. Coat chicken with the butter mixture and place in a shallow pan.
4. Drizzle oil over chicken and roast for 25 minutes.
5. Flip chicken and roast for another 20 minutes.
6. Flip chicken one more time and roast for a final 15 minutes.
- **Nutrition Info:** Calories: 392, Sodium: 551 mg, Dietary Fiber: 0 g, Total Fat: 18.4 g, Total Carbs: 0.6 g, Protein: 55.4 g.

169.Basic Roasted Tofu

Servings: 4
Cooking Time: 45 Minutes
Ingredients:
- 1 or more (16-ounce) containers extra-firm tofu
- 1 tablespoon sesame oil
- 1 tablespoon soy sauce

- 1 tablespoon rice vinegar
- 1 tablespoon water

Directions:
1. Start by drying the tofu: first pat dry with paper towels, then lay on another set of paper towels or a dish towel.
2. Put a plate on top of the tofu then put something heavy on the plate (like a large can of vegetables). Leave it there for at least 20 minutes.
3. While tofu is being pressed, whip up marinade by combining oil, soy sauce, vinegar, and water in a bowl and set aside.
4. Cut the tofu into squares or sticks. Place the tofu in the marinade for at least 30 minutes.
5. Preheat toaster oven to 350°F. Line a pan with parchment paper and add as many pieces of tofu as you can, giving each piece adequate space.
6. Bake 20–45 minutes; tofu is done when the outside edges look golden brown. Time will vary depending on tofu size and shape.
- **Nutrition Info:** Calories: 114, Sodium: 239 mg, Dietary Fiber: 1.1 g, Total Fat: 8.1 g, Total Carbs: 2.2 g, Protein: 9.5 g.

170.Fried Paprika Tofu

Servings:
Cooking Time: 12 Minutes
Ingredients:
- 1 block extra firm tofu; pressed to remove excess water and cut into cubes
- 1/4 cup cornstarch
- 1 tablespoon smoked paprika
- salt and pepper to taste

Directions:
1. Line the Air Fryer basket with aluminum foil and brush with oil. Preheat the Air Fryer to 370 - degrees Fahrenheit.
2. Mix all ingredients in a bowl. Toss to combine. Place in the Air Fryer basket and cook for 12 minutes.

171.Zucchini Stew

Servings: 4
Cooking Time: 12 Minutes
Ingredients:
- 8 zucchinis, roughly cubed
- ¼ cup tomato sauce
- 1 tbsp. olive oil
- ½ tsp. basil; chopped.
- ¼ tsp. rosemary; dried
- Salt and black pepper to taste.

Directions:
1. Grease a pan that fits your air fryer with the oil, add all the ingredients, toss, introduce the pan in the fryer and cook at 350°F for 12 minutes
2. Divide into bowls and serve.

- **Nutrition Info:** Calories: 200; Fat: 6g; Fiber: 2g; Carbs: 4g; Protein: 6g

172.Coriander Artichokes(3)

Servings: 4
Cooking Time: 12 Minutes
Ingredients:
- 12 oz. artichoke hearts
- 1 tbsp. lemon juice
- 1 tsp. coriander, ground
- ½ tsp. cumin seeds
- ½ tsp. olive oil
- Salt and black pepper to taste.

Directions:
1. In a pan that fits your air fryer, mix all the ingredients, toss, introduce the pan in the fryer and cook at 370°F for 15 minutes
2. Divide the mix between plates and serve as a side dish.
- **Nutrition Info:** Calories: 200; Fat: 7g; Fiber: 2g; Carbs: 5g; Protein: 8g

173.Delicious Chicken Burgers

Servings: 4
Cooking Time: 30 Minutes
Ingredients:
- 4 boneless, skinless chicken breasts
- 1¾ ounces plain flour
- 2 eggs
- 4 hamburger buns, split and toasted
- 4 mozzarella cheese slices
- 1 teaspoon mustard powder
- ½ teaspoon paprika
- 1 teaspoon Worcestershire sauce
- ¼ teaspoon dried parsley
- ¼ teaspoon dried tarragon
- ¼ teaspoon dried oregano
- 1 teaspoon dried garlic
- 1 teaspoon chicken seasoning
- ½ teaspoon cayenne pepper
- Salt and black pepper, as required

Directions:
1. Preheat the Air fryer to 355 degree F and grease an Air fryer basket.
2. Put the chicken breasts, mustard, paprika, Worcestershire sauce, salt, and black pepper in a food processor and pulse until minced.
3. Make 4 equal-sized patties from the mixture.
4. Place the flour in a shallow bowl and whisk the egg in a second bowl.
5. Combine dried herbs and spices in a third bowl.
6. Coat each chicken patty with flour, dip into whisked egg and then coat with breadcrumb mixture.
7. Arrange the chicken patties into the Air fryer basket in a single layer and cook for about 30 minutes, flipping once in between.

8. Place half bun in a plate, layer with lettuce leaf, patty and cheese slice.
9. Cover with bun top and dish out to serve warm.
- **Nutrition Info:** Calories: 562, Fat: 20.3g, Carbohydrates: 33g, Sugar: 3.3g, Protein: 58.7g, Sodium: 560mg

174. Country Comfort Corn Bread

Servings: 12
Cooking Time: 20 Minutes
Ingredients:
- 1 cup yellow cornmeal
- 1-1/2 cups oatmeal
- 1/4 teaspoon salt
- 1/4 cup granulated sugar
- 2 teaspoons baking powder
- 1 cup milk
- 1 large egg
- 1/2 cup applesauce

Directions:
1. Start by blending oatmeal into a fine powder.
2. Preheat toaster oven to 400°F.
3. Mix oatmeal, cornmeal, salt, sugar, and baking powder, and stir to blend.
4. Add milk, egg, and applesauce, and mix well.
5. Pour into a pan and bake for 20 minutes.
- **Nutrition Info:** Calories: 113, Sodium: 71 mg, Dietary Fiber: 1.9 g, Total Fat: 1.9 g, Total Carbs: 21.5 g, Protein: 3.4 g.

175. Duck Rolls

Servings: 3
Cooking Time: 40 Minutes
Ingredients:
- 1 pound duck breast fillet, each cut into 2 pieces
- 3 tablespoons fresh parsley, finely chopped
- 1 small red onion, finely chopped
- 1 garlic clove, crushed
- 1½ teaspoons ground cumin
- 1 teaspoon ground cinnamon
- ½ teaspoon red chili powder
- Salt, to taste
- 2 tablespoons olive oil

Directions:
1. Preheat the Air fryer to 355 degree F and grease an Air fryer basket.
2. Mix the garlic, parsley, onion, spices, and 1 tablespoon of olive oil in a bowl.
3. Make a slit in each duck piece horizontally and coat with onion mixture.
4. Roll each duck piece tightly and transfer into the Air fryer basket.
5. Cook for about 40 minutes and cut into desired size slices to serve.

- **Nutrition Info:** Calories: 239, Fats: 8.2g, Carbohydrates: 3.2g, Sugar: 0.9g, Proteins: 37.5g, Sodium: 46mg

176. Turkey And Mushroom Stew

Servings: 4
Cooking Time: 12 Minutes
Ingredients:
- ½ lb. brown mushrooms; sliced
- 1 turkey breast, skinless, boneless; cubed and browned
- ¼ cup tomato sauce
- 1 tbsp. parsley; chopped.
- Salt and black pepper to taste.

Directions:
1. In a pan that fits your air fryer, mix the turkey with the mushrooms, salt, pepper and tomato sauce, toss, introduce in the fryer and cook at 350°F for 25 minutes
2. Divide into bowls and serve for lunch with parsley sprinkled on top.
- **Nutrition Info:** Calories: 220; Fat: 12g; Fiber: 2g; Carbs: 5g; Protein: 12g

177. Okra Casserole

Servings: 4
Cooking Time: 12 Minutes
Ingredients:
- 2 red bell peppers; cubed
- 2 tomatoes; chopped.
- 3 garlic cloves; minced
- 3 cups okra
- ½ cup cheddar; shredded
- ¼ cup tomato puree
- 1 tbsp. cilantro; chopped.
- 1 tsp. olive oil
- 2 tsp. coriander, ground
- Salt and black pepper to taste.

Directions:
1. Grease a heat proof dish that fits your air fryer with the oil, add all the ingredients except the cilantro and the cheese and toss them really gently
2. Sprinkle the cheese and the cilantro on top, introduce the dish in the fryer and cook at 390°F for 20 minutes.
3. Divide between plates and serve for lunch.
- **Nutrition Info:** Calories: 221; Fat: 7g; Fiber: 2g; Carbs: 4g; Protein: 9g

178. Herb-roasted Turkey Breast

Servings: 8
Cooking Time: 60 Minutes
Ingredients:
- 3 lb turkey breast
- Rub Ingredients:
- 2 tbsp olive oil
- 2 tbsp lemon juice
- 1 tbsp minced Garlic

- 2 tsp ground mustard
- 2 tsp kosher salt
- 1 tsp pepper
- 1 tsp dried rosemary
- 1 tsp dried thyme
- 1 tsp ground sage

Directions:
1. Take a small bowl and thoroughly combine the Rub Ingredients: in it. Rub this on the outside of the turkey breast and under any loose skin.
2. Place the coated turkey breast keeping skin side up on a cooking tray.
3. Place the drip pan at the bottom of the cooking chamber of the Instant Pot Duo Crisp Air Fryer. Select Air Fry option, post this, adjust the temperature to 360°F and the time to one hour, then touch start.
4. When preheated, add the food to the cooking tray in the lowest position. Close the lid for cooking.
5. When the Air Fry program is complete, check to make sure that the thickest portion of the meat reads at least 160°F, remove the turkey and let it rest for 10 minutes before slicing and serving.
- **Nutrition Info:** Calories 214, Total Fat 10g, Total Carbs 2g, Protein 29g

179.Kalamta Mozarella Pita Melts

Servings: 2
Cooking Time: 5 Minutes
Ingredients:
- 2 (6-inch) whole wheat pitas
- 1 teaspoon extra-virgin olive oil
- 1 cup grated part-skim mozzarella cheese
- 1/4 small red onion
- 1/4 cup pitted Kalamata olives
- 2 tablespoons chopped fresh herbs such as parsley, basil, or oregano

Directions:
1. Start by preheating toaster oven to 425°F.
2. Brush the pita on both sides with oil and warm in the oven for one minute.
3. Dice onions and halve olives.
4. Sprinkle mozzarella over each pita and top with onion and olive.
5. Return to the oven for another 5 minutes or until the cheese is melted.
6. Sprinkle herbs over the pita and serve.
- **Nutrition Info:** Calories: 387, Sodium: 828 mg, Dietary Fiber: 7.4 g, Total Fat: 16.2 g, Total Carbs: 42.0 g, Protein: 23.0 g.

180.Moroccan Pork Kebabs

Servings: 4
Cooking Time: 45 Minutes
Ingredients:
- 1/4 cup orange juice

- 1 tablespoon tomato paste
- 1 clove chopped garlic
- 1 tablespoon ground cumin
- 1/8 teaspoon ground cinnamon
- 4 tablespoons olive oil
- 1-1/2 teaspoons salt
- 3/4 teaspoon black pepper
- 1-1/2 pounds boneless pork loin
- 1 small eggplant
- 1 small red onion
- Pita bread (optional)
- 1/2 small cucumber
- 2 tablespoons chopped fresh mint
- Wooden skewers

Directions:
1. Start by placing wooden skewers in water to soak.
2. Cut pork loin and eggplant into 1- to 1-1/2-inch chunks.
3. Preheat toaster oven to 425°F.
4. Cut cucumber and onions into pieces and chop the mint.
5. In a large bowl, combine the orange juice, tomato paste, garlic, cumin, cinnamon, 2 tablespoons of oil, 1 teaspoon of salt, and 1/2 teaspoon of pepper.
6. Add the pork to this mixture and refrigerate for at least 30 minutes, but up to 8 hours.
7. Mix together vegetables, remaining oil, and salt and pepper.
8. Skewer the vegetables and bake for 20 minutes.
9. Add the pork to the skewers and bake for an additional 25 minutes.
10. Remove ingredients from skewers and sprinkle with mint; serve with flatbread if using.
- **Nutrition Info:** Calories: 465, Sodium: 1061 mg, Dietary Fiber: 5.6 g, Total Fat: 20.8 g, Total Carbs: 21.9 g, Protein: 48.2 g.

181.Sweet Potato And Eggplant Mix

Servings: 4
Cooking Time: 20 Minutes
Ingredients:
- 2 sweet potatoes, peeled and cut into medium wedges
- 2 eggplants, roughly cubed
- 1 tablespoon avocado oil
- Juice of 1 lemon
- 4 garlic cloves, minced
- 1 teaspoon nutmeg, ground
- Salt and black pepper to the taste
- 1 tablespoon rosemary, chopped

Directions:
1. In your air fryer, combine the potatoes with the eggplants and the other Ingredients:, toss and cook at 370 degrees F for 20 minutes.

2. Divide the mix between plates and serve as a side dish.
- **Nutrition Info:** Calories 182, fat 6, fiber 3, carbs 11, protein 5

182.Roasted Mini Peppers

Servings: 6
Cooking Time: 15 Minutes
Ingredients:
- 1 bag mini bell peppers
- Cooking spray
- Salt and pepper to taste

Directions:
1. Start by preheating toaster oven to 400°F.
2. Wash and dry the peppers, then place flat on a baking sheet.
3. Spray peppers with cooking spray and sprinkle with salt and pepper.
4. Roast for 15 minutes.
- **Nutrition Info:** Calories: 19, Sodium: 2 mg, Dietary Fiber: 1.3 g, Total Fat: 0.3 g, Total Carbs: 3.6 g, Protein: 0.6 g.

183.Onion Omelet

Servings: 2
Cooking Time: 15 Minutes
Ingredients:
- 4 eggs
- ¼ teaspoon low-sodium soy sauce
- Ground black pepper, as required
- 1 teaspoon butter
- 1 medium yellow onion, sliced
- ¼ cup Cheddar cheese, grated

Directions:
1. In a skillet, melt the butter over medium heat and cook the onion and cook for about 8-10 minutes.
2. Remove from the heat and set aside to cool slightly.
3. Meanwhile, in a bowl, add the eggs, soy sauce and black pepper and beat well.
4. Add the cooked onion and gently, stir to combine.
5. Place the zucchini mixture into a small baking pan.
6. Press "Power Button" of Air Fry Oven and turn the dial to select the "Air Fry" mode.
7. Press the Time button and again turn the dial to set the cooking time to 5 minutes.
8. Now push the Temp button and rotate the dial to set the temperature at 355 degrees F.
9. Press "Start/Pause" button to start.
10. When the unit beeps to show that it is preheated, open the lid.
11. Arrange pan over the "Wire Rack" and insert in the oven.
12. Cut the omelet into 2 portions and serve hot.
- **Nutrition Info:** Calories: 222 Cal Total Fat: 15.4 g Saturated Fat: 6.9 g Cholesterol: 347

mg Sodium: 264 mg Total Carbs: 6.1 g Fiber: 1.2 g Sugar: 3.1 g Protein: 15.3 g

184.Air Fried Steak Sandwich

Servings: 4
Cooking Time: 16 Minutes
Ingredients:
- Large hoagie bun, sliced in half
- 6 ounces of sirloin or flank steak, sliced into bite-sized pieces
- ½ tablespoon of mustard powder
- ½ tablespoon of soy sauce
- 1 tablespoon of fresh bleu cheese, crumbled
- 8 medium-sized cherry tomatoes, sliced in half
- 1 cup of fresh arugula, rinsed and patted dry

Directions:
1. Preparing the ingredients. In a small mixing bowl, combine the soy sauce and onion powder; stir with a fork until thoroughly combined.
2. Lay the raw steak strips in the soy-mustard mixture, and fully immerse each piece to marinate.
3. Set the instant crisp air fryer to 320 degrees for 10 minutes.
4. Arrange the soy-mustard marinated steak pieces on a piece of tin foil, flat and not overlapping, and set the tin foil on one side of the instant crisp air fryer basket. The foil should not take up more than half of the surface.
5. Lay the hoagie-bun halves, crusty-side up and soft-side down, on the other half of the air-fryer.
6. Air frying. Close air fryer lid.
7. After 10 minutes, the instant crisp air fryer will shut off; the hoagie buns should be starting to crisp and the steak will have begun to cook.
8. Carefully, flip the hoagie buns so they are now crusty-side down and soft-side up; crumble a layer of the bleu cheese on each hoagie half.
9. With a long spoon, gently stir the marinated steak in the foil to ensure even coverage.
10. Set the instant crisp air fryer to 360 degrees for 6 minutes.
11. After 6 minutes, when the fryer shuts off, the bleu cheese will be perfectly melted over the toasted bread, and the steak will be juicy on the inside and crispy on the outside.
12. Remove the cheesy hoagie halves first, using tongs, and set on a serving plate; then cover one side with the steak, and top with the cherry-tomato halves and the arugula. Close with the other cheesy hoagie-half, slice into two pieces, and enjoy.

- **Nutrition Info:** Calories 284 Total fat 7.9 g Saturated fat 1.4 g Cholesterol 36 mg Sodium 704 mg Total carbs 46 g Fiber 3.6 g Sugar 5.5 g Protein 17.9 g

185.Sweet Potato Rosti

Servings: 2
Cooking Time: 15 Minutes
Ingredients:
- ½ lb. sweet potatoes, peeled, grated and squeezed
- 1 tablespoon fresh parsley, chopped finely
- Salt and ground black pepper, as required
- 2 tablespoons sour cream

Directions:
1. In a large bowl, mix together the grated sweet potato, parsley, salt, and black pepper.
2. Press "Power Button" of Air Fry Oven and turn the dial to select the "Air Fry" mode.
3. Press the Time button and again turn the dial to set the cooking time to 15 minutes.
4. Now push the Temp button and rotate the dial to set the temperature at 355 degrees F.
5. Press "Start/Pause" button to start.
6. When the unit beeps to show that it is preheated, open the lid and lightly, grease the sheet pan.
7. Arrange the sweet potato mixture into the "Sheet Pan" and shape it into an even circle.
8. Insert the "Sheet Pan" in the oven.
9. Cut the potato rosti into wedges.
10. Top with the sour cream and serve immediately.
- **Nutrition Info:** Calories: 160 Cal Total Fat: 2.7 g Saturated Fat: 1.6 g Cholesterol: 5 mg Sodium: 95 mg Total Carbs: 32.3 g Fiber: 4.7 g Sugar: 0.6 g Protein: 2.2 g

186.Air Fryer Fish

Servings: 4
Cooking Time: 17 Minutes
Ingredients:
- 4-6 Whiting Fish fillets cut in half
- Oil to mist
- Fish Seasoning
- ¾ cup very fine cornmeal
- ¼ cup flour
- 2 tsp old bay
- 1 ½ tsp salt
- 1 tsp paprika
- ½ tsp garlic powder
- ½ tsp black pepper

Directions:
1. Put the Ingredients: for fish seasoning in a Ziplock bag and shake it well. Set aside.
2. Rinse and pat dry the fish fillets with paper towels. Make sure that they still are damp.
3. Place the fish fillets in a ziplock bag and shake until they are completely covered with seasoning.
4. Place the fillets on a baking rack to let any excess flour to fall off.
5. Grease the bottom of the Instant Pot Duo Crisp Air Fryer basket tray and place the fillets on the tray. Close the lid, select the Air Fry option and cook filets on 400°F for 10 minutes.
6. Open the Air Fryer lid and spray the fish with oil on the side facing up before flipping it over, ensure that the fish is fully coated. Flip and cook another side of the fish for 7 minutes. Remove the fish and serve.
- **Nutrition Info:** Calories 193, Total Fat 1g, Total Carbs 27g, Protein 19g

DINNER RECIPES

187.Almond Asparagus

Servings: 3
Cooking Time: 6 Minutes
Ingredients:
- 1 pound asparagus
- 1/3 cup almonds, sliced
- 2 tablespoons olive oil
- 2 tablespoons balsamic vinegar
- Salt and black pepper, to taste

Directions:
1. Preheat the Air fryer to 400 ºF and grease an Air fryer basket.
2. Mix asparagus, oil, vinegar, salt, and black pepper in a bowl and toss to coat well.
3. Arrange asparagus into the Air fryer basket and sprinkle with the almond slices.
4. Cook for about 6 minutes and dish out to serve hot.
- **Nutrition Info:** Calories: 173, Fat: 14.8g, Carbohydrates: 8.2g, Sugar: 3.3g, Protein: 5.6g, Sodium: 54mg

188.Roasted Lamb

Servings: 4
Cooking Time: 1 Hour 30 Minutes
Ingredients:
- 2½ pounds half lamb leg roast, slits carved
- 2 garlic cloves, sliced into smaller slithers
- 1 tablespoon dried rosemary
- 1 tablespoon olive oil
- Cracked Himalayan rock salt and cracked peppercorns, to taste

Directions:
1. Preheat the Air fryer to 400 degree F and grease an Air fryer basket.
2. Insert the garlic slithers in the slits and brush with rosemary, oil, salt, and black pepper.
3. Arrange the lamb in the Air fryer basket and cook for about 15 minutes.
4. Set the Air fryer to 350 degree F on the Roast mode and cook for 1 hour and 15 minutes.
5. Dish out the lamb chops and serve hot.
- **Nutrition Info:** Calories: 246, Fat: 7.4g, Carbohydrates: 9.4g, Sugar: 6.5g, Protein: 37.2g, Sodium: 353mg

189.Rice And Tuna Puff

Servings: 6
Cooking Time: 60 Minutes
Ingredients:
- 2/3 cup uncooked white rice
- 1 1/3 cups water
- 1/3 cup butter
- 1/4 cup all-purpose flour
- 1 teaspoon salt
- 1/4 teaspoon ground black pepper
- 1 1/2 cups milk
- 2 egg yolks
- 1 (12 ounces) can tuna, undrained
- 2 tablespoons grated onion
- 1 tablespoon lemon juice
- 2 egg whites

Directions:
1. In a saucepan, bring water to a boil. Stir in rice, cover, and cook on low heat until liquid is fully absorbed, around 20 minutes.
2. In another saucepan over medium heat, melt butter. Stir in pepper, salt, and flour. Cook for 2 minutes, whisking constantly and slowly adding milk. Continue cooking and stirring until thickened.
3. In a medium bowl, whisk egg yolks. Slowly whisk in half of the thickened milk mixture. Add to a pan of remaining milk and continue cooking and stirring for 2 more minutes. Stir in lemon juice, onion, tuna, and rice.
4. Place the instant pot air fryer lid on, lightly grease baking pan of the instant pot with cooking spray. And transfer rice mixture into it.
5. Beat egg whites until stiff peak forms. Slowly fold into rice mixture.
6. Cover pan with foil, place the baking pan in the instant pot and close the air fryer lid.
7. Cook at 360 ºF for 20 minutes.
8. Cook for 15 minutes at 390 ºF until tops are lightly browned and the middle has set.
9. Serve and enjoy.
- **Nutrition Info:** Calories: 302; Carbs: 24.1g; Protein: 20.6g; Fat: 13.6g

190.Broiled Tilapia With Parmesan And Herbs

Servings: 4
Cooking Time: 8 Minutes
Ingredients:
- 4 (6- to 8-ounce) farm-raised tilapia filets
- 1/2 cup freshly grated parmesan cheese
- 2 tablespoons low-fat mayonnaise
- 2 tablespoons light sour cream
- 2 tablespoons melted unsalted butter
- 2 tablespoons lemon juice
- 1/2 teaspoon dried basil
- 1/2 teaspoon dried tarragon
- 1/8 teaspoon onion powder
- Salt and pepper to taste

Directions:
1. Mix together 1/4 cup parmesan and all other ingredients, except tilapia.
2. Place mixture in a plastic zipper bag, add fish and toss.

3. Pour fish mixture into a shallow pan and set aside to marinate for 20 minutes.
4. Place the fish in a broiler pan, top with a few spoonful of marinade, and sprinkle the rest of the parmesan over the fish.
5. Broil until lightly browned, around 8 minutes.
- **Nutrition Info:** Calories: 369, Sodium: 459 mg, Dietary Fiber: 0 g, Total Fat: 17.7 g, Total Carbs: 2.0 g, Protein: 51.6 g.

191.Summer Fish Packets

Servings: 2
Cooking Time: 20 Minutes
Ingredients:
- 2 snapper fillets
- 1 shallot, peeled and sliced
- 2 garlic cloves, halved
- 1 bell pepper, sliced
- 1 small-sized serrano pepper, sliced
- 1 tomato, sliced
- 1 tablespoon olive oil
- 1/4 teaspoon freshly ground black pepper
- 1/2 teaspoon paprika
- Sea salt, to taste
- 2 bay leaves

Directions:
1. Place two parchment sheets on a working surface. Place the fish in the center of one side of the parchment paper.
2. Top with the shallot, garlic, peppers, and tomato. Drizzle olive oil over the fish and vegetables. Season with black pepper, paprika, and salt. Add the bay leaves.
3. Fold over the other half of the parchment. Now, fold the paper around the edges tightly and create a half moon shape, sealing the fish inside.
4. Cook in the preheated Air Fryer at 390 degrees F for 15 minutes. Serve warm.
- **Nutrition Info:** 329 Calories; 8g Fat; 17g Carbs; 47g Protein; 4g Sugars; 8g Fiber

192.Rich Meatloaf With Mustard And Peppers

Servings: 5
Cooking Time: 20 Minutes
Ingredients:
- 1 pound beef, ground
- 1/2 pound veal, ground
- 1 egg
- 4 tablespoons vegetable juice
- 1/2 cup pork rinds
- 2 bell peppers, chopped
- 1 onion, chopped
- 2 garlic cloves, minced
- 2 tablespoons tomato paste
- 2 tablespoons soy sauce
- 1 (1-ouncepackage ranch dressing mix

- Sea salt, to taste
- 1/2 teaspoon ground black pepper, to taste
- 7 ounces tomato puree
- 1 tablespoon Dijon mustard

Directions:
1. Start by preheating your Air Fryer to 330 degrees F.
2. In a mixing bowl, thoroughly combine the ground beef, veal, egg, vegetable juice, pork rinds, bell peppers, onion, garlic, tomato paste, soy sauce, ranch dressing mix, salt, and ground black pepper.
3. Mix until everything is well incorporated and press into a lightly greased meatloaf pan.
4. Cook approximately 25 minutes in the preheated Air Fryer. Whisk the tomato puree with the mustard and spread the topping over the top of your meatloaf.
5. Continue to cook 2 minutes more. Let it stand on a cooling rack for 6 minutes before slicing and serving. Enjoy!
- **Nutrition Info:** 398 Calories; 24g Fat; 9g Carbs; 32g Protein; 3g Sugars; 6g Fiber

193.Crispy Scallops

Servings: 4
Cooking Time: 6 Minutes
Ingredients:
- 18 sea scallops, cleaned and patted very dry
- 1/8 cup all-purpose flour
- 1 tablespoon 2% milk
- ½ egg
- ¼ cup cornflakes, crushed
- ½ teaspoon paprika
- Salt and black pepper, as required

Directions:
1. Preheat the Air fryer to 400 degree F and grease an Air fryer basket.
2. Mix flour, paprika, salt, and black pepper in a bowl.
3. Whisk egg with milk in another bowl and place the cornflakes in a third bowl.
4. Coat each scallop with the flour mixture, dip into the egg mixture and finally, dredge in the cornflakes.
5. Arrange scallops in the Air fryer basket and cook for about 6 minutes.
6. Dish out the scallops in a platter and serve hot.
- **Nutrition Info:** Calories: 150, Fat: 1.7g, Carbohydrates: 8g, Sugar: 0.4g, Protein: 24g, Sodium: 278mg

194.Shrimp Casserole Louisiana Style

Servings: 2
Cooking Time: 35 Minutes
Ingredients:
- 3/4 cup uncooked instant rice

- 3/4 cup water
- 1/2 pound small shrimp, peeled and deveined
- 1 tablespoon butter
- 1/2 (4 ounces) can sliced mushrooms, drained
- 1/2 (8 ounces) container sour cream
- 1/3 cup shredded Cheddar cheese

Directions:
1. Place the instant pot air fryer lid on, lightly grease baking pan of the instant pot with cooking spray. Add rice, water, mushrooms, and butter. Cover with foil and place the baking pan in the instant pot.
2. Close the air fryer lid and cook at 360 ºF for 20 minutes.
3. Open foil cover, stir in shrimps, return foil and let it rest for 5 minutes.
4. Remove foil completely and stir in sour cream. Mix well and evenly spread rice. Top with cheese.
5. Cook for 7 minutes at 390 ºF until tops are lightly browned.
6. Serve and enjoy.
- **Nutrition Info:** Calories: 569; Carbs: 38.5g; Protein: 31.8g; Fat: 31.9g

195.Corned Beef With Carrots

Servings: 3
Cooking Time: 35 Minutes
Ingredients:
- 1 tbsp beef spice
- 1 whole onion, chopped
- 4 carrots, chopped
- 12 oz bottle beer
- 1½ cups chicken broth
- 4 pounds corned beef

Directions:
1. Preheat your air fryer to 380 f. Cover beef with beer and set aside for 20 minutes. Place carrots, onion and beef in a pot and heat over high heat. Add in broth and bring to a boil. Drain boiled meat and veggies; set aside.
2. Top with beef spice. Place the meat and veggies in your air fryer's cooking basket and cook for 30 minutes.
- **Nutrition Info:** Calories: 464 Cal Total Fat: 17 g Saturated Fat: 6.8 g Cholesterol: 91.7 mg Sodium: 1904.2 mg Total Carbs: 48.9 g Fiber: 7.2 g Sugar: 5.8 g Protein: 30.6 g

196.Bbq Pork Ribs

Servings: 2 To 3
Cooking Time: 5 Hrs 30 Minutes
Ingredients:
- 1 lb pork ribs
- 1 tsp soy sauce
- Salt and black pepper to taste
- 1 tsp oregano
- 1 tbsp + 1 tbsp maple syrup
- 3 tbsp barbecue sauce
- 2 cloves garlic, minced
- 1 tbsp cayenne pepper
- 1 tsp sesame oil

Directions:
1. Put the chops on a chopping board and use a knife to cut them into smaller pieces of desired sizes. Put them in a mixing bowl, add the soy sauce, salt, pepper, oregano, one tablespoon of maple syrup, barbecue sauce, garlic, cayenne pepper, and sesame oil. Mix well and place the pork in the fridge to marinate in the spices for 5 hours.
2. Preheat the Air Fryer to 350 F. Open the Air Fryer and place the ribs in the fryer basket. Slide the fryer basket in and cook for 15 minutes. Open the Air fryer, turn the ribs using tongs, apply the remaining maple syrup with a brush, close the Air Fryer, and continue cooking for 10 minutes.
- **Nutrition Info:** 346 Calories; 11g Fat; 4g Carbs; 32g Protein; 1g Sugars; 1g Fiber

197.Okra With Green Beans

Servings: 2
Cooking Time: 20 Minutes
Ingredients:
- ½, 10-ouncesbag frozen cut okra
- ½, 10-ouncesbag frozen cut green beans
- ¼ cup nutritional yeast
- 3 tablespoons balsamic vinegar
- Salt and black pepper, to taste

Directions:
1. Preheat the Air fryer to 400 ºF and grease an Air fryer basket.
2. Mix the okra, green beans, nutritional yeast, vinegar, salt, and black pepper in a bowl and toss to coat well.
3. Arrange the okra mixture into the Air fryer basket and cook for about 20 minutes.
4. Dish out in a serving dish and serve hot.
- **Nutrition Info:** Calories: 126, Fat: 1.3g, Carbohydrates: 19.7g, Sugar: 2.1g, Protein: 11.9g, Sodium: 100mg

198.Lobster Lasagna Maine Style

Servings: 6
Cooking Time: 50 Minutes
Ingredients:
- 1/2 (15 ounces) container ricotta cheese
- 1 egg
- 1 cup shredded Cheddar cheese
- 1/2 cup shredded mozzarella cheese
- 1/2 cup grated Parmesan cheese
- 1/2 medium onion, minced
- 1-1/2 teaspoons minced garlic
- 1 tablespoon chopped fresh parsley

- 1/2 teaspoon freshly ground black pepper
- 1 (16 ounces) jar Alfredo pasta sauce
- 8 no-boil lasagna noodles
- 1 pound cooked and cubed lobster meat
- 5-ounce package baby spinach leaves

Directions:
1. Mix well half of Parmesan, half of the mozzarella, half of cheddar, egg, and ricotta cheese in a medium bowl. Stir in pepper, parsley, garlic, and onion.
2. Place the instant pot air fryer lid on, lightly grease baking pan of the instant pot with cooking spray.
3. On the bottom of the pan, spread ½ of the Alfredo sauce, top with a single layer of lasagna noodles. Followed by 1/3 of lobster meat, 1/3 of ricotta cheese mixture, 1/3 of spinach. Repeat layering process until all ingredients are used up.
4. Sprinkle remaining cheese on top. Shake pan to settle lasagna and burst bubbles. Cover pan with foil and place the baking pan in the instant pot.
5. Close the air fryer lid and cook at 360 ºF for 30 minutes
6. Remove foil and cook for 10 minutes at 390 ºF until tops are lightly browned.
7. Let it stand for 10 minutes.
8. Serve and enjoy.
- **Nutrition Info:** Calories: 558; Carbs: 20.4g; Protein: 36.8g; Fat: 36.5g

199.Coconut Crusted Shrimp

Servings: 3
Cooking Time: 40 Minutes
Ingredients:
- 8 ounces coconut milk
- ½ cup sweetened coconut, shredded
- ½ cup panko breadcrumbs
- 1 pound large shrimp, peeled and deveined
- Salt and black pepper, to taste

Directions:
1. Preheat the Air fryer to 350-degree F and grease an Air fryer basket.
2. Place the coconut milk in a shallow bowl.
3. Mix coconut, breadcrumbs, salt, and black pepper in another bowl.
4. Dip each shrimp into coconut milk and finally, dredge in the coconut mixture.
5. Arrange half of the shrimps into the Air fryer basket and cook for about 20 minutes.
6. Dish out the shrimps onto serving plates and repeat with the remaining mixture to serve.
- **Nutrition Info:** Calories: 408, Fats: 23.7g, Carbohydrates: 11.7g, Sugar: 3.4g, Proteins: 31g, Sodium: 253mg

200.Fish Cakes With Horseradish Sauce

Servings: 4
Cooking Time: 20 Minutes
Ingredients:
- Halibut Cakes:
- 1 pound halibut
- 2 tablespoons olive oil
- 1/2 teaspoon cayenne pepper
- 1/4 teaspoon black pepper
- Salt, to taste
- 2 tablespoons cilantro, chopped
- 1 shallot, chopped
- 2 garlic cloves, minced
- 1 cup Romano cheese, grated
- 1 egg, whisked
- 1 tablespoon Worcestershire sauce
- Mayo Sauce:
- 1 teaspoon horseradish, grated
- 1/2 cup mayonnaise

Directions:
1. Start by preheating your Air Fryer to 380 degrees F. Spritz the Air Fryer basket with cooking oil.
2. Mix all ingredients for the halibut cakes in a bowl; knead with your hands until everything is well incorporated.
3. Shape the mixture into equally sized patties. Transfer your patties to the Air Fryer basket. Cook the fish patties for 10 minutes, turning them over halfway through.
4. Mix the horseradish and mayonnaise. Serve the halibut cakes with the horseradish mayo.
- **Nutrition Info:** 532 Calories; 32g Fat; 3g Carbs; 28g Protein; 3g Sugars; 6g Fiber

201.Marinated Cajun Beef

Servings: 2
Cooking Time: 20 Minutes
Ingredients:
- 1/3 cup beef broth
- 2 tablespoons Cajun seasoning, crushed
- 1/2 teaspoon garlic powder
- 3/4 pound beef tenderloins
- ½ tablespoon pear cider vinegar
- 1/3 teaspoon cayenne pepper
- 1 ½ tablespoon olive oil
- 1/2 teaspoon freshly ground black pepper
- 1 teaspoon salt

Directions:
1. Firstly, coat the beef tenderloins with salt, cayenne pepper, and black pepper.
2. Mix the remaining items in a medium-sized bowl; let the meat marinate for 40 minutes in this mixture.
3. Roast the beef for about 22 minutes at 385 degrees F, turning it halfway through the cooking time.

- **Nutrition Info:** 483 Calories; 23g Fat; 5g Carbs; 53g Protein; 6g Sugars; 4g Fiber

202.Red Wine Infused Mushrooms

Servings: 6
Cooking Time: 30 Minutes
Ingredients:
- 1 tablespoon butter
- 2 pounds fresh mushrooms, quartered
- 2 teaspoons Herbs de Provence
- ½ teaspoon garlic powder
- 2 tablespoons red wine

Directions:
1. Preheat the Air fryer to 325 ºF and grease an Air fryer pan.
2. Mix the butter, Herbs de Provence, and garlic powder in the Air fryer pan and toss to coat well.
3. Cook for about 2 minutes and stir in the mushrooms and red wine.
4. Cook for about 28 minutes and dish out in a platter to serve hot.
- **Nutrition Info:** Calories: 54, Fat: 2.4g, Carbohydrates: 5.3g, Sugar: 2.7g, Protein: 4.8g, Sodium: 23mg

203.Shrimp Scampi

Servings: 6
Cooking Time: 7 Minutes
Ingredients:
- 4 tablespoons salted butter
- 1 pound shrimp, peeled and deveined
- 2 tablespoons fresh basil, chopped
- 1 tablespoon fresh chives, chopped
- 1 tablespoon fresh lemon juice
- 1 tablespoon garlic, minced
- 2 teaspoons red pepper flakes, crushed
- 2 tablespoons dry white wine

Directions:
1. Preheat the Air fryer to 325 ºF and grease an Air fryer pan.
2. Heat butter, lemon juice, garlic, and red pepper flakes in a pan and return the pan to Air fryer basket.
3. Cook for about 2 minutes and stir in shrimp, basil, chives and wine.
4. Cook for about 5 minutes and dish out the mixture onto serving plates.
5. Serve hot.
- **Nutrition Info:** Calories: 250, Fat: 13.7g, Carbohydrates: 3.3g, Sugar: 0.3g, Protein: 26.3g, Sodium: 360mg

204.Sirloin Steak With Cremini Mushroom Sauce

Servings: 5
Cooking Time: 20 Minutes
Ingredients:
- 2 tablespoons butter

- 2 pounds sirloin, cut into four pieces
- Salt and cracked black pepper, to taste
- 1 teaspoon cayenne pepper
- 1/2 teaspoon dried rosemary
- 1/2 teaspoon dried dill
- 1/4 teaspoon dried thyme
- 1 pound Cremini mushrooms, sliced
- 1 cup sour cream
- 1 teaspoon mustard
- 1/2 teaspoon curry powder

Directions:
1. Start by preheating your Air Fryer to 396 degrees F. Grease a baking pan with butter.
2. Add the sirloin, salt, black pepper, cayenne pepper, rosemary, dill, and thyme to the baking pan. Cook for 9 minutes.
3. Next, stir in the mushrooms, sour cream, mustard, and curry powder. Continue to cook another 5 minutes or until everything is heated through.
4. Spoon onto individual serving plates.
- **Nutrition Info:** 349 Calories; 12g Fat; 4g Carbs; 49g Protein; 6g Sugars; 4g Fiber

205.Chat Masala Grilled Snapper

Servings: 5
Cooking Time: 25 Minutes
Ingredients:
- 2 ½ pounds whole fish
- Salt to taste
- 1/3 cup chat masala
- 3 tablespoons fresh lime juice
- 5 tablespoons olive oil

Directions:
1. Place the instant pot air fryer lid on and preheat the instant pot at 390 degrees F.
2. Place the grill pan accessory in the instant pot.
3. Season the fish with salt, chat masala and lime juice.
4. Brush with oil
5. Place the fish on a foil basket and place it inside the grill.
6. Close the air fryer lid and cook for 25 minutes.
- **Nutrition Info:** Calories:308; Carbs: 0.7g; Protein: 35.2g; Fat: 17.4g

206.Lemongrass Pork Chops

Servings: 3
Cooking Time: 2 Hrs 20 Minutes
Ingredients:
- 3 slices pork chops
- 2 garlic cloves, minced
- 1 ½ tbsp sugar
- 4 stalks lemongrass, trimmed and chopped
- 2 shallots, chopped
- 2 tbsp olive oil
- 1 ¼ tsp soy sauce

- 1 ¼ tsp fish sauce
- 1 ½ tsp black pepper

Directions:
1. In a bowl, add the garlic, sugar, lemongrass, shallots, olive oil, soy sauce, fish sauce, and black pepper; mix well. Add the pork chops, coat them with the mixture and allow to marinate for around 2 hours to get nice and savory.
2. Preheat the Air Fryer to 400 F. Cooking in 2 to 3 batches, remove and shake each pork chop from the marinade and place it in the fryer basket. Cook it for 7 minutes. Turn the pork chops with kitchen tongs and cook further for 5 minutes. Remove the chops and serve with a side of sautéed asparagus.
- **Nutrition Info:** 346 Calories; 11g Fat; 4g Carbs; 32g Protein; 1g Sugars; 1g Fiber

207. Morning Ham And Cheese Sandwich

Servings: 4
Cooking Time: 15 Minutes
Ingredients:
- 8 slices whole wheat bread
- 4 slices lean pork ham
- 4 slices cheese
- 8 slices tomato

Directions:
1. Preheat your air fryer to 360 f. Lay four slices of bread on a flat surface. Spread the slices with cheese, tomato, turkey and ham. Cover with the remaining slices to form sandwiches. Add the sandwiches to the air fryer cooking basket and cook for 10 minutes.
- **Nutrition Info:** Calories: 361 Cal Total Fat: 16.7 g Saturated Fat: 0 g Cholesterol: 0 mg Sodium: 1320 mg Total Carbs: 32.5 g Fiber: 2.3 g Sugar: 5.13 g Protein: 19.3 g

208. Indian Meatballs With Lamb

Servings: 8
Cooking Time: 14 Minutes
Ingredients:
- 1 garlic clove
- 1 tablespoon butter
- 4 oz chive stems
- ¼ tablespoon turmeric
- 1/3 teaspoon cayenne pepper
- 1 teaspoon ground coriander
- ¼ teaspoon bay leaf
- 1 teaspoon salt
- 1-pound ground lamb
- 1 egg
- 1 teaspoon ground black pepper

Directions:
1. Peel the garlic clove and mince it
2. Combine the minced garlic with the ground lamb.

3. Then sprinkle the meat mixture with the turmeric, cayenne pepper, ground coriander, bay leaf, salt, and ground black pepper.
4. Beat the egg in the forcemeat.
5. Then grate the chives and add them in the lamb forcemeat too.
6. Mix it up to make the smooth mass.
7. Then preheat the air fryer to 400 F.
8. Put the butter in the air fryer basket tray and melt it.
9. Then make the meatballs from the lamb mixture and place them in the air fryer basket tray.
10. Cook the dish for 14 minutes.
11. Stir the meatballs twice during the cooking.
12. Serve the cooked meatballs immediately.
13. Enjoy!
- **Nutrition Info:** calories 134, fat 6.2, fiber 0.4, carbs 1.8, protein 16.9

209. Spicy Cauliflower Rice

Servings: 2
Cooking Time: 22 Minutes
Ingredients:
- 1 cauliflower head, cut into florets 1/2 tsp cumin
- 1/2 tsp chili powder
- 6 onion spring, chopped 2 jalapenos, chopped
- 4 tbsp olive oil
- 1 zucchini, trimmed and cut into cubes 1/2 tsp paprika
- 1/2 tsp garlic powder 1/2 tsp cayenne pepper 1/2 tsp pepper
- 1/2 tsp salt

Directions:
1. Preheat the air fryer to 370 F.
2. Add cauliflower florets into the food processor and process until it looks like rice.
3. Transfer cauliflower rice into the air fryer baking pan and drizzle with half oil.
4. Place pan in the air fryer and cook for 12 minutes, stir halfway through.
5. Heat remaining oil in a small pan over medium heat.
6. Add zucchini and cook for 5-8 minutes.
7. Add onion and jalapenos and cook for 5 minutes.
8. Add spices and stir well. Set aside.
9. Add cauliflower rice in the zucchini mixture and stir well.
10. Serve and enjoy.
- **Nutrition Info:** Calories 254 Fat 28 g Carbohydrates 12.3 g Sugar 5 g

210. Baked Egg And Veggies

Servings: 2
Cooking Time: 20 Minutes
Ingredients:

- 1 cup fresh spinach; chopped
- 1 small zucchini, sliced lengthwise and quartered
- 1 medium Roma tomato; diced
- ½ medium green bell pepper; seeded and diced
- 2 large eggs.
- 2 tbsp. salted butter
- ¼ tsp. garlic powder.
- ¼ tsp. onion powder.
- ½ tsp. dried basil
- ¼ tsp. dried oregano.

Directions:
1. Grease two (4-inchramekins with 1 tbsp. butter each.
2. Take a large bowl, toss zucchini, bell pepper, spinach and tomatoes. Divide the mixture in two and place half in each ramekin.
3. Crack an egg on top of each ramekin and sprinkle with onion powder, garlic powder, basil and oregano. Place into the air fryer basket. Adjust the temperature to 330 Degrees F and set the timer for 10 minutes. Serve immediately.
- **Nutrition Info:** Calories: 150; Protein: 3g; Fiber: 2g; Fat: 10g; Carbs: 6g

211.Asparagus Frittata

Servings: 4
Cooking Time: 10 Minutes
Ingredients:
- 6 eggs
- 3 mushrooms, sliced
- 10 asparagus, chopped 1/4 cup half and half
- 2 tsp butter, melted
- 1 cup mozzarella cheese, shredded 1 tsp pepper
- 1 tsp salt

Directions:
1. Toss mushrooms and asparagus with melted butter and add into the air fryer basket.
2. Cook mushrooms and asparagus at 350 F for 5 minutes. Shake basket twice.
3. Meanwhile, in a bowl, whisk together eggs, half and half, pepper, and salt.
4. Transfer cook mushrooms and asparagus into the air fryer baking dish.
5. Pour egg mixture over mushrooms and asparagus.
6. Place dish in the air fryer and cook at 350 F for 5 minutes or until eggs are set.
7. Slice and serve.
- **Nutrition Info:** Calories 211 Fat 13 g Carbohydrates 4 g Sugar 1 g Protein 16 g Cholesterol 272 mg

212.Pork Chops With Keto Gravy

Servings: 4

Cooking Time: 17 Minutes
Ingredients:
- 1-pound pork chops
- 1 teaspoon kosher salt
- ½ teaspoon ground cinnamon
- 1 teaspoon ground white pepper
- 1 cup heavy cream
- 6 oz. white mushrooms
- 1 tablespoon butter
- ½ teaspoon ground ginger
- 1 teaspoon ground turmeric
- 4 oz chive stems
- 1 garlic clove, chopped

Directions:
1. Sprinkle the pork chops with the kosher salt, ground cinnamon, ground white pepper, and ground turmeric.
2. Preheat the air fryer to 375 F.
3. Pour the heavy cream in the air fryer basket tray.
4. Then slice the white mushrooms and add them in the heavy cream.
5. After this, add butter, ground ginger, chopped chives, and chopped garlic.
6. Cook the gravy for 5 minutes.
7. Then stir the cream gravy and add the pork chops.
8. Cook the pork chops at 400 F for 12 minutes.
9. When the time is over stir the pork chops gently and transfer them to the serving plates.
10. Enjoy!
- **Nutrition Info:** calories 518, fat 42.4, fiber 1.5, carbs 6.2, protein 28

213.Green Beans And Mushroom Casserole

Servings: 6
Cooking Time: 12 Minutes
Ingredients:
- 24 ounces fresh green beans, trimmed
- 2 cups fresh button mushrooms, sliced
- 1/3 cup French fried onions
- 3 tablespoons olive oil
- 2 tablespoons fresh lemon juice
- 1 teaspoon ground sage
- 1 teaspoon garlic powder
- 1 teaspoon onion powder
- Salt and black pepper, to taste

Directions:
1. Preheat the Air fryer to 400 ºF and grease an Air fryer basket.
2. Mix the green beans, mushrooms, oil, lemon juice, sage, and spices in a bowl and toss to coat well.
3. Arrange the green beans mixture into the Air fryer basket and cook for about 12 minutes.

4. Dish out in a serving dish and top with fried onions to serve.
- **Nutrition Info:** Calories: 65, Fat: 1.6g, Carbohydrates: 11g, Sugar: 2.4g, Protein: 3g, Sodium: 52mg

214.Kale And Brussels Sprouts

Servings: 8
Cooking Time: 7 Minutes
Ingredients:
- 1 lb. Brussels sprouts, trimmed
- 3 oz. mozzarella, shredded
- 2 cups kale, torn
- 1 tbsp. olive oil
- Salt and black pepper to taste.

Directions:
1. In a pan that fits the air fryer, combine all the Ingredients: except the mozzarella and toss.
2. Put the pan in the air fryer and cook at 380°F for 15 minutes
3. Divide between plates, sprinkle the cheese on top and serve.
- **Nutrition Info:** Calories: 170; Fat: 5g; Fiber: 3g; Carbs: 4g; Protein: 7g

215.Grilled Tasty Scallops

Servings: 2
Cooking Time: 10 Minutes
Ingredients:
- 1 pound sea scallops, cleaned and patted dry
- Salt and pepper to taste
- 3 dried chilies
- 2 tablespoon dried thyme
- 1 tablespoon dried oregano
- 1 tablespoon ground coriander
- 1 tablespoon ground fennel
- 2 teaspoons chipotle pepper

Directions:
1. Place the instant pot air fryer lid on and preheat the instant pot at 390 degrees F.
2. Place the grill pan accessory in the instant pot.
3. Mix all ingredients in a bowl.
4. Dump the scallops on the grill pan, close the air fryer lid and cook for 10 minutes.
- **Nutrition Info:** Calories:291 ; Carbs: 20.7g; Protein: 48.6g; Fat: 2.5g

216.Rigatoni With Roasted Broccoli And Chick Peas

Servings: 4
Cooking Time: 10 Minutes
Ingredients:
- 1 can anchovies packed in oil
- 4 cloves garlic, chopped
- 1 can chickpeas
- 1 chicken bouillon cube
- 1 pound broccoli, cut into small florets
- 1/2 pound whole wheat rigatoni
- 1/2 cup grated Romano cheese

Directions:
1. Drain and chop anchovies (set aside oil for later use), and cut broccoli into small florets.
2. Preheat toaster oven to 450°F.
3. In a shallow sauce pan, sauté anchovies in their oil, with garlic, until the garlic browns.
4. Drain the chickpeas, saving the canned liquid.
5. Add the chickpea liquid and bouillon to the anchovies, stir until bouillon dissolves.
6. Pour anchovy mix into a roasting pan and add broccoli and chickpeas.
7. Roast for 20 minutes.
8. While the veggies roast, cook rigatoni per package directions; drain the pasta, saving one cup of water.
9. Add the pasta to the anchovy mix and roast for another 10 minutes. Add reserved water, stirring in a little at a time until the pasta reaches the desired consistency.
10. Top with Romano and serve.
- **Nutrition Info:** Calories: 574, Sodium: 1198 mg, Dietary Fiber: 13.7 g, Total Fat: 14.0 g, Total Carbs: 81.1 g, Protein: 31.1 g.

217.Lamb Skewers

Servings: 4
Cooking Time: 20 Minutes
Ingredients:
- 2 lb. lamb meat; cubed
- 2 red bell peppers; cut into medium pieces
- ¼ cup olive oil
- 2 tbsp. lemon juice
- 1 tbsp. oregano; dried
- 1 tbsp. red vinegar
- 1 tbsp. garlic; minced
- ½ tsp. rosemary; dried
- A pinch of salt and black pepper

Directions:
1. Take a bowl and mix all the ingredients and toss them well.
2. Thread the lamb and bell peppers on skewers, place them in your air fryer's basket and cook at 380°F for 10 minutes on each side. Divide between plates and serve with a side salad
- **Nutrition Info:** Calories: 274; Fat: 12g; Fiber: 3g; Carbs: 6g; Protein: 16g

218.Cheddar Pork Meatballs

Servings: 4 To 6
Cooking Time: 25 Minutes
Ingredients:
- 1 lb ground pork
- 1 large onion, chopped
- ½ tsp maple syrup

- 2 tsp mustard
- ½ cup chopped basil leaves
- Salt and black pepper to taste
- 2 tbsp. grated cheddar cheese

Directions:
1. In a mixing bowl, add the ground pork, onion, maple syrup, mustard, basil leaves, salt, pepper, and cheddar cheese; mix well. Use your hands to form bite-size balls. Place in the fryer basket and cook at 400 f for 10 minutes.
2. Slide out the fryer basket and shake it to toss the meatballs. Cook further for 5 minutes. Remove them onto a wire rack and serve with zoodles and marinara sauce.
- **Nutrition Info:** Calories: 300 Cal Total Fat: 24 g Saturated Fat: 9 g Cholesterol: 70 mg Sodium: 860 mg Total Carbs: 3 g Fiber: 0 g Sugar: 0 g Protein: 16 g

219.Pork Belly With Honey

Servings: 8
Cooking Time: 35 Minutes
Ingredients:
- 2 pounds pork belly
- ½ tsp pepper
- 1 tbsp olive oil
- 1 tbsp salt
- 3 tbsp honey

Directions:
1. Preheat your air fryer to 400 f. Season the pork belly with salt and pepper. Grease the basket with oil. Add seasoned meat and cook for 15 minutes. Add honey and cook for 10 minutes more. Serve with green salad.
- **Nutrition Info:** Calories: 274 Cal Total Fat: 18 g Saturated Fat: 0 g Cholesterol: 0 mg Sodium: 0 mg Total Carbs: 8 g Fiber: 0 g Sugar: 0 g Protein: 18 g

220.Greek Souvlaki With Eggplant

Servings: 4
Cooking Time: 20 Minutes
Ingredients:
- 1 ½ pounds beef stew meat cubes
- 1/4 cup mayonnaise
- 1/4 cup sour cream
- 1 tablespoon yellow mustard
- 1 tablespoon Worcestershire sauce
- 1 cup pearl onions
- 1 small-sized eggplant, 1 ½-inch cubes
- Sea salt and ground black pepper, to taste

Directions:
1. In a mixing bowl, toss all ingredients until everything is well coated.
2. Place in your refrigerator, cover, and let it marinate for 1 hour.
3. Soak wooden skewers in water for 15 minutes

4. Thread the beef cubes, pearl onions and eggplant onto skewers. Cook in preheated Air Fryer at 395 degrees F for 12 minutes, flipping halfway through the cooking time. Serve warm.
- **Nutrition Info:** 372 Calories; 22g Fat; 2g Carbs; 33g Protein; 6g Sugars; 7g Fiber

221.Beef Roast

Servings: 4
Cooking Time:x
Ingredients:
- 2 lbs. beef roast
- 1 tbsp. smoked paprika
- 3 tbsp. garlic; minced
- 3 tbsp. olive oil
- Salt and black pepper to taste

Directions:
1. In a bowl, combine all the ingredients and coat the roast well.
2. Place the roast in your air fryer and cook at 390°F for 55 minutes. Slice the roast, divide it between plates and serve with a side salad

222.Cod With Avocado Mayo Sauce

Servings: 2
Cooking Time: 20 Minutes
Ingredients:
- 2 cod fish fillets
- 1 egg
- Sea salt, to taste
- 2 teaspoons olive oil
- 1/2 avocado, peeled, pitted, and mashed
- 1 tablespoon mayonnaise
- 3 tablespoons sour cream
- 1/2 teaspoon yellow mustard
- 1 teaspoon lemon juice
- 1 garlic clove, minced
- 1/4 teaspoon black pepper
- 1/4 teaspoon salt
- 1/4 teaspoon hot pepper sauce

Directions:
1. Start by preheating your Air Fryer to 360 degrees F. Spritz the Air Fryer basket with cooking oil.
2. Pat dry the fish fillets with a kitchen towel. Beat the egg in a shallow bowl. Add in the salt and olive oil.
3. Dip the fish into the egg mixture, making sure to coat thoroughly. Cook in the preheated Air Fryer approximately 12 minutes.
4. Meanwhile, make the avocado sauce by mixing the remaining ingredients in a bowl. Place in your refrigerator until ready to serve.
5. Serve the fish fillets with chilled avocado sauce on the side.

- **Nutrition Info:** 344 Calories; 27g Fat; 8g Carbs; 21g Protein; 8g Sugars; 7g Fiber

223.Ham Pinwheels

Servings: 4
Cooking Time: 11 Minutes
Ingredients:
- 1 puff pastry sheet
- 10 ham slices
- 1 cup Gruyere cheese, shredded plus more for sprinkling
- 4 teaspoons Dijon mustard

Directions:
1. Preheat the Air fryer to 375 degree F and grease an Air fryer basket.
2. Place the puff pastry onto a smooth surface and spread evenly with the mustard.
3. Top with the ham and ¾ cup cheese and roll the puff pastry.
4. Wrap the roll in plastic wrap and freeze for about 30 minutes.
5. Remove from the freezer and slice into ½-inch rounds.
6. Arrange the pinwheels in the Air fryer basket and cook for about 8 minutes.
7. Top with remaining cheese and cook for 3 more minutes.
8. Dish out in a platter and serve warm.
- **Nutrition Info:** Calories: 294, Fat: 19.4g, Carbohydrates: 8.4g, Sugar: 0.2g, Protein: 20.8g, Sodium: 1090mg

224.Award Winning Breaded Chicken

Servings: 4
Cooking Time: 20 Minutes
Ingredients:
- 1 1/2 tsp.s olive oil
- 1 tsp. red pepper flakes, crushed 1/3 tsp. chicken bouillon granules 1/3 tsp. shallot powder
- 1 1/2 tablespoons tamari soy sauce 1/3 tsp. cumin powder
- 1½ tablespoons mayo 1 tsp. kosher salt
- For the chicken:
- 2 beaten eggs Breadcrumbs
- 1½ chicken breasts, boneless and skinless 1 ½ tablespoons plain flour

Directions:
1. Margarine fly the chicken breasts, and then, marinate them for at least 55 minutes. Coat the chicken with plain flour; then, coat with the beaten eggs; finally, roll them in the breadcrumbs.
2. Lightly grease the cooking basket. Air-fry the breaded chicken at 345 °F for 12 minutes, flipping them halfway.
- **Nutrition Info:** 262 Calories; 14.9g Fat; 2.7g Carbs; 27.5g Protein; 0.3g Sugars

225.Zingy Dilled Salmon

Servings: 2
Cooking Time: 20 Minutes
Ingredients:
- 2 salmon steaks
- Coarse sea salt, to taste
- 1/4 teaspoon freshly ground black pepper, or more to taste
- 1 tablespoon sesame oil
- Zest of 1 lemon
- 1 tablespoon fresh lemon juice
- 1 teaspoon garlic, minced
- 1/2 teaspoon smoked cayenne pepper
- 1/2 teaspoon dried dill

Directions:
1. Preheat your Air Fryer to 380 degrees F. Pat dry the salmon steaks with a kitchen towel.
2. In a ceramic dish, combine the remaining ingredients until everything is well whisked.
3. Add the salmon steaks to the ceramic dish and let them sit in the refrigerator for 1 hour. Now, place the salmon steaks in the cooking basket. Reserve the marinade.
4. Cook for 12 minutes, flipping halfway through the cooking time.
5. Meanwhile, cook the marinade in a small sauté pan over a moderate flame. Cook until the sauce has thickened.
6. Pour the sauce over the steaks and serve.
- **Nutrition Info:** 476 Calories; 18g Fat; 2g Carbs; 47g Protein; 8g Sugars; 4g Fiber

226.Sage Beef

Servings: 4
Cooking Time: 30 Minutes
Ingredients:
- 2pounds beef stew meat, cubed
- 1tablespoon sage, chopped
- 2tablespoons butter, melted
- ½ teaspoon coriander, ground
- ½ tablespoon garlic powder
- 1teaspoon Italian seasoning
- Salt and black pepper to the taste

Directions:
1. In the air fryer's pan, mix the beef with the sage, melted butter and the other ingredients, introduce the pan in the fryer and cook at 360 degrees F for 30 minutes.
2. Divide everything between plates and serve.
- **Nutrition Info:** Calories 290, Fat 11, Fiber 6, Carbs 20, Protein 29

227.Cheese And Garlic Stuffed Chicken Breasts

Servings: 2
Cooking Time: 20 Minutes
Ingredients:
- 1/2 cup Cottage cheese 2 eggs, beaten

- 2 medium-sized chicken breasts, halved
- 2 tablespoons fresh coriander, chopped 1tsp. fine sea salt
- Seasoned breadcrumbs
- 1/3 tsp. freshly ground black pepper, to savor 3 cloves garlic, finely minced

Directions:
1. Firstly, flatten out the chicken breast using a meat tenderizer.
2. In a medium-sized mixing dish, combine the Cottage cheese with the garlic, coriander, salt, and black pepper.
3. Spread 1/3 of the mixture over the first chicken breast. Repeat with the remaining ingredients. Roll the chicken around the filling; make sure to secure with toothpicks.
4. Now, whisk the egg in a shallow bowl. In another shallow bowl, combine the salt, ground black pepper, and seasoned breadcrumbs.
5. Coat the chicken breasts with the whisked egg; now, roll them in the breadcrumbs.
6. Cook in the air fryer cooking basket at 365 °F for 22 minutes. Serve immediately.
- **Nutrition Info:** 424 Calories; 24.5g Fat; 7.5g Carbs; 43.4g Protein; 5.3g Sugars

228.Prawn Burgers

Servings: 2
Cooking Time: 6 Minutes
Ingredients:
- ½ cup prawns, peeled, deveined and finely chopped
- ½ cup breadcrumbs
- 2-3 tablespoons onion, finely chopped
- 3 cups fresh baby greens
- ½ teaspoon ginger, minced
- ½ teaspoon garlic, minced
- ½ teaspoon red chili powder
- ½ teaspoon ground cumin
- ¼ teaspoon ground turmeric
- Salt and ground black pepper, as required

Directions:
1. Preheat the Air fryer to 390 degree F and grease an Air fryer basket.
2. Mix the prawns, breadcrumbs, onion, ginger, garlic, and spices in a bowl.
3. Make small-sized patties from the mixture and transfer to the Air fryer basket.
4. Cook for about 6 minutes and dish out in a platter.
5. Serve immediately warm alongside the baby greens.
- **Nutrition Info:** Calories: 240, Fat: 2.7g, Carbohydrates: 37.4g, Sugar: 4g, Protein: 18g, Sodium: 371mg

229.Lemon Garlic Shrimps

Servings: 2

Cooking Time: 8 Minutes
Ingredients:
- ¾ pound medium shrimp, peeled and deveined
- 1½ tablespoons fresh lemon juice
- 1 tablespoon olive oil
- 1 teaspoon lemon pepper
- ¼ teaspoon paprika
- ¼ teaspoon garlic powder

Directions:
1. Preheat the Air fryer to 400 degree F and grease an Air fryer basket.
2. Mix lemon juice, olive oil, lemon pepper, paprika and garlic powder in a large bowl.
3. Stir in the shrimp and toss until well combined.
4. Arrange shrimp into the Air fryer basket in a single layer and cook for about 8 minutes.
5. Dish out the shrimp in serving plates and serve warm.
- **Nutrition Info:** Calories: 260, Fat: 12.4g, Carbohydrates: 0.3g, Sugar: 0.1g, Protein: 35.6g, Sodium: 619mg

230.Crumbly Oat Meatloaf

Servings: 8
Cooking Time: 60 Minutes
Ingredients:
- 2 lbs. ground beef
- 1 cup of salsa
- 3/4 cup Quaker Oats
- 1/2 cup chopped onion
- 1 large egg, beaten
- 1 tablespoon Worcestershire sauce
- Salt and black pepper to taste

Directions:
1. Thoroughly mix ground beef with salsa, oats, onion, egg, and all the ingredients in a bowl.
2. Grease a meatloaf pan with oil or butter and spread the minced beef in the pan.
3. Press "Power Button" of Air Fry Oven and turn the dial to select the "Bake" mode.
4. Press the Time button and again turn the dial to set the cooking time to 60 minutes.
5. Now push the Temp button and rotate the dial to set the temperature at 350 degrees F.
6. Once preheated, place the beef baking pan in the oven and close its lid.
7. Slice and serve.
- **Nutrition Info:** Calories: 412 Cal Total Fat: 24.8 g Saturated Fat: 12.4 g Cholesterol: 3 mg Sodium: 132 mg Total Carbs: 43.8 g Fiber: 3.9 g Sugar: 2.5 g Protein: 18.9 g

231.Steak With Cascabel-garlic Sauce

Servings: 4
Cooking Time: 20 Minutes
Ingredients:

- 2 teaspoons brown mustard
- 2 tablespoons mayonnaise
- 1 ½ pounds beef flank steak, trimmed and cubed
- 2 teaspoons minced cascabel
- ½ cup scallions, finely chopped
- 1/3 cup Crème fraîche
- 2 teaspoons cumin seeds
- 3 cloves garlic, pressed
- Pink peppercorns to taste, freshly cracked
- 1 teaspoon fine table salt
- 1/3 teaspoon black pepper, preferably freshly ground

Directions:
1. Firstly, fry the cumin seeds just about 1 minute or until they pop.
2. After that, season your beef flank steak with fine table salt, black pepper and the fried cumin seeds; arrange the seasoned beef cubes on the bottom of your baking dish that fits in the air fryer.
3. Throw in the minced cascabel, garlic, and scallions; air-fry approximately 8 minutes at 390 degrees F.
4. Once the beef cubes start to tender, add your favorite mayo, Crème fraîche, freshly cracked pink peppercorns and mustard; air-fry 7 minutes longer. Serve over hot wild rice.
- **Nutrition Info:** 329 Calories; 16g Fat; 8g Carbs; 37g Protein; 9g Sugars; 6g Fiber

232.Rice Flour Coated Shrimp

Servings: 3
Cooking Time: 20 Minutes
Ingredients:
- 3 tablespoons rice flour
- 1 pound shrimp, peeled and deveined
- 2 tablespoons olive oil
- 1 teaspoon powdered sugar
- Salt and black pepper, as required

Directions:
1. Preheat the Air fryer to 325 ºF and grease an Air fryer basket.
2. Mix rice flour, olive oil, sugar, salt, and black pepper in a bowl.
3. Stir in the shrimp and transfer half of the shrimp to the Air fryer basket.
4. Cook for about 10 minutes, flipping once in between.
5. Dish out the mixture onto serving plates and repeat with the remaining mixture.
- **Nutrition Info:** Calories: 299, Fat: 12g, Carbohydrates: 11.1g, Sugar: 0.8g, Protein: 35g, Sodium: 419mg

233.Veggie Stuffed Bell Peppers

Servings: 6
Cooking Time: 25 Minutes

Ingredients:
- 6 large bell peppers, tops and seeds removed
- 1 carrot, peeled and finely chopped
- 1 potato, peeled and finely chopped
- ½ cup fresh peas, shelled
- 1/3 cup cheddar cheese, grated
- 2 garlic cloves, minced
- Salt and black pepper, to taste

Directions:
1. Preheat the Air fryer to 350 ºF and grease an Air fryer basket.
2. Mix vegetables, garlic, salt and black pepper in a bowl.
3. Stuff the vegetable mixture in each bell pepper and arrange in the Air fryer pan.
4. Cook for about 20 minutes and top with cheddar cheese.
5. Cook for about 5 more minutes and dish out to serve warm.
- **Nutrition Info:** Calories: 101, Fat: 2.5g, Carbohydrates: 17.1g, Sugar: 7.4g, Protein: 4.1g, Sodium: 51mg

234.Pesto & White Wine Salmon

Servings: 4
Cooking Time: 10 Minutes
Ingredients:
- 1-1/4 pounds salmon filet
- 2 tablespoons white wine
- 2 tablespoons pesto
- 1 lemon

Directions:
1. Cut the salmon into 4 pieces and place on a greased baking sheet.
2. Slice the lemon into quarters and squeeze 1 quarter over each piece of salmon.
3. Drizzle wine over salmon and set aside to marinate while preheating the toaster oven on broil.
4. Spread pesto over each piece of salmon.
5. Broil for at least 10 minutes, or until the fish is cooked to desired doneness and the pesto is browned.
- **Nutrition Info:** Calories: 236, Sodium: 111 mg, Dietary Fiber: 0.9 g, Total Fat: 12.1 g, Total Carbs: 3.3 g, Protein: 28.6 g.

235.Irish Whisky Steak

Servings: 6
Cooking Time: 20 Minutes
Ingredients:
- 2 pounds sirloin steaks
- 1 ½ tablespoons tamari sauce
- 1/3 teaspoon cayenne pepper
- 1/3 teaspoon ground ginger
- 2 garlic cloves, thinly sliced
- 2 tablespoons Irish whiskey
- 2 tablespoons olive oil

- Fine sea salt, to taste

Directions:
1. Firstly, add all the ingredients, minus the olive oil and the steak, to a resealable plastic bag.
2. Throw in the steak and let it marinate for a couple of hours. After that, drizzle the sirloin steaks with 2 tablespoons olive oil.
3. Roast for approximately 22 minutes at 395 degrees F, turning it halfway through the time.

- **Nutrition Info:** 260 Calories; 17g Fat; 8g Carbs; 35g Protein; 2g Sugars; 1g Fiber

236.Delicious Beef Roast With Red Potatoes

Servings: 3
Cooking Time: 25 Minutes
Ingredients:
- 2 tbsp olive oil
- 4 pound top round roast beef
- 1 tsp salt
- ¼ tsp fresh ground black pepper
- 1 tsp dried thyme
- ½ tsp fresh rosemary, chopped
- 3 pounds red potatoes, halved
- Olive oil, black pepper and salt for garnish

Directions:
1. Preheat your Air Fryer to 360 F. In a small bowl, mix rosemary, salt, pepper and thyme; rub oil onto beef. Season with the spice mixture. Place the prepared meat in your Air Fryer's cooking basket and cook for 20 minutes.
2. Give the meat a turn and add potatoes, more pepper and oil. Cook for 20 minutes more. Take the steak out and set aside to cool for 10 minutes. Cook the potatoes in your Air Fryer for 10 more minutes at 400 F. Serve hot.

- **Nutrition Info:** 346 Calories; 11g Fat; 4g Carbs; 32g Protein; 1g Sugars; 1g Fiber

237.Baked Veggie Egg Rolls

Servings: 2
Cooking Time: 20 Minutes
Ingredients:
- 1/2 tablespoon olive or vegetable oil
- 2 cups thinly-sliced chard
- 1/4 cup grated carrot
- 1/2 cup chopped pea pods
- 3 shiitake mushrooms
- 2 scallions
- 2 medium cloves garlic
- 1/2 tablespoon fresh ginger
- 1/2 tablespoon soy sauce
- 6 egg roll wrappers
- Olive oil spray for cookie sheet and egg rolls

Directions:

1. Start by mincing mushrooms, garlic, and ginger and slicing scallions.
2. Heat oil on medium heat in a medium skillet and char peas, carrots, scallions, and mushrooms.
3. Cook 3 minutes, then add ginger. Stir in soy sauce and remove from heat.
4. Preheat toaster oven to 400°F and spray cookie sheet. Spoon even portions of vegetable mix over each egg roll wrapper, and wrap them up.
5. Place egg rolls on cookie sheet and spray with olive oil. Bake for 20 minutes until egg roll shells are browned.

- **Nutrition Info:** Calories: 421, Sodium: 1166 mg, Dietary Fiber: 8.2 g, Total Fat: 7.7 g, Total Carbs: 76.9 g, Protein: 13.7 g.

238.Miso-glazed Salmon

Servings: 4
Cooking Time: 5 Minutes
Ingredients:
- 1/4 cup red or white miso
- 1/3 cup sake
- 1 tablespoon soy sauce
- 2 tablespoons vegetable oil
- 1/4 cup sugar
- 4 skinless salmon filets

Directions:
1. In a shallow bowl, mix together the miso, sake, oil, soy sauce, and sugar.
2. Toss the salmon in the mixture until thoroughly coated on all sides.
3. Preheat your toaster oven to "high" on broil mode.
4. Place salmon in a broiling pan and broil until the top is well charred—about 5 minutes.

- **Nutrition Info:** Calories: 401, Sodium: 315 mg, Dietary Fiber: 0 g, Total Fat: 19.2 g, Total Carbs: 14.1 g, Protein: 39.2 g.

239.Sage Sausages Balls

Servings: 4
Cooking Time: 20 Minutes
Ingredients:
- 3 ½ oz sausages, sliced
- Salt and black pepper to taste
- 1 cup onion, chopped
- 3 tbsp breadcrumbs
- ½ tsp garlic puree
- 1 tsp sage

Directions:
1. Preheat your air fryer to 340 f. In a bowl, mix onions, sausage meat, sage, garlic puree, salt and pepper. Add breadcrumbs to a plate. Form balls using the mixture and roll them in breadcrumbs. Add onion balls in your air

fryer's cooking basket and cook for 15 minutes. Serve and enjoy!

- **Nutrition Info:** Calories: 162 Cal Total Fat: 12.1 g Saturated Fat: 0 g Cholesterol: 25 mg Sodium: 324 mg Total Carbs: 7.3 g Fiber: 0 g Sugar: 0 g Protein: 6 g

240.Beef Sausage With Grilled Broccoli

Servings: 4
Cooking Time: 20 Minutes
Ingredients:

- 1 pound beef Vienna sausage
- 1/2 cup mayonnaise
- 1 teaspoon yellow mustard
- 1 tablespoon fresh lemon juice
- 1 teaspoon garlic powder
- 1/4 teaspoon black pepper
- 1 pound broccoli

Directions:

1. Start by preheating your Air Fryer to 380 degrees F. Spritz the grill pan with cooking oil.
2. Cut the sausages into serving sized pieces. Cook the sausages for 15 minutes, shaking the basket occasionally to get all sides browned. Set aside.
3. In the meantime, whisk the mayonnaise with mustard, lemon juice, garlic powder, and black pepper. Toss the broccoli with the mayo mixture.
4. Turn up temperature to 400 degrees F. Cook broccoli for 6 minutes, turning halfway through the cooking time.
5. Serve the sausage with the grilled broccoli on the side.

- **Nutrition Info:** 477 Calories; 42g Fat; 3g Carbs; 19g Protein; 7g Sugars; 6g Fiber

241.Garlic Butter Pork Chops

Servings: 4
Cooking Time: 8 Minutes
Ingredients:

- 4 pork chops
- 1 tablespoon coconut butter
- 2 teaspoons parsley
- 1 tablespoon coconut oil
- 2 teaspoons garlic, grated
- Salt and black pepper, to taste

Directions:

1. Preheat the Air fryer to 350 degree F and grease an Air fryer basket.
2. Mix all the seasonings, coconut oil, garlic, butter, and parsley in a bowl and coat the pork chops with it.
3. Cover the chops with foil and refrigerate to marinate for about 1 hour.
4. Remove the foil and arrange the chops in the Air fryer basket.

5. Cook for about 8 minutes and dish out in a bowl to serve warm.

- **Nutrition Info:** Calories: 311, Fat: 25.5g, Carbohydrates: 1.4g, Sugar: 0.3g, Protein: 18.4g, Sodium: 58mg

242.Five Spice Pork

Servings: 4
Cooking Time: 20 Minutes
Ingredients:

- 1-pound pork belly
- 2 tablespoons swerve
- 2 tablespoons dark soy sauce
- 1 tablespoon Shaoxing: cooking wine
- 2 teaspoons garlic, minced
- 2 teaspoons ginger, minced
- 1 tablespoon hoisin sauce
- 1 teaspoon Chinese Five Spice

Directions:

1. Preheat the Air fryer to 390 degree F and grease an Air fryer basket.
2. Mix all the ingredients in a bowl and place in the Ziplock bag.
3. Seal the bag, shake it well and refrigerate to marinate for about 1 hour.
4. Remove the pork from the bag and arrange it in the Air fryer basket.
5. Cook for about 15 minutes and dish out in a bowl to serve warm.

- **Nutrition Info:** Calories: 604, Fat: 30.6g, Carbohydrates: 1.4g, Sugar: 20.3g, Protein: 19.8g, Sodium: 834mg

243.Korean Beef Bowl

Servings: 4
Cooking Time: 18 Minutes
Ingredients:

- 1 tablespoon minced garlic
- 1 teaspoon ground ginger
- 4 oz chive stems, chopped
- 2 tablespoon apple cider vinegar
- 1 teaspoon stevia extract
- 1 tablespoon flax seeds
- 1 teaspoon olive oil
- 1 teaspoon olive oil
- 1-pound ground beef
- 4 tablespoon chicken stock

Directions:

1. Sprinkle the ground beef with the apple cider vinegar and stir the meat with the help of the spoon.
2. After this, sprinkle the ground beef with the ground ginger, minced garlic, and olive oil.
3. Mix it up.
4. Preheat the air fryer to 370 F.
5. Put the ground beef in the air fryer basket tray and cook it for 8 minutes.

6. After this, stir the ground beef carefully and sprinkle with the chopped chives, flax seeds, olive oil, and chicken stock.
7. Mix the dish up and cook it for 10 minutes more.
8. When the time is over – stir the dish carefully.
9. Serve Korean beef bowl immediately.
10. Enjoy!
- **Nutrition Info:** calories 258, fat 10.1, fiber 1.2, carbs 4.2, protein 35.3

244.Almond Pork Bites

Servings: 10
Cooking Time: 40 Minutes
Ingredients:
- 16 oz sausage meat
- 1 whole egg, beaten
- 3 ½ oz onion, chopped
- 2 tbsp dried sage
- 2 tbsp almonds, chopped
- ½ tsp pepper
- 3 ½ oz apple, sliced
- ½ tsp salt

Directions:
1. Preheat your air fryer to 350 f. In a bowl, mix onion, almonds, sliced apples, egg, pepper and salt. Add the almond mixture and sausage in a ziploc bag. Mix to coat well and set aside for 15 minutes.
2. Use the mixture to form cutlets. Add cutlets to your fryer's basket and cook for 25 minutes. Serve with heavy cream and enjoy!
- **Nutrition Info:** Calories: 491.7 Cal Total Fat: 25.9 g Saturated Fat: 4.4 g Cholesterol: 42 mg Sodium: 364.3 mg Total Carbs: 40.4 g Fiber: 3.3 g Sugar: 0.7 g Protein: 21.8 g

245.Garlic Lamb Shank

Servings: 5
Cooking Time: 24 Minutes
Ingredients:
- 17 oz. lamb shanks
- 2 tablespoon garlic, peeled
- 1 teaspoon kosher salt
- 1 tablespoon dried parsley
- 4 oz chive stems, chopped
- ½ cup chicken stock
- 1 teaspoon butter
- 1 teaspoon dried rosemary
- 1 teaspoon nutmeg
- ½ teaspoon ground black pepper

Directions:
1. Chop the garlic roughly.
2. Make the cuts in the lamb shank and fill the cuts with the chopped garlic.
3. Then sprinkle the lamb shank with the kosher salt, dried parsley, dried rosemary, nutmeg, and ground black pepper.

4. Stir the spices on the lamb shank gently.
5. Then put the butter and chicken stock in the air fryer basket tray.
6. Preheat the air fryer to 380 F.
7. Put the chives in the air fryer basket tray.
8. Add the lamb shank and cook the meat for 24 minutes.
9. When the lamb shank is cooked – transfer it to the serving plate and sprinkle with the remaining liquid from the cooked meat.
10. Enjoy!
- **Nutrition Info:** calories 205, fat 8.2, fiber 0.8, carbs 3.8, protein 27.2

246.Scallops With Capers Sauce

Servings: 2
Cooking Time: 6 Minutes
Ingredients:
- 10: 1-ouncesea scallops, cleaned and patted very dry
- 2 tablespoons fresh parsley, finely chopped
- 2 teaspoons capers, finely chopped
- Salt and ground black pepper, as required
- ¼ cup extra-virgin olive oil
- 1 teaspoon fresh lemon zest, finely grated
- ½ teaspoon garlic, finely chopped

Directions:
1. Preheat the Air fryer to 390 degree F and grease an Air fryer basket.
2. Season the scallops evenly with salt and black pepper.
3. Arrange the scallops in the Air fryer basket and cook for about 6 minutes.
4. Mix parsley, capers, olive oil, lemon zest and garlic in a bowl.
5. Dish out the scallops in a platter and top with capers sauce.
- **Nutrition Info:** Calories: 344, Fat: 26.3g, Carbohydrates: 4.2g, Sugar: 0.1g, Protein: 24g, Sodium: 393mg

247.Broccoli And Tomato Sauce

Servings: 4
Cooking Time: 7 Minutes
Ingredients:
- 1 broccoli head, florets separated
- ¼ cup scallions; chopped
- ½ cup tomato sauce
- 1 tbsp. olive oil
- 1 tbsp. sweet paprika
- Salt and black pepper to taste.

Directions:
1. In a pan that fits the air fryer, combine the broccoli with the rest of the Ingredients: toss.
2. Put the pan in the fryer and cook at 380°F for 15 minutes
3. Divide between plates and serve.

- **Nutrition Info:** Calories: 163; Fat: 5g; Fiber: 2g; Carbs: 4g; Protein: 8g

248.Creamy Lemon Turkey

Servings: 4
Cooking Time: 20 Minutes
Ingredients:
- 1/3 cup sour cream
- 2 cloves garlic, finely minced 1/3 tsp. lemon zest
- 2 small-sized turkey breasts, skinless and cubed 1/3 cup thickened cream
- 2 tablespoons lemon juice
- 1 tsp. fresh marjoram, chopped
- Salt and freshly cracked mixed peppercorns, to taste 1/2 cup scallion, chopped
- 1/2 can tomatoes, diced
- 1½ tablespoons canola oil

Directions:
1. Firstly, pat dry the turkey breast. Mix the remaining items; marinate the turkey for 2 hours.
2. Set the air fryer to cook at 355 °F. Brush the turkey with a nonstick spray; cook for 23 minutes, turning once. Serve with naan and enjoy!

- **Nutrition Info:** 260 Calories; 15.3g Fat; 8.9g Carbs; 28.6g Protein; 1.9g Sugars

MEAT RECIPES

249.Italian Sausages And Red Grapes

Servings:6
Cooking Time: 20 Minutes
Ingredients:

- 2 pounds (905 g) seedless red grapes
- 3 shallots, sliced
- 2 teaspoons fresh thyme
- 2 tablespoons olive oil
- ½ teaspoon kosher salt
- Freshly ground black pepper, to taste
- 6 links (about 1½ pounds / 680 g) hot Italian sausage
- 3 tablespoons balsamic vinegar

Directions:

1. Place the grapes in a large bowl. Add the shallots, thyme, olive oil, salt, and pepper. Gently toss. Place the grapes in the baking pan. Arrange the sausage links evenly in the pan.
2. Slide the baking pan into Rack Position 2, select Roast, set temperature to 375ºF (190ºC), and set time to 20 minutes.
3. After 10 minutes, remove the pan. Turn over the sausages and sprinkle the vinegar over the sausages and grapes. Gently toss the grapes and move them to one side of the pan. Return the pan to the oven and continue cooking.
4. When cooking is complete, the grapes should be very soft and the sausages browned. Serve immediately.

250.Country Fried Steak

Servings: 2
Cooking Time: 12 Minutes
Ingredients:

- 1 tsp. pepper
- 2 C. almond milk
- 2 tbsp. almond flour
- 6 ounces ground sausage meat
- 1 tsp. pepper
- 1 tsp. salt
- 1 tsp. garlic powder
- 1 tsp. onion powder
- 1 C. panko breadcrumbs
- 1 C. almond flour
- 3 beaten eggs
- 6 ounces sirloin steak, pounded till thin

Directions:

1. Preparing the Ingredients. Season panko breadcrumbs with spices.
2. Dredge steak in flour, then egg, and then seasoned panko mixture.
3. Place into air fryer rack/basket.
4. Air Frying. Set temperature to 370°F, and set time to 12 minutes.

5. To make sausage gravy, cook sausage and drain off fat, but reserve 2 tablespoons.
6. Add flour to sausage and mix until incorporated. Gradually mix in milk over medium to high heat till it becomes thick.
7. Season mixture with pepper and cook 3 minutes longer.
8. Serve steak topped with gravy and enjoy!
- **Nutrition Info:** CALORIES: 395; FAT: 11G; PROTEIN:39G; SUGAR:5G

251.Minced Venison Grandma's Easy To Cook Wontons With Garlic Paste

Servings:x
Cooking Time:x
Ingredients:

- 1 ½ cup all-purpose flour
- ½ tsp. salt
- 2 tsp. soya sauce
- 5 tbsp. water
- 2 cups minced venison
- 2 tbsp. oil
- 2 tsp. ginger-garlic paste
- 2 tsp. vinegar

Directions:

1. Squeeze the dough and cover it with plastic wrap and set aside. Next, cook the ingredients for the filling and try to ensure that the venison is covered well with the sauce. Roll the dough and place the filling in the center.
2. Now, wrap the dough to cover the filling and pinch the edges together. Pre heat the oven at 200° F for 5 minutes.
3. Place the wontons in the fry basket and close it. Let them cook at the same temperature for another 20 minutes. Recommended sides are chili sauce or ketchup.

252.Parmesan Chicken Fingers With Plum Sauce

Servings: 2
Cooking Time: 20 Minutes
Ingredients:

- 2 chicken breasts, cut in strips
- 3 tbsp Parmesan cheese, grated
- ¼ tbsp fresh chives, chopped
- ⅓ cup breadcrumbs
- 1 egg white
- 2 tbsp plum sauce, optional
- ½ tbsp fresh thyme, chopped
- ½ tbsp black pepper
- 1 tbsp water

Directions:

1. Preheat on Air Fry function to 360 F. Mix the chives, Parmesan cheese, thyme, pepper

and breadcrumbs. In another bowl, whisk the egg white and mix with the water. Dip the chicken strips into the egg mixture and then in the breadcrumb mixture. Place the strips in the greased basket and fit in the baking tray. Cook for 10 minutes, flipping once. Serve with plum sauce.

253.Caraway Crusted Beef Steaks

Servings:4
Cooking Time: 10 Minutes
Ingredients:
- 4 beef steaks
- 2 teaspoons caraway seeds
- 2 teaspoons garlic powder
- Sea salt and cayenne pepper, to taste
- 1 tablespoon melted butter
- $^1/_3$ cup almond flour
- 2 eggs, beaten

Directions:
1. Add the beef steaks to a large bowl and toss with the caraway seeds, garlic powder, salt and pepper until well coated.
2. Stir together the melted butter and almond flour in a bowl. Whisk the eggs in a different bowl.
3. Dredge the seasoned steaks in the eggs, then dip in the almond and butter mixture.
4. Arrange the coated steaks in the basket.
5. Put the air fryer basket on the baking pan and slide into Rack Position 2, select Air Fry, set temperature to 355ºF (179ºC) and set time to 10 minutes.
6. Flip the steaks once halfway through to ensure even cooking.
7. When cooking is complete, the internal temperature of the beef steaks should reach at least 145ºF (63ºC) on a meat thermometer.
8. Transfer the steaks to plates. Let cool for 5 minutes and serve hot.

254.Pork Tandoor

Servings:x
Cooking Time:x
Ingredients:
- 2 cup fresh green coriander
- ½ cup mint leaves
- 4 tsp. fennel
- 2 tbsp. ginger-garlic paste
- 1 small onion
- 2 cups sliced pork belly
- 1 big capsicum (Cut this capsicum into big cubes)
- 1 onion (Cut it into quarters. Now separate the layers carefully.)
- 5 tbsp. gram flour
- A pinch of salt to taste
- 6-7 flakes garlic (optional)

- Salt to taste
- 3 tbsp. lemon juice

Directions:
1. You will first need to make the sauce. Add the ingredients to a blender and make a thick paste. Slit the pieces of pork and stuff half the paste into the cavity obtained. Take the remaining paste and add it to the gram flour and salt. Toss the pieces of Pork in this mixture and set aside. Apply a little bit of the mixture on the capsicum and onion.
2. Place these on a stick along with the pork pieces. Pre heat the oven at 290 Fahrenheit for around 5 minutes. Open the basket. Arrange the satay sticks properly.
3. Close the basket. Keep the sticks with the pork at 180 degrees for around half an hour while the sticks with the vegetables are to be kept at the same temperature for only 7 minutes. Turn the sticks in between so that one side does not get burnt and also to provide a uniform cook.

255.Easy Lamb Chops With Asparagus

Servings:4
Cooking Time: 15 Minutes
Ingredients:
- 4 asparagus spears, trimmed
- 2 tablespoons olive oil, divided
- 1 pound (454 g) lamb chops
- 1 garlic clove, minced
- 2 teaspoons chopped fresh thyme, for serving
- Salt and ground black pepper, to taste

Directions:
1. Spritz the air fryer basket with cooking spray.
2. On a large plate, brush the asparagus with 1 tablespoon olive oil, then sprinkle with salt. Set aside.
3. On a separate plate, brush the lamb chops with remaining olive oil and sprinkle with salt and ground black pepper.
4. Arrange the lamb chops in the pan.
5. Put the air fryer basket on the baking pan and slide into Rack Position 2, select Air Fry, set temperature to 400ºF (205ºC) and set time to 15 minutes.
6. Flip the lamb chops and add the asparagus and garlic halfway through.
7. When cooking is complete, the lamb should be well browned and the asparagus should be tender.
8. Serve them on a plate with thyme on top.

256.Mom's Meatballs

Servings:4
Cooking Time: 20 Minutes
Ingredients:
- 1 lb ground beef

- 2 tbsp olive oil
- 1 red onion, chopped
- 1 garlic clove, minced
- 2 whole eggs, beaten
- Salt and black pepper to taste

Directions:
1. Warm olive oil in a pan over medium heat and sauté onion and garlic for 3 minutes until tender; transfer to a bowl. Add in ground beef and egg and mix well. Season with salt and pepper.
2. Preheat oven to 360 F on AirFry function. Mold the mixture into golf-size ball shapes. Place the balls in the greased frying basket and cook for 12-14 minutes. Serve.

257. Italian Steak And Spinach Rolls

Servings:4
Cooking Time: 9 Minutes
Ingredients:
- 2 teaspoons dried Italian seasoning
- 2 cloves garlic, minced
- 1 tablespoon vegetable oil
- 1 teaspoon kosher salt
- 1 teaspoon ground black pepper
- 1 pound (454 g) flank steak, ¼ to ½ inch thick
- 1 (10-ounce / 284-g) package frozen spinach, thawed and squeezed dry
- ½ cup diced jarred roasted red pepper
- 1 cup shredded Mozzarella cheese
- Cooking spray

Directions:
1. Combine the Italian seasoning, garlic, vegetable oil, salt, and ground black pepper in a large bowl. Stir to mix well.
2. Dunk the steak in the seasoning mixture and toss to coat well. Wrap the bowl in plastic and marinate under room temperature for at least 30 minutes.
3. Spritz the air fryer basket with cooking spray.
4. Remove the marinated steak from the bowl and unfold on a clean work surface, then spread the top of the steak with a layer of spinach, a layer of red pepper and a layer of cheese. Leave a ¼-inch edge uncovered.
5. Roll the steak up to wrap the filling, then secure with 3 toothpicks. Cut the roll in half and transfer the rolls in the prepared basket, seam side down.
6. Put the air fryer basket on the baking pan and slide into Rack Position 2, select Air Fry, set temperature to 400ºF (205ºC) and set time to 9 minutes.
7. Flip the rolls halfway through the cooking.
8. When cooking is complete, the steak should be lightly browned and the internal temperature reaches at least 145ºF (63ºC).

9. Remove the rolls from the oven and slice to serve.

258. Honey And Wine Chicken Breasts

Servings: 4
Cooking Time: 15 Minutes
Ingredients:
- 2 chicken breasts, rinsed and halved
- 1 tablespoon melted butter
- 1/2 teaspoon freshly ground pepper, or to taste
- 3/4 teaspoon sea salt, or to taste
- 1 teaspoon paprika
- 1 teaspoon dried rosemary
- 2 tablespoons dry white wine
- 1 tablespoon honey

Directions:
1. Preparing the Ingredients. Firstly, pat the chicken breasts dry. Lightly coat them with the melted butter.
2. Then, add the remaining ingredients.
3. Air Frying. Transfer them to the air fryer rack/basket; bake about 15 minutes at 330 degrees F. Serve warm and enjoy
- **Nutrition Info:** CALORIES: 189; FAT: 14G; PROTEIN:11G; SUGAR:1

259. Juicy Baked Chicken Breast

Servings: 4
Cooking Time: 25 Minutes
Ingredients:
- 4 chicken breasts
- 1 tbsp fresh parsley, chopped
- 1/4 tsp red pepper flakes
- 1/2 tsp black pepper
- 1 tsp Italian seasoning
- 2 tbsp olive oil
- 1/4 cup balsamic vinegar
- 1 tsp kosher salt

Directions:
1. Fit the oven with the rack in position
2. Place chicken breasts into the mixing bowl.
3. Mix together remaining ingredients and pour over chicken breasts and coat well and let marinate for 30 minutes.
4. Arrange marinated chicken breasts into a greased baking dish.
5. Set to bake at 425 F for 30 minutes. After 5 minutes place the baking dish in the preheated oven.
6. Slice and serve.
- **Nutrition Info:** Calories 345 Fat 18.2 g Carbohydrates 0.6 g Sugar 0.2 g Protein 42.3 g Cholesterol 131 mg

260. Hot Chicken Wings

Servings: 2
Cooking Time: 20 Minutes + Chilling Time
Ingredients:

- 8 chicken wings
- 1 tbsp water
- 2 tbsp potato starch
- 2 tbsp hot curry paste
- ½ tbsp baking powder

Directions:
1. Combine hot curry paste and water in a small bowl. Add in the wings toss to coat. Cover the bowl with plastic wrap and refrigerate for 30 minutes.
2. Preheat on Air Fry function to 370 degrees. In a bowl, mix the baking powder with potato starch. Remove the wings from the fridge and dip them in the starch mixture.
3. Place on a lined baking dish and cook in your for 7 minutes. Flip over and cook for 5 minutes.

261.Morning Ham & Cheese Sandwich

Servings: 4
Cooking Time: 15 Minutes
Ingredients:
- 8 slices whole wheat bread
- 4 slices lean pork ham
- 4 slices cheese
- 8 slices tomato

Directions:
1. Lay four slices of bread on a flat surface. Spread the slices with cheese, tomato, turkey, and ham. Cover with the remaining slices to form sandwiches. Add the sandwiches to the cooking basket and cook for 10 minutes at 360 F on Air Fry function. Serve.

262.Beef Chimichangas

Servings: 4
Cooking Time: 10 Minutes
Ingredients:
- 1 lb. ground beef
- 1 tbsp. taco seasoning
- 1/3 cup salsa
- 4 flour tortillas
- 16 oz. refried beans
- 1 cup Mexican cheese blend, grated
- 1 cup lettuce, shredded
- 1 tbsp. olive oil

Directions:
1. Heat a medium skillet over medium heat. Add beef and taco seasoning and cook, breaking up with spatula, until meat is no longer pink. Stir in salsa and remove from heat.
2. Place tortillas, one at a time, on work surface and spread with 1/3 cup beans, leaving a 1-inch border.
3. Top with beef mixture, cheese and lettuce. Fold one edge of the tortilla to the middle, then the opposite edge so they overlap

slightly. Fold other two ends towards middle until you have a rectangular pocket.
4. Place the baking pan in position 2 of the oven. Lightly brush Chimichangas with oil and place in fryer basket. Place on baking pan.
5. Set oven to air fry on 400°F for 10 minutes. Cook until Chimichangas are golden brown and crispy. Serve immediately with your favorite toppings.
- **Nutrition Info:** Calories 638, Total Fat 22g, Saturated Fat 9g, Total Carbs 58g, Net Carbs 42g, Protein 52g, Sugar 3g, Fiber 12g, Sodium 928mg, Potassium 1045mg, Phosphorus 650mg

263.Peppercorn Pork Chops

Servings:x
Cooking Time:x
Ingredients:
- 4 (8-to 10-oz) pork chops, about 1-inch thick, at room temperature
- 1 Tbsp coarsely crushed black peppercorns
- 2 Tbsp extra-virgin olive oil
- 1 (16-oz) bag frozen French-style green beans
- Salt and freshly ground black pepper, to taste

Directions:
1. Pat the chops dry. Rub each of the pork chops on both sides with the peppercorns, pressing hard.
2. In oven, heat the olive oil until hot.
3. Add the pork chops and cook, uncovered, for 6 to 8 minutes on each side.
4. Turn off the heat and let them rest in the pot for 5 minutes before transferring them to a plate.
5. Add the green beans to oven over medium-high heat and cook until tender, about 5 minutes. Season with salt and pepper, and serve over the pork chops.

264.Baked Sweet & Tangy Pork Chops

Servings: 2
Cooking Time: 35 Minutes
Ingredients:
- 2 pork chops
- 2 tbsp brown sugar
- 2 tbsp ketchup
- 2 onion sliced
- Pepper
- Salt

Directions:
1. Fit the oven with the rack in position
2. Season pork chops with pepper and salt.
3. Place pork chops in a baking dish.
4. Mix ketchup and brown sugar and pour over pork chops.

5. Top with onion slices.
6. Set to bake at 375 F for 40 minutes. After 5 minutes place the baking dish in the preheated oven.
7. Serve and enjoy.
- **Nutrition Info:** Calories 308 Fat 19.9 g Carbohydrates 13.5 g Sugar 12.5 g Protein 18.4 g Cholesterol 69 mg

265. Lamb Chili With Red Chili Sauce

Servings:x
Cooking Time:x
Ingredients:
- 1 lb. lamb (Cut into cubes)
- 2 ½ tsp. ginger-garlic paste
- 1 tsp. red chili sauce
- 2 tbsp. tomato ketchup
- 2 tsp. soya sauce
- 1-2 tbsp. honey
- ¼ tsp. Ajinomoto
- 1-2 tsp. red chili flakes
- ¼ tsp. salt
- ¼ tsp. red chili powder/black pepper
- A few drops of edible orange food coloring
- For sauce:
- 2 tbsp. olive oil
- 1 ½ tsp. ginger garlic paste
- ½ tbsp. red chili sauce

Directions:
1. Mix all the ingredients for the marinade and put the lamb cubes inside and let it rest overnight. Mix the breadcrumbs, oregano and red chili flakes well and place the marinated Oregano Fingers on this mixture. Cover it with plastic wrap and leave it till right before you serve to cook.
2. Pre heat the oven at 160 degrees Fahrenheit for 5 minutes. Place the Oregano Fingers in the fry basket and close it. Let them cook at the same temperature for another 15 minutes or so.
3. Toss the Oregano Fingers well so that they are cooked uniformly.

266. Lamb Skewered Momo's Recipe

Servings:x
Cooking Time:x
Ingredients:
- 2 cups minced lamb
- 2 tbsp. oil
- 1 ½ cup all-purpose flour
- ½ tsp. salt
- 5 tbsp. water
- 2 tsp. ginger-garlic paste
- 2 tsp. soya sauce
- 2 tsp. vinegar

Directions:
1. Squeeze the dough and cover it with plastic wrap and set aside. Next, cook the

ingredients for the filling and try to ensure that the lamb is covered well with the sauce. Roll the dough and cut it into a square. Place the filling in the center.
2. Now, wrap the dough to cover the filling and pinch the edges together. Pre heat the oven at 200° F for 5 minutes. Place the wontons in the fry basket and close it. Let them cook at the same temperature for another 20 minutes. Recommended sides are chili sauce or ketchup.

267. Duck Breasts With Marmalade Balsamic Glaze

Servings:4
Cooking Time: 13 Minutes
Ingredients:
- 4 (6-ounce / 170-g) skin-on duck breasts
- 1 teaspoon salt
- ¼ cup orange marmalade
- 1 tablespoon white balsamic vinegar
- ¾ teaspoon ground black pepper

Directions:
1. Cut 10 slits into the skin of the duck breasts, then sprinkle with salt on both sides.
2. Place the breasts in the air fryer basket, skin side up.
3. Put the air fryer basket on the baking pan and slide into Rack Position 2, select Air Fry, set temperature to 400ºF (205ºC) and set time to 10 minutes.
4. Meanwhile, combine the remaining ingredients in a small bowl. Stir to mix well.
5. When cooking is complete, brush the duck skin with the marmalade mixture. Flip the breast and air fry for 3 more minutes or until the skin is crispy and the breast is well browned.
6. Serve immediately.

268. Duck Liver Fries

Servings:x
Cooking Time:x
Ingredients:
- A pinch of salt to taste
- 1 tbsp. lemon juice
- For the garnish:
- 1 cup melted cheddar cheese
- 1 lb. duck liver (Cut in to long Oregano Fingers)
- ingredients for the marinade:
- 1 tbsp. olive oil
- 1 tsp. mixed herbs
- ½ tsp. red chili flakes

Directions:
1. Take all the ingredients mentioned under the heading "For the marinade" and mix them well.

2. Cook the duck liver Oregano Fingers and soak them in the marinade.
3. Pre heat the oven for around 5 minutes at 300 Fahrenheit. Take out the basket of the fryer and place the chicken Oregano Fingers in them. Close the basket.
4. Now keep the fryer at 220 Fahrenheit for 20 or 25 minutes. In between the process, toss the fries twice or thrice so that they get cooked properly.
5. Towards the end of the cooking process (the last 2 minutes or so), sprinkle the cut coriander leaves on the fries. Add the melted cheddar cheese over the fries and serve hot.

269.Sweet Pork Belly

Servings:6
Cooking Time: 35 Minutes
Ingredients:
- 2 pounds pork belly
- Salt and black pepper to taste
- 3 tbsp olive oil
- 3 tbsp honey

Directions:
1. Season the pork belly with salt and pepper. Grease a baking dish with olive oil. Add in the meat and place in the oven. Select Bake function, adjust the temperature to 400 F, and press Start. Cook for 15 minutes. Brush with honey and cook for 10 more minutes. Serve with green salad.

270.Air Fried Crispy Venison

Servings:4
Cooking Time: 10 Minutes
Ingredients:
- 2 eggs
- ¼ cup milk
- 1 cup whole wheat flour
- ½ teaspoon salt
- ¼ teaspoon ground black pepper
- 1 pound (454 g) venison backstrap, sliced
- Cooking spray

Directions:
1. Spritz the air fryer basket with cooking spray.
2. Whisk the eggs with milk in a large bowl. Combine the flour with salt and ground black pepper in a shallow dish.
3. Dredge the venison in the flour first, then into the egg mixture. Shake the excess off and roll the venison back over the flour to coat well.
4. Arrange the venison in the pan and spritz with cooking spray.
5. Put the air fryer basket on the baking pan and slide into Rack Position 2, select Air Fry,

set temperature to 360ºF (182ºC) and set time to 10 minutes.
6. Flip the venison halfway through.
7. When cooking is complete, the internal temperature of the venison should reach at least 145ºF (63ºC) for medium rare.
8. Serve immediately.

271.Seafood Grandma's Easy To Cook Wontons

Servings:x
Cooking Time:x
Ingredients:
- 1 ½ cup all-purpose flour
- ½ tsp. salt
- 5 tbsp. water
- For filling:
- 2 cups minced seafood (prawns, shrimp, oysters, scallops)
- 2 tbsp. oil
- 2 tsp. ginger-garlic paste
- 2 tsp. soya sauce
- 2 tsp. vinegar

Directions:
1. Squeeze the dough and cover it with plastic wrap and set aside. Next, cook the ingredients for the filling and try to ensure that the seafood is covered well with the sauce. Roll the dough and place the filling in the center. Now, wrap the dough to cover the filling and pinch the edges together. Pre heat the oven at 200° F for 5 minutes.
2. Place the wontons in the fry basket and close it. Let them cook at the same temperature for another 20 minutes. Recommended sides are chili sauce or ketchup.

272.Fried Pork Scotch Egg

Servings: 2
Cooking Time: 25 Minutes
Ingredients:
- 3 soft-boiled eggs, peeled
- 8 ounces of raw minced pork, or sausage outside the casings
- 2 teaspoons of ground rosemary
- 2 teaspoons of garlic powder
- Pinch of salt and pepper
- 2 raw eggs
- 1 cup of breadcrumbs (Panko, but other brands are fine, or home-made bread crumbs work too)

Directions:
1. Preparing the Ingredients. Cover the basket of the air fryer oven with a lining of tin foil, leaving the edges uncovered to allow air to circulate through the basket. Preheat the air fryer oven to 350 degrees.

2. In a mixing bowl, combine the raw pork with the rosemary, garlic powder, salt, and pepper. This will probably be easiest to do with your masher or bare hands (though make sure to wash thoroughly after handling raw meat!); combine until all the spices are evenly spread throughout the meat.
3. Divide the meat mixture into three equal portions in the mixing bowl, and form each into balls with your hands.
4. Lay a large sheet of plastic wrap on the countertop, and flatten one of the balls of meat on top of it, to form a wide, flat meat-circle.
5. Place one of the peeled soft-boiled eggs in the center of the meat-circle and then, using the ends of the plastic wrap, pull the meat-circle so that it is fully covering and surrounding the soft-boiled egg.
6. Tighten and shape the plastic wrap covering the meat so that if forms a ball, and make sure not to squeeze too hard lest you squish the soft-boiled egg at the center of the ball! Set aside.
7. Repeat steps 5-7 with the other two soft-boiled eggs and portions of meat-mixture.
8. In a separate mixing bowl, beat the two raw eggs until fluffy and until the yolks and whites are fully combined.
9. One by one, remove the plastic wrap and dunk the pork-covered balls into the raw egg, and then roll them in the bread crumbs, covering fully and generously.
10. Place each of the bread-crumb covered meat-wrapped balls onto the foil-lined surface of the air fryer oven. Three of them should fit nicely, without touching.
11. Air Frying. Set the air fryer oven timer to 25 minutes.
12. About halfway through the cooking time, shake the handle of the air-fryer vigorously, so that the scotch eggs inside roll around and ensure full coverage.
13. After 25 minutes, the air fryer oven will shut off, and the scotch eggs should be perfect – the meat fully cooked, the egg-yolks still runny on the inside, and the outsides crispy and golden-brown. Using tongs, place them on serving plates, slice in half, and enjoy

273.Mini Pot Pies

Servings: 16
Cooking Time: 20 Minutes
Ingredients:
- 2 cans large flaky biscuits, refrigerated
- 6 oz. turkey, cooked & chopped fine
- 3 ½ cups turkey gravy
- 2 cups mixed vegetables

- 1 cup cheddar cheese, grated

Directions:
1. Place baking pan in position 1 of the oven. Spray 3 6-cup muffin tins with cooking spray.
2. Gently pull each biscuit until it is double in size. Press into prepared tins, pressing up the sides until edge is at, or above, the top of the cup.
3. In a large bowl, stir together turkey, gravy, and vegetables. Spoon mixture into biscuits. Top with cheese.
4. Set oven to bake on 350°F for 25 minutes. After 5 minutes, place muffin tin, one at a time, in the oven and bake until golden brown, about 20-22 minutes. Repeat with remaining tins. Serve warm.
- **Nutrition Info:** Calories 324, Total Fat 8g, Saturated Fat 2g, Total Carbs 24g, Net Carbs 23g, Protein 9g, Sugar 1g, Fiber 1g, Sodium 790mg, Potassium 210mg, Phosphorus 232mg

274.Pork Grandma's Easy To Cook Wontons

Servings:x
Cooking Time:x
Ingredients:
- 1 ½ cup all-purpose flour
- ½ tsp. salt
- 2 tsp. soya sauce
- 2 tbsp. oil
- 2 tsp. ginger-garlic paste
- 2 tsp. vinegar
- 5 tbsp. water
- 2 cups minced pork

Directions:
1. Squeeze the dough and cover it with plastic wrap and set aside. Next, cook the ingredients for the filling and try to ensure that the pork is covered well with the sauce. Roll the dough and place the filling in the center.
2. Now, wrap the dough to cover the filling and pinch the edges together. Pre heat the oven at 200° F for 5 minutes. Place the wontons in the fry basket and close it.
3. Let them cook at the same temperature for another 20 minutes. Recommended sides are chili sauce or ketchup.

275.Pork Sausages Bites With Almonds & Apples

Servings:6
Cooking Time: 25 Minutes
Ingredients:
- 16 oz sausage meat
- 1 whole egg, beaten
- 3 ½ oz onion, chopped

- 2 tbsp dried sage
- 2 tbsp almonds, chopped
- ½ tsp pepper
- 3 ½ oz apple, sliced
- ½ tsp salt

Directions:
1. Preheat oven to 350 F on AirFry function. In a bowl, mix onion, almonds, apples, egg, pepper, and salt. Add in the sausages and mix well with your hands. Form bite-size shapes from the mixture and add them to the frying basket. Cook for 20 minutes until golden. Serve warm.

276.Cheesy Turkey Burgers

Servings:4
Cooking Time: 25 Minutes
Ingredients:
- 2 medium yellow onions
- 1 tablespoon olive oil
- 1½ teaspoons kosher salt, divided
- 1¼ pound (567 g) ground turkey
- $^1/_3$ cup mayonnaise
- 1 tablespoon Dijon mustard
- 2 teaspoons Worcestershire sauce
- 4 slices sharp Cheddar cheese (about 4 ounces / 113 g in total)
- 4 hamburger buns, sliced

Directions:
1. Trim the onions and cut them in half through the root. Cut one of the halves in half. Grate one quarter. Place the grated onion in a large bowl. Thinly slice the remaining onions and place in a medium bowl with the oil and ½ teaspoon of kosher salt. Toss to coat. Place the onions in a single layer in the baking pan.
2. Slide the baking pan into Rack Position 2, select Roast, set temperature to 350ºF (180ºC), and set time to 10 minutes.
3. While the onions are cooking, add the turkey to the grated onion. Add the remaining kosher salt, mayonnaise, mustard, and Worcestershire sauce. Mix just until combined, being careful not to overwork the turkey. Divide the mixture into 4 patties, each about ¾-inch thick.
4. When cooking is complete, remove from the oven. Move the onions to one side of the pan and place the burgers on the pan. Poke your finger into the center of each burger to make a deep indentation.
5. Select Convection Broil, set temperature to High, and set time to 12 minutes.
6. After 6 minutes, remove the pan. Turn the burgers and stir the onions. Return the pan to the oven and continue cooking. After about 4 minutes, remove the pan and place the cheese slices on the burgers. Return the pan to the oven and continue cooking for about 1 minute, or until the cheese is melted and the center of the burgers has reached at least 165ºF (74ºC) on a meat thermometer.
7. When cooking is complete, remove from the oven. Loosely cover the burgers with foil.
8. Lay out the buns, cut-side up, on the oven rack. Select Convection Broil; set temperature to High, and set time to 3 minutes. Check the buns after 2 minutes; they should be lightly browned.
9. Remove the buns from the oven. Assemble the burgers and serve.

277.Gold Livers

Servings:4
Cooking Time: 10 Minutes
Ingredients:
- 2 eggs
- 2 tablespoons water
- ¾ cup flour
- 2 cups panko bread crumbs
- 1 teaspoon salt
- ½ teaspoon ground black pepper
- 20 ounces (567 g) chicken livers
- Cooking spray

Directions:
1. Spritz the air fryer basket with cooking spray.
2. Whisk the eggs with water in a large bowl. Pour the flour in a separate bowl. Pour the panko on a shallow dish and sprinkle with salt and pepper.
3. Dredge the chicken livers in the flour. Shake the excess off, then dunk the livers in the whisked eggs, and then roll the livers over the panko to coat well.
4. Arrange the livers in the basket and spritz with cooking spray.
5. Put the air fryer basket on the baking pan and slide into Rack Position 2, select Air Fry, set temperature to 390ºF (199ºC) and set time to 10 minutes.
6. Flip the livers halfway through.
7. When cooking is complete, the livers should be golden and crispy.
8. Serve immediately.

278.Delicious Lamb Patties

Servings: 4
Cooking Time: 15 Minutes
Ingredients:
- 1 lb ground lamb
- 1 tsp ground coriander
- 1 tsp ground cumin
- 1/4 cup fresh parsley, chopped
- 1/4 cup onion, minced
- 1 tbsp garlic, minced

- 1/4 tsp cayenne pepper
- 1/2 tsp ground allspice
- 1 tsp ground cinnamon
- 1/4 tsp pepper
- 1 tsp kosher salt

Directions:
1. Fit the oven with the rack in position
2. Add all ingredients into the mixing bowl and mix until well combined.
3. Make small patties from meat mixture and place onto the parchment-lined baking pan.
4. Set to bake at 450 F for 20 minutes. After 5 minutes place the baking pan in the preheated oven.
5. Serve and enjoy.
- **Nutrition Info:** Calories 223 Fat 8.5 g Carbohydrates 2.6 g Sugar 0.4 g Protein 32.3 g Cholesterol 102 mg

279.Korean-style Chicken Wings

Servings: 4
Cooking Time: 20 Minutes
Ingredients:
- 1 pound chicken wings
- 8 oz flour
- 8 oz breadcrumbs
- 3 beaten eggs
- 4 tbsp canola oil
- Salt and black pepper to taste
- 2 tbsp sesame seeds
- 2 tbsp Korean red pepper paste
- 1 tbsp apple cider vinegar
- 2 tbsp honey
- 1 tbsp soy sauce
- Sesame seeds, to serve

Directions:
1. Separate the chicken wings into winglets and drumettes. In a bowl, mix salt, olive oil, and pepper. Coat the chicken with flour followed by eggs and breadcrumbs. Place in the basket and fit in the baking tray. Oil with cooking spray and cook for 15 minutes on Air Fry mode at 350 F.
2. Mix red pepper paste, apple cider vinegar, soy sauce, honey, and ¼ cup of water in a saucepan and bring to a boil over medium heat. Simmer until the sauce thickens, about 3-4 minutes. Pour the sauce over the chicken pieces. Garnish with sesame seeds and serve.

280.Worcestershire Ribeye Steaks

Servings:2 To 4
Cooking Time: 10 To 12 Minutes
Ingredients:
- 2 (8-ounce / 227-g) boneless ribeye steaks
- 4 teaspoons Worcestershire sauce
- ½ teaspoon garlic powder
- Salt and ground black pepper, to taste
- 4 teaspoons olive oil

Directions:
1. Brush the steaks with Worcestershire sauce on both sides. Sprinkle with garlic powder and coarsely ground black pepper. Drizzle the steaks with olive oil. Allow steaks to marinate for 30 minutes.
2. Transfer the steaks into the basket.
3. Put the air fryer basket on the baking pan and slide into Rack Position 2, select Roast, set the temperature to 400ºF (205ºC) and set time to 4 minutes.
4. After 2 minutes, remove from the oven. Flip the steaks. Return to the oven and continue cooking.
5. When cooking is complete, the steaks should be well browned.
6. Remove the steaks from the basket and let sit for 5 minutes. Salt and serve.

281.Honey Glazed Chicken Breasts

Servings:4
Cooking Time: 10 Minutes
Ingredients:
- 4 (4-ounce / 113-g) boneless, skinless chicken breasts
- Chicken seasoning or rub, to taste
- Salt and ground black pepper, to taste
- ¼ cup honey
- 2 tablespoons soy sauce
- 2 teaspoons grated fresh ginger
- 2 garlic cloves, minced
- Cooking spray

Directions:
1. Spritz the air fryer basket with cooking spray.
2. Rub the chicken breasts with chicken seasoning, salt, and black pepper on a clean work surface.
3. Arrange the chicken breasts in the basket and spritz with cooking spray.
4. Put the air fryer basket on the baking pan and slide into Rack Position 2, select Air Fry, set temperature to 400ºF (205ºC) and set time to 10 minutes.
5. Flip the chicken breasts halfway through.
6. When cooking is complete, the internal temperature of the thickest part of the chicken should reach at least 165ºF (74ºC).
7. Meanwhile, combine the honey, soy sauce, ginger, and garlic in a saucepan and heat over medium-high heat for 3 minutes or until thickened. Stir constantly.
8. Remove the chicken from the oven and serve with the honey glaze.

282.Pheasant Chili

Servings:x
Cooking Time:x
Ingredients:

- 1 lb. cubed pheasant
- 2 ½ tsp. ginger-garlic paste
- 1 tsp. red chili sauce
- ¼ tsp. salt
- ¼ tsp. red chili powder/black pepper
- A few drops of edible orange food coloring
- For sauce:
- 2 tbsp. olive oil
- 1 ½ tsp. ginger garlic paste
- ½ tbsp. red chili sauce
- 2 tbsp. tomato ketchup
- 2 tsp. soya sauce
- 1-2 tbsp. honey
- ¼ tsp. Ajinomoto
- 1-2 tsp. red chili flakes

Directions:
1. Mix all the ingredients for the marinade and put the pheasant cubes inside and let it rest overnight. Mix the breadcrumbs, oregano and red chili flakes well and place the marinated Oregano Fingers on this mixture.
2. Cover it with plastic wrap and leave it till right before you serve to cook. Pre heat the oven at 160 degrees Fahrenheit for 5 minutes. Place the Oregano Fingers in the fry basket and close it. Let them cook at the same temperature for another 15 minutes or so. Toss the Oregano Fingers well so that they are cooked uniformly.

283.Calf's Liver Golden Strips

Servings:4
Cooking Time: 4 To 5 Minutes
Ingredients:
- 1 pound (454 g) sliced calf's liver, cut into about ½-inch-wide strips
- Salt and ground black pepper, to taste
- 2 eggs
- 2 tablespoons milk
- ½ cup whole wheat flour
- 1½ cups panko bread crumbs
- ½ cup plain bread crumbs
- ½ teaspoon salt
- ¼ teaspoon ground black pepper
- Cooking spray

Directions:
1. Sprinkle the liver strips with salt and pepper.
2. Beat together the egg and milk in a bowl. Place wheat flour in a shallow dish. In a second shallow dish, mix panko, plain bread crumbs, ½ teaspoon salt, and ¼ teaspoon pepper.
3. Dip liver strips in flour, egg wash, and then bread crumbs, pressing in coating slightly to make crumbs stick.
4. Spritz the air fryer basket with cooking spray. Place strips in a single layer in the basket.

5. Put the air fryer basket on the baking pan and slide into Rack Position 2, select Air Fry, set the temperature to 400ºF (205ºC) and set the time to 4 minutes.
6. After 2 minutes, remove from the oven. Flip the strips with tongs. Return to the oven and continue cooking.
7. When cooking is complete, the liver strips should be crispy and golden.
8. Serve immediately.

284.Hot Curried Chicken Wings

Servings:2
Cooking Time: 20 Minutes + Marinating Time
Ingredients:
- 8 chicken wings
- 1 tbsp water
- 4 tbsp potato starch
- 2 tbsp hot curry paste
- ½ tbsp baking powder

Directions:
1. In a bowl, combine curry paste with 1 tbsp of water. Add in the wings and toss to coat. Cover the bowl with cling film and refrigerate for 2 hours.
2. Preheat on AirFry function to 370 degrees. In a bowl, mix baking powder and potato starch. Dip in the wings. Transfer to a lined baking dish, press Start, and cook for 14 minutes.

285.Saucy Grilled Chicken

Servings:2
Cooking Time: 25 Minutes + Marinating Time
Ingredients:
- 2 chicken breasts, cubed
- 1 garlic clove, minced
- ½ cup ketchup
- ½ tbsp fresh ginger, minced
- ½ cup soy sauce
- 2 tbsp sherry
- ½ cup pineapple juice
- 2 tbsp apple cider vinegar
- ½ cup brown sugar

Directions:
1. In a saucepan over low heat, mix ketchup, pineapple juice, sugar, vinegar, soy sauce, sherry, and ginger and stir until heated. Pour the hot sauce over the chicken. Marinate for 15 minutes.
2. Preheat on Bake function to 360 F. Transfer the chicken in a baking dish and press Start. Bake for 15 -20 minutes. Serve warm.

286.Hearty Mushroom And Sausage Calzones

Servings:4
Cooking Time: 24 Minutes
Ingredients:

- 2 links Italian sausages (about ½ pound / 227 g)
- 1 pound (454 g) pizza dough, thawed
- 3 tablespoons olive oil, divided
- ¼ cup Marinara sauce
- ½ cup roasted mushrooms
- 1 cup shredded Mozzarella cheese

Directions:
1. Place the sausages in the baking pan.
2. Slide the baking pan into Rack Position 2, select Roast, set temperature to 375ºF (190ºC), and set time to 12 minutes.
3. After 6 minutes, remove from the oven and turn over the sausages. Return to the oven and continue cooking.
4. While the sausages cook, divide the pizza dough into 4 equal pieces. One at a time, place a piece of dough onto a square of parchment paper 9 inches in diameter. Brush the dough on both sides with ¾ teaspoon of olive oil, then top the dough with another piece of parchment. Press the dough into a 7-inch circle. Remove the top piece of parchment and set aside. Repeat with the remaining pieces of dough.
5. When cooking is complete, remove from the oven. Place the sausages on a cutting board. Let them cool for several minutes, then slice into ¼-inch rounds and cut each round into 4 pieces.
6. One at a time, spread a tablespoon of marinara sauce over half of a dough circle, leaving a ½-inch border at the edges. Cover with a quarter of the sausage pieces and add a quarter of the mushrooms. Sprinkle with ¼ cup of cheese. Pull the other side of the dough over the filling and pinch the edges together to seal. Transfer from the parchment to the baking pan. Repeat with the other rounds of dough, sauce, sausage, mushrooms, and cheese.
7. Brush the tops of the calzones with 1 tablespoon of olive oil.
8. Select Roast, set temperature to 450ºF (235ºC), and set time to 12 minutes.
9. After 6 minutes, remove from the oven. The calzones should be golden brown. Turn over the calzones and brush the tops with the remaining olive oil. Return the pan to the oven and continue cooking.
10. When cooking is complete, the crust should be a deep golden brown on both sides. Remove from the oven. The center should be molten; let cool for several minutes before serving.

287.Beer Corned Beef With Carrots

Servings:4
Cooking Time: 35 Minutes
Ingredients:

- 1 tbsp beef spice
- 1 white onion, chopped
- 2 carrots, chopped
- 12 oz bottle beer
- 1 ½ cups chicken broth
- 4 pounds corned beef

Directions:
1. Cover beef with beer and let sit in the fridge for 30 minutes. Transfer to a pot over medium heat and add in chicken broth, carrots, and onion. Bring to a boil and simmer for 10 minutes. Drain boiled meat and veggies and place them in a baking dish. Sprinkle with beef spice. Select Bake function, adjust the temperature to 400 F, and press Start. Cook for 30 minutes.

288.Pork Wonton Wonderful

Servings: 3
Cooking Time: 25 Minutes
Ingredients:

- 8 wanton wrappers (Leasa brand works great, though any will do)
- 4 ounces of raw minced pork
- 1 medium-sized green apple
- 1 cup of water, for wetting the wanton wrappers
- 1 tablespoon of vegetable oil
- ½ tablespoon of oyster sauce
- 1 tablespoon of soy sauce
- Large pinch of ground white pepper

Directions:
1. Preparing the Ingredients. Cover the basket of the air fryer oven with a lining of tin foil, leaving the edges uncovered to allow air to circulate through the basket. Preheat the air fryer oven to 350 degrees.
2. In a small mixing bowl, combine the oyster sauce, soy sauce, and white pepper, then add in the minced pork and stir thoroughly. Cover and set in the fridge to marinate for at least 15 minutes. Core the apple, and slice into small cubes – smaller than bite-sized chunks.
3. Add the apples to the marinating meat mixture, and combine thoroughly. Spread the wonton wrappers, and fill each with a large spoonful of the filling. Wrap the wontons into triangles, so that the wrappers fully cover the filling, and seal with a drop of the water.
4. Coat each filled and wrapped wonton thoroughly with the vegetable oil, to help ensure a nice crispy fry. Place the wontons on the foil-lined air-fryer rack/basket. Place the Rack on the middle-shelf of the air fryer oven.
5. Air Frying. Set the air fryer oven timer to 25 minutes. Halfway through cooking time,

shake the handle of the air fryer rack/basket vigorously to jostle the wontons and ensure even frying. After 25 minutes, when the air fryer oven shuts off, the wontons will be crispy golden-brown on the outside and juicy and delicious on the inside. Serve directly from the Oven rack/basket and enjoy while hot.

289.Teriyaki Pork Rolls

Servings: 6
Cooking Time: 8 Minutes
Ingredients:
- 1 tsp. almond flour
- 4 tbsp. low-sodium soy sauce
- 4 tbsp. mirin
- 4 tbsp. brown sugar
- Thumb-sized amount of ginger, chopped
- Pork belly slices
- Enoki mushrooms

Directions:
1. Preparing the Ingredients. Mix brown sugar, mirin, soy sauce, almond flour, and ginger together until brown sugar dissolves.
2. Take pork belly slices and wrap around a bundle of mushrooms. Brush each roll with teriyaki sauce. Chill half an hour.
3. Preheat your air fryer oven to 350 degrees and add marinated pork rolls.
4. Air Frying. Set temperature to 350°F, and set time to 8 minutes.
- **Nutrition Info:** CALORIES: 412; FAT: 9G; PROTEIN:19G; SUGAR:4G

290.Cayenne Chicken Drumsticks

Servings: 4
Cooking Time: 50 Minutes
Ingredients:
- 8 chicken drumsticks
- 2 tbsp oregano
- 2 tbsp thyme
- 2 oz oats
- ¼ cup milk
- ¼ steamed cauliflower florets
- 1 egg
- 1 tbsp ground cayenne pepper
- Salt and black pepper to taste

Directions:
1. Preheat on Air Fry function to 350 F. Season the drumsticks with salt and pepper; rub them with the milk. Place all the other ingredients except the egg in a food processor. Process until smooth. Dip drumsticks in the egg first and then in the oat mixture. Arrange on the greased AitjrFryer basket and fit in the baking tray. Cook for 20 minutes until golden brown.

291.Meatballs(7)

Servings: 4
Cooking Time: 10 Minutes
Ingredients:
- 2 eggs
- 1 tsp sesame oil
- 1 tsp ginger, minced
- 1 tsp garlic, minced
- 1/2 cup breadcrumbs
- 2 lbs ground pork
- 1/3 tsp red chili pepper flakes
- 1 tbsp scallions, diced
- 1 tsp soy sauce
- Pepper
- Salt

Directions:
1. Fit the oven with the rack in position 2.
2. Add all ingredients into the large bowl and mix until well combined.
3. Make small balls from meat mixture and place in the air fryer basket then place the air fryer basket in the baking pan.
4. Place a baking pan on the oven rack. Set to air fry at 400 F for 10 minutes.
5. Serve and enjoy.
- **Nutrition Info:** Calories 423 Fat 12 g Carbohydrates 10.7 g Sugar 1.1 g Protein 64.1 g Cholesterol 247 mg

292.Meatballs(16)

Servings: 6
Cooking Time: 12 Minutes
Ingredients:
- 1 egg
- 20 oz ground beef
- 1/2 cup parmesan cheese, grated
- 8 tbsp almond milk
- 6 garlic cloves, minced
- 3/4 cups almond meal
- 2 tbsp basil, chopped
- 2 tbsp parsley, chopped
- 1 tsp black pepper
- 1 tsp salt

Directions:
1. Fit the oven with the rack in position
2. Add all ingredients into the mixing bowl and mix until well combined.
3. Make small balls from the meat mixture and place it into the parchment-lined baking pan.
4. Set to bake at 350 F for 17 minutes. After 5 minutes place the baking pan in the preheated oven.
5. Serve and enjoy.
- **Nutrition Info:** Calories 331 Fat 19 g Carbohydrates 5.3 g Sugar 1.3 g Protein 35.3 g Cholesterol 117 mg

293.Chicken & Cheese Enchilada

Servings:4
Cooking Time: 35 Minutes
Ingredients:
- 1 lb chicken breasts, chopped
- 2 cups cheddar cheese, grated
- ½ cup salsa
- 1 can green chilies, chopped
- 12 flour tortillas
- 2 cups enchilada sauce

Directions:
1. In a bowl, mix salsa and enchilada sauce. Toss in the chopped chicken to coat. Place the chicken on the tortillas and roll; top with cheese. Place the prepared tortillas in a baking tray and press Start. Cook for 25-30 minutes at 400 F on Bake function. Serve with guacamole and hot dips!

294.Cayenne Turkey Breasts

Servings:4
Cooking Time: 25 Minutes
Ingredients:
- 1 lb turkey breast, boneless and skinless
- 2 cups panko breadcrumbs
- Cayenne pepper and salt to taste
- 1 stick butter, melted

Directions:
1. Preheat on AirFry function to 350 F. In a bowl, mix breadcrumbs, cayenne pepper, and salt. Brush the butter onto the turkey and coat with the breadcrumbs. Cook for 15 minutes.

295.Chicken Shawarma

Servings:4
Cooking Time: 18 Minutes
Ingredients:
- 1½ pounds (680 g) boneless, skinless chicken thighs
- 1¼ teaspoon kosher salt, divided
- 2 tablespoons plus 1 teaspoon olive oil, divided
- $^2/_3$ cup plus 2 tablespoons plain Greek yogurt, divided
- 2 tablespoons freshly squeezed lemon juice (about 1 medium lemon)
- 4 garlic cloves, minced, divided
- 1 tablespoon Shawarma Seasoning
- 4 pita breads, cut in half
- 2 cups cherry tomatoes
- ½ small cucumber, peeled, deseeded, and chopped
- 1 tablespoon chopped fresh parsley

Directions:
1. Sprinkle the chicken thighs on both sides with 1 teaspoon of kosher salt. Place in a resealable plastic bag and set aside while you make the marinade.

2. In a small bowl, mix 2 tablespoons of olive oil, 2 tablespoons of yogurt, the lemon juice, 3 garlic cloves, and Shawarma Seasoning until thoroughly combined. Pour the marinade over the chicken. Seal the bag, squeezing out as much air as possible. And massage the chicken to coat it with the sauce. Set aside.
3. Wrap 2 pita breads each in two pieces of aluminum foil and place in the baking pan.
4. Slide the baking pan into Rack Position 1, select Convection Bake, set temperature to 300ºF (150ºC), and set time to 6 minutes.
5. After 3 minutes, remove the pan from the oven and turn over the foil packets. Return the pan to the oven and continue cooking. When cooking is complete, remove the pan from the oven and place the foil-wrapped pitas on the top of the oven to keep warm.
6. Remove the chicken from the marinade, letting the excess drip off into the bag. Place them in the baking pan. Arrange the tomatoes around the sides of the chicken. Discard the marinade.
7. Slide the baking pan into Rack Position 2, select Convection Broil, set temperature to High, and set time to 12 minutes.
8. After 6 minutes, remove the pan from the oven and turn over the chicken. Return the pan to the oven and continue cooking.
9. Wrap the cucumber in a paper towel to remove as much moisture as possible. Place them in a small bowl. Add the remaining yogurt, kosher salt, olive oil, garlic clove, and parsley. Whisk until combined.
10. When cooking is complete, the chicken should be browned, crisp along its edges, and sizzling. Remove from the oven and place the chicken on a cutting board. Cut each thigh into several pieces. Unwrap the pitas. Spread a tablespoon of sauce into a pita half. Add some chicken and add 2 roasted tomatoes. Serve.

296.Pheasant Marinade Cutlet

Servings:x
Cooking Time:x
Ingredients:
- 2 cups sliced pheasant
- 1 big capsicum (Cut this capsicum into big cubes)
- 1 onion (Cut it into quarters. Now separate the layers carefully.)
- 5 tbsp. gram flour
- A pinch of salt to taste
- For the filling:
- 2 cup fresh green coriander
- ½ cup mint leaves
- 4 tsp. fennel
- 2 tbsp. ginger-garlic paste

- 1 small onion
- 6-7 flakes garlic (optional)
- Salt to taste
- 3 tbsp. lemon juice

Directions:
1. You will first need to make the sauce. Add the ingredients to a blender and make a thick paste. Slit the pieces of pheasant and stuff half the paste into the cavity obtained. Take the remaining paste and add it to the gram flour and salt.
2. Toss the pieces of pheasant in this mixture and set aside. Apply a little bit of the mixture on the capsicum and onion. Place these on a stick along with the pheasant pieces. Pre heat the oven at 290 Fahrenheit for around 5 minutes. Open the basket. Arrange the satay sticks properly. Close the basket.
3. Keep the sticks with the mutton at 180 degrees for around half an hour while the sticks with the vegetables are to be kept at the same temperature for only 7 minutes. Turn the sticks in between so that one side does not get burnt and also to provide a uniform cook.

297.Chicken Madeira

Servings:x
Cooking Time:x
Ingredients:
- 2 cups Madeira wine
- 2 cups beef broth
- ½ cup shredded Mozzarella cheese
- 4 boneless, skinless chicken breasts
- 1 Tbsp salt
- Salt and freshly ground black pepper, to taste
- 6 cups water
- ½ lb. asparagus, trimmed
- 2 Tbsp extra-virgin olive oil
- 2 Tbsp chopped fresh parsley

Directions:
1. Lay the chicken breasts on a cutting board, and cover each with a piece of plastic wrap. Use a mallet or a small, heavy frying pan to pound them to ¼ inch thick. Discard the plastic wrap and season with salt and pepper on both sides of the chicken.
2. Fill oven with the water, bring to a boil, and add the salt.
3. Add the asparagus and boil, uncovered, until crisp, tender, and bright green, 2 to 3 minutes. Remove immediately and set aside. Pour out the water.
4. In oven over medium heat, heat the olive oil. Cook the chicken for 4 to 5 minutes on each side. Remove and set aside.

5. Add the Madeira wine and beef broth. Bring to a boil, reduce to a simmer, and cook for 10 to 12 minutes.
6. Return the chicken to the pot, turning it to coat in the sauce.
7. Lay the asparagus and cheese on top of the chicken. Then transfer oven to the oven broiler and broil for 3 to 4 minutes. Garnish with the parsley, if using, and serve.

298.Bacon-wrapped Sausage With Tomato Relish

Servings:4
Cooking Time: 32 Minutes
Ingredients:
- 8 pork sausages
- 8 bacon strips
- Relish:
- 8 large tomatoes, chopped
- 1 small onion, peeled
- 1 clove garlic, peeled
- 1 tablespoon white wine vinegar
- 3 tablespoons chopped parsley
- 1 teaspoon smoked paprika
- 2 tablespoons sugar
- Salt and ground black pepper, to taste

Directions:
1. Purée the tomatoes, onion, and garlic in a food processor until well mixed and smooth.
2. Pour the purée in a saucepan and drizzle with white wine vinegar. Sprinkle with salt and ground black pepper. Simmer over medium heat for 10 minutes.
3. Add the parsley, paprika, and sugar to the saucepan and cook for 10 more minutes or until it has a thick consistency. Keep stirring during the cooking. Refrigerate for an hour to chill.
4. Wrap the sausage with bacon strips and secure with toothpicks, then place them in the basket.
5. Put the air fryer basket on the baking pan and slide into Rack Position 2, select Air Fry, set temperature to 350ºF (180ºC) and set time to 12 minutes.
6. Flip the bacon-wrapped sausage halfway through.
7. When cooking is complete, the bacon should be crispy and browned.
8. Transfer the bacon-wrapped sausage on a plate and baste with the relish or just serve with the relish alongside.

299.Beef And Spinach Meatloaves

Servings:2
Cooking Time: 45 Minutes
Ingredients:
- 1 large egg, beaten
- 1 cup frozen spinach

- $^{1}/_{3}$ cup almond meal
- ¼ cup chopped onion
- ¼ cup plain Greek milk
- ¼ teaspoon salt
- ¼ teaspoon dried sage
- 2 teaspoons olive oil, divided
- Freshly ground black pepper, to taste
- ½ pound (227 g) extra-lean ground beef
- ¼ cup tomato paste
- 1 tablespoon granulated stevia
- ¼ teaspoon Worcestershire sauce
- Cooking spray

Directions:
1. Coat a shallow baking pan with cooking spray.
2. In a large bowl, combine the beaten egg, spinach, almond meal, onion, milk, salt, sage, 1 teaspoon of olive oil, and pepper.
3. Crumble the beef over the spinach mixture. Mix well to combine. Divide the meat mixture in half. Shape each half into a loaf. Place the loaves in the prepared pan.
4. In a small bowl, whisk together the tomato paste, stevia, Worcestershire sauce, and remaining 1 teaspoon of olive oil. Spoon half of the sauce over each meatloaf.
5. Slide the baking pan into Rack Position 1, select Convection Bake, set the temperature to 350ºF (180ºC) and set the time to 40 minutes.
6. When cooking is complete, an instant-read thermometer inserted in the center of the meatloaves should read at least 165ºF (74ºC).
7. Serve immediately.

300.Swedish Meatballs

Servings: 4
Cooking Time: 14 Minutes
Ingredients:
- For the meatballs
- 1 pound 93% lean ground beef
- 1 (1-ounce) packet Lipton Onion Recipe Soup & Dip Mix
- ⅓ cup bread crumbs
- 1 egg, beaten
- Salt
- Pepper
- For the gravy
- 1 cup beef broth
- ⅓ cup heavy cream
- 1 tablespoons all-purpose flour

Directions:
1. Preparing the Ingredients. In a large bowl, combine the ground beef, onion soup mix, bread crumbs, egg, and salt and pepper to taste. Mix thoroughly.
2. Using 2 tablespoons of the meat mixture, create each meatball by rolling the beef

mixture around in your hands. This should yield about 10 meatballs.
3. Air Frying. Place the meatballs in the air fryer oven. It is okay to stack them. Cook for 14 minutes.
4. While the meatballs cook, prepare the gravy. Heat a saucepan over medium-high heat.
5. Add the beef broth and heavy cream. Stir for 1 to 2 minutes.
6. Add the flour and stir. Cover and allow the sauce to simmer for 3 to 4 minutes, or until thick.
7. Drizzle the gravy over the meatballs and serve.
- **Nutrition Info:** CALORIES: 178; FAT: 14G; PROTEIN:9G; FIBER:0

301.Buffalo Chicken Tenders

Servings: 5
Cooking Time: 25 Minutes
Ingredients:
- Nonstick cooking spray
- 2/3 cup panko bread crumbs
- ½ tsp cayenne pepper
- ½ tsp paprika
- ½ tsp garlic powder
- ½ tsp salt
- 3 chicken breasts, boneless, skinless & cut in 10 strips
- ½ cup butter, melted
- ½ cup hot sauce

Directions:
1. Line a baking sheet with foil and spray with cooking spray.
2. In a shallow dish combine, bread crumbs and seasonings.
3. Dip chicken in crumb mixture to coat all sides. Lay on prepared pan and refrigerate 1 hour.
4. In a small bowl, whisk together butter and hot sauce.
5. Place baking pan in position 2 of the oven. Lightly spray the fryer basket with cooking spray.
6. Dip each piece of chicken in the butter mixture and place in basket. Place the basket on the baking pan.
7. Set oven to air fry on 400°F for 25 minutes. Cook until outside is crispy and golden brown and chicken is no longer pink. Turn chicken over halfway through cooking time. Serve immediately.
- **Nutrition Info:** Calories 371, Total Fat 23g, Saturated Fat 12g, Total Carbs 10g, Net Carbs 9g, Protein 31g, Sugar 1g, Fiber 1g, Sodium 733mg, Potassium 505mg, Phosphorus 310mg

302.Gnocchi With Chicken And Spinach

Servings:4
Cooking Time: 13 Minutes
Ingredients:
- 1 (1-pound / 454-g) package shelf-stable gnocchi
- 1¼ cups chicken stock
- ½ teaspoon kosher salt
- 1 pound (454 g) chicken breast, cut into 1-inch chunks
- 1 cup heavy whipping cream
- 2 tablespoons sun-dried tomato purée
- 1 garlic clove, minced
- 1 cup frozen spinach, thawed and drained
- 1 cup grated Parmesan cheese

Directions:
1. Place the gnocchi in an even layer in the baking pan. Pour the chicken stock over the gnocchi.
2. Slide the baking pan into Rack Position 1, select Convection Bake, set temperature to 450ºF (235ºC), and set time to 7 minutes.
3. While the gnocchi are cooking, sprinkle the salt over the chicken pieces. In a small bowl, mix the cream, tomato purée, and garlic.
4. When cooking is complete, blot off any remaining stock, or drain the gnocchi and return it to the pan. Top the gnocchi with the spinach and chicken. Pour the cream mixture over the ingredients in the pan.
5. Slide the baking pan into Rack Position 2, select Roast, set temperature to 400ºF (205ºC), and set time to 6 minutes.
6. After 4 minutes, remove from the oven and gently stir the ingredients. Return to the oven and continue cooking.
7. When cooking is complete, the gnocchi should be tender and the chicken should be cooked through. Remove from the oven. Stir in the Parmesan cheese until it's melted and serve.

303.Ham & Cheese Stuffed Chicken Breasts

Servings: 4
Cooking Time: 40 Minutes
Ingredients:
- 4 skinless and boneless chicken breasts
- 4 slices ham
- 4 slices Swiss cheese
- 3 tbsp all-purpose flour
- 4 tbsp butter
- 1 tbsp paprika
- 1 tbsp chicken bouillon granules
- ½ cup dry white wine
- 1 cup heavy whipping cream

Directions:
1. Preheat on Air Fry function to 380 F. Pound the chicken breasts and top with a slice of ham and Swiss cheese. Fold the edges of the chicken over the filling and secure the borders with toothpicks. In a medium bowl, combine the paprika and flour and coat in the chicken rolls. Fry the chicken in your for 20 minutes, turning once.
2. In a large skillet over low heat, melt the butter and add the heavy cream, bouillon granules, and wine; bring to a boil. Add in the chicken and let simmer for around 5-10 minutes. Serve.

304.Lahmacun (turkish Pizza)

Servings:4
Cooking Time: 10 Minutes
Ingredients:
- 4 (6-inch) flour tortillas
- For the Meat Topping:
- 4 ounces (113 g) ground lamb or 85% lean ground beef
- ¼ cup finely chopped green bell pepper
- ¼ cup chopped fresh parsley
- 1 small plum tomato, deseeded and chopped
- 2 tablespoons chopped yellow onion
- 1 garlic clove, minced
- 2 teaspoons tomato paste
- ¼ teaspoon sweet paprika
- ¼ teaspoon ground cumin
- ⅛ to ¼ teaspoon red pepper flakes
- ⅛ teaspoon ground allspice
- ⅛ teaspoon kosher salt
- ⅛ teaspoon black pepper
- For Serving:
- ¼ cup chopped fresh mint
- 1 teaspoon extra-virgin olive oil
- 1 lemon, cut into wedges

Directions:
1. Combine all the ingredients for the meat topping in a medium bowl until well mixed.
2. Lay the tortillas on a clean work surface. Spoon the meat mixture on the tortillas and spread all over.
3. Place the tortillas in the basket.
4. Put the air fryer basket on the baking pan and slide into Rack Position 2, select Air Fry, set temperature to 400ºF (205ºC) and set time to 10 minutes.
5. When cooking is complete, the edge of the tortilla should be golden and the meat should be lightly browned.
6. Transfer them to a serving dish. Top with chopped fresh mint and drizzle with olive oil. Squeeze the lemon wedges on top and serve.

305.Carne Asada

Servings:4
Cooking Time: 15 Minutes

Ingredients:
- 3 chipotle peppers in adobo, chopped
- $1/3$ cup chopped fresh oregano
- $1/3$ cup chopped fresh parsley
- 4 cloves garlic, minced
- Juice of 2 limes
- 1 teaspoon ground cumin seeds
- $1/3$ cup olive oil
- 1 to 1½ pounds (454 g to 680 g) flank steak
- Salt, to taste

Directions:
1. Combine the chipotle, oregano, parsley, garlic, lime juice, cumin, and olive oil in a large bowl. Stir to mix well.
2. Dunk the flank steak in the mixture and press to coat well. Wrap the bowl in plastic and marinate under room temperature for at least 30 minutes.
3. Discard the marinade and place the steak in the basket. Sprinkle with salt.
4. Put the air fryer basket on the baking pan and slide into Rack Position 2, select Air Fry, set temperature to 390ºF (199ºC) and set time to 15 minutes.
5. Flip the steak halfway through the cooking time.
6. When cooking is complete, the steak should be medium-rare or reach your desired doneness.
7. Remove the steak from the oven and slice to serve.

306.Air Fryer Herb Pork Chops

Servings: 4
Cooking Time: 15 Minutes
Ingredients:
- 4 pork chops
- 2 tsp oregano
- 2 tsp thyme
- 2 tsp sage
- 1 tsp garlic powder
- 1 tsp paprika
- 1 tsp rosemary
- Pepper
- Salt

Directions:
1. Fit the oven with the rack in position 2.
2. Line the air fryer basket with parchment paper.
3. Mix garlic powder, paprika, rosemary, oregano, thyme, sage, pepper, and salt and rub over pork chops.
4. Place pork chops in the air fryer basket then place an air fryer basket in the baking pan.
5. Place a baking pan on the oven rack. Set to air fry at 360 F for 15 minutes.
6. Serve and enjoy.

- **Nutrition Info:** Calories 266 Fat 20.2 g Carbohydrates 2 g Sugar 0.3 g Protein 18.4 g Cholesterol 69 mg

307.Pesto & Spinach Beef Rolls

Servings:4
Cooking Time: 30 Minutes
Ingredients:
- 2 lb beef steak, thinly sliced
- Salt and black pepper to taste
- 3 tbsp pesto
- ½ cup mozzarella cheese, shredded
- 1 cup spinach, chopped
- 1 bell pepper, deseeded and sliced

Directions:
1. Preheat oven to 400 F on Bake function. Place the beef slices between 2 baking paper sheets and flatten them with a rolling pin to about a fifth of an inch thick. Lay the slices on a clean surface and spread them with the pesto. Top with mozzarella, spinach, and bell pepper.
2. Roll up the slices and secure using a toothpick. Season with salt and pepper. Place the slices in the greased basket and Bake for 15 minutes. Serve immediately!

308.Chicken Parm

Servings: 4
Cooking Time: 35 Minutes
Ingredients:
- Nonstick cooking spray
- ½ cup flour
- 2 eggs
- 2/3 cup panko bread crumbs
- 2/3 cup Italian seasoned bread crumbs
- 1/3 + ¼ cup parmesan cheese, divided
- 2 tbsp. fresh parsley, chopped
- ½ tsp salt
- ¼ tsp pepper
- 4 chicken breast halves, skinless & boneless
- 24 oz. marinara sauce
- 1 cup mozzarella cheese, grated

Directions:
1. Place the baking pan in position 2 of the oven. Lightly spray the fryer basket with cooking spray.
2. Place flour in a shallow dish.
3. In a separate shallow dish, beat the eggs.
4. In a third shallow dish, combine both bread crumbs, 1/3 cup parmesan cheese, 2 tablespoons parsley, salt, and pepper.
5. Place chicken between two sheets of plastic wrap and pound to ½-inch thick.
6. Dip chicken first in flour, then eggs, and bread crumb mixture to coat. Place in basket and place the basket on the baking pan.

7. Set oven to air fry on 375°F for 10 minutes. Turn chicken over halfway through cooking time.
8. Remove chicken and baking pan from the oven. Place the rack in position 1. Set oven to bake on 425°F for 30 minutes.
9. Pour 1 ½ cups marinara in the bottom of 8x11-inch baking dish. Place chicken over sauce and add another 2 tablespoons marinara to tops of chicken. Top chicken with mozzarella and parmesan cheese.
10. Once oven preheats for 5 minutes, place the dish in the oven and bake 20-25 minutes until bubbly and cheese is golden brown. Serve.
- **Nutrition Info:** Calories 529, Total Fat 13g, Saturated Fat 5g, Total Carbs 52g, Net Carbs 47g, Protein 51g, Sugar 9g, Fiber 5g, Sodium 1437mg, Potassium 1083mg, Phosphorus 709mg

309.Cheesy Chicken Escallops

Servings: 4
Cooking Time: 10 Minutes
Ingredients:
- 4 skinless chicken breasts
- 2 ½ oz panko breadcrumbs
- 1 ounce Parmesan cheese, grated
- 6 sage leaves, chopped
- 1 ¼ ounces flour
- 2 beaten eggs

Directions:
1. Place the chicken breasts between a cling film, beat well using a rolling pin until a ½ inch thickness is achieved.
2. In a bowl, add Parmesan cheese, sage, and breadcrumbs. Dredge the chicken into the seasoned flour and then into the eggs. Finally, coat in the breadcrumbs.
3. Spray the chicken breasts with cooking spray and cook in your oven for 14-16 minutes at 350 F on Air Fry function.

310.Duck Oregano Fingers

Servings:x
Cooking Time:x
Ingredients:
- 2 tsp. salt
- 1 tsp. pepper powder
- 1 tsp. red chili powder
- 6 tbsp. corn flour
- 1 lb. boneless duck (Cut into Oregano Fingers)
- 2 cup dry breadcrumbs
- 2 tsp. oregano
- 2 tsp. red chili flakes
- 1 ½ tbsp. ginger-garlic paste
- 4 tbsp. lemon juice
- 4 eggs

Directions:
1. Mix all the ingredients for the marinade and put the duck Oregano Fingers inside and let it rest overnight.
2. Mix the breadcrumbs, oregano and red chili flakes well and place the marinated Oregano Fingers on this mixture. Cover it with plastic wrap and leave it till right before you serve to cook.
3. Pre heat the oven at 160 degrees Fahrenheit for 5 minutes. Place the Oregano Fingers in the fry basket and close it. Let them cook at the same temperature for another 15 minutes or so. Toss the Oregano Fingers well so that they are cooked uniformly.

FISH & SEAFOOD RECIPES

311.Paprika Shrimp

Servings:4
Cooking Time: 10 Minutes
Ingredients:

- 1 pound (454 g) tiger shrimp
- 2 tablespoons olive oil
- ½ tablespoon old bay seasoning
- ¼ tablespoon smoked paprika
- ¼ teaspoon cayenne pepper
- A pinch of sea salt

Directions:

1. Toss all the ingredients in a large bowl until the shrimp are evenly coated.
2. Arrange the shrimp in the air fryer basket.
3. Put the air fryer basket on the baking pan and slide into Rack Position 2, select Air Fry, set temperature to 380ºF (193ºC), and set time to 10 minutes.
4. When cooking is complete, the shrimp should be pink and cooked through. Remove from the oven and serve hot.

312.Spinach Scallops

Servings: 2
Cooking Time: 10 Minutes
Ingredients:

- 8 sea scallops
- 1 tbsp fresh basil, chopped
- 1 tbsp tomato paste
- 3/4 cup heavy cream
- 12 oz frozen spinach, thawed and drained
- 1 tsp garlic, minced
- 1/2 tsp pepper
- 1/2 tsp salt

Directions:

1. Fit the oven with the rack in position
2. Layer spinach in the baking dish.
3. Spray scallops with cooking spray and season with pepper and salt.
4. Place scallops on top of spinach.
5. In a small bowl, mix garlic, basil, tomato paste, whipping cream, pepper, and salt and pour over scallops and spinach.
6. Set to bake at 350 F for 15 minutes. After 5 minutes place the baking dish in the preheated oven.
7. Serve and enjoy.
- **Nutrition Info:** Calories 310 Fat 18.3 g Carbohydrates 12.6 g Sugar 1.7 g Protein 26.5 g Cholesterol 101 mg

313.Glazed Tuna And Fruit Kebabs

Servings:4
Cooking Time: 10 Minutes
Ingredients:

- Kebabs:
- 1 pound (454 g) tuna steaks, cut into 1-inch cubes
- ½ cup canned pineapple chunks, drained, juice reserved
- ½ cup large red grapes
- Marinade:
- 1 tablespoon honey
- 1 teaspoon olive oil
- 2 teaspoons grated fresh ginger
- Pinch cayenne pepper
- Special Equipment:
- 4 metal skewers

Directions:

1. Make the kebabs: Thread, alternating tuna cubes, pineapple chunks, and red grapes, onto the metal skewers.
2. Make the marinade: Whisk together the honey, olive oil, ginger, and cayenne pepper in a small bowl. Brush generously the marinade over the kebabs and allow to sit for 10 minutes.
3. When ready, transfer the kebabs to the air fryer basket.
4. Put the air fryer basket on the baking pan and slide into Rack Position 2, select Air Fry, set temperature to 370ºF (188ºC), and set time to 10 minutes.
5. After 5 minutes, remove from the oven and flip the kebabs and brush with the remaining marinade. Return the pan to the oven and continue cooking for an additional 5 minutes.
6. When cooking is complete, the kebabs should reach an internal temperature of 145ºF (63ºC) on a meat thermometer. Remove from the oven and discard any remaining marinade. Serve hot.

314.Parmesan-crusted Salmon Patties

Servings:4
Cooking Time: 13 Minutes
Ingredients:

- 1 pound (454 g) salmon, chopped into ½-inch pieces
- 2 tablespoons coconut flour
- 2 tablespoons grated Parmesan cheese
- 1½ tablespoons milk
- ½ white onion, peeled and finely chopped
- ½ teaspoon butter, at room temperature
- ½ teaspoon chipotle powder
- ½ teaspoon dried parsley flakes
- $1/3$ teaspoon ground black pepper
- $1/3$ teaspoon smoked cayenne pepper
- 1 teaspoon fine sea salt

Directions:

1. Put all the ingredients for the salmon patties in a bowl and stir to combine well.

2. Scoop out 2 tablespoons of the salmon mixture and shape into a patty with your palm, about ½ inch thick. Repeat until all the mixture is used. Transfer to the refrigerator for about 2 hours until firm.
3. When ready, arrange the salmon patties in the baking pan.
4. Slide the baking pan into Rack Position 1, select Convection Bake, set temperature to 395ºF (202ºC), and set time to 13 minutes.
5. Flip the patties halfway through the cooking time.
6. When cooking is complete, the patties should be golden brown. Remove from the oven and cool for 5 minutes before serving.

315. Speedy Fried Scallops

Servings: 4
Cooking Time: 5 Minutes
Ingredients:
- 12 fresh scallops
- 3 tbsp flour
- Salt and black pepper to taste
- 1 egg, lightly beaten
- 1 cup breadcrumbs

Directions:
1. Coat the scallops with flour. Dip into the egg, then into the breadcrumbs. Spray with olive oil and arrange them on the basket. Fit in the baking tray and cook for 6 minutes at 360 F on Air Fry function, turning once halfway through cooking. Serve.

316. Baked Pesto Salmon

Servings: 4
Cooking Time: 15 Minutes
Ingredients:
- 4 salmon fillets
- 1/3 cup parmesan cheese, grated
- 1/3 cup breadcrumbs
- 6 tbsp pesto

Directions:
1. Fit the oven with the rack in position
2. Place fish fillets into the baking dish.
3. Pour pesto over fish fillets.
4. Mix together breadcrumbs and parmesan cheese and sprinkle over fish.
5. Set to bake at 325 F for 20 minutes. After 5 minutes place the baking dish in the preheated oven.
6. Serve and enjoy.
- **Nutrition Info:** Calories 396 Fat 22.8 g Carbohydrates 8.3 g Sugar 2.1 g Protein 40.4 g Cholesterol 89 mg

317. Mustard-crusted Sole Fillets

Servings:4
Cooking Time: 10 Minutes
Ingredients:

- 5 teaspoons low-sodium yellow mustard
- 1 tablespoon freshly squeezed lemon juice
- 4 (3.5-ounce / 99-g) sole fillets
- 2 teaspoons olive oil
- ½ teaspoon dried marjoram
- ½ teaspoon dried thyme
- ⅛ teaspoon freshly ground black pepper
- 1 slice low-sodium whole-wheat bread, crumbled

Directions:
1. Whisk together the mustard and lemon juice in a small bowl until thoroughly mixed and smooth. Spread the mixture evenly over the sole fillets, then transfer the fillets to the baking pan.
2. In a separate bowl, combine the olive oil, marjoram, thyme, black pepper, and bread crumbs and stir to mix well. Gently but firmly press the mixture onto the top of fillets, coating them completely.
3. Slide the baking pan into Rack Position 1, select Convection Bake, set temperature to 320ºF (160ºC), and set time to 10 minutes.
4. When cooking is complete, the fish should reach an internal temperature of 145ºF (63ºC) on a meat thermometer. Remove from the oven and serve on a plate.

318. Air Fry Prawns

Servings: 4
Cooking Time: 6 Minutes
Ingredients:
- 24 prawns
- 6 tbsp mayonnaise
- 1 1/2 tsp chili powder
- 2 tbsp vinegar
- 2 tbsp ketchup
- 1 tsp red chili flakes
- 1/2 tsp sea salt

Directions:
1. Fit the oven with the rack in position 2.
2. In a bowl, toss prawns with chili flakes, chili powder, and salt.
3. Add shrimp to the air fryer basket then place an air fryer basket in the baking pan.
4. Place a baking pan on the oven rack. Set to air fry at 350 F for 6 minutes.
5. In a small bowl, mix mayonnaise, vinegar, and ketchup and serve with shrimp.
- **Nutrition Info:** Calories 255 Fat 9.8 g Carbohydrates 9.8 g Sugar 3.2 g Protein 30.5 g Cholesterol 284 mg

319. Sticky Hoisin Tuna

Servings:4
Cooking Time: 5 Minutes
Ingredients:
- ½ cup hoisin sauce
- 2 tablespoons rice wine vinegar

- 2 teaspoons sesame oil
- 2 teaspoons dried lemongrass
- 1 teaspoon garlic powder
- ¼ teaspoon red pepper flakes
- ½ small onion, quartered and thinly sliced
- 8 ounces (227 g) fresh tuna, cut into 1-inch cubes
- Cooking spray
- 3 cups cooked jasmine rice

Directions:
1. In a small bowl, whisk together the hoisin sauce, vinegar, sesame oil, lemongrass, garlic powder, and red pepper flakes.
2. Add the sliced onion and tuna cubes and gently toss until the fish is evenly coated.
3. Arrange the coated tuna cubes in the air fryer basket in a single layer.
4. Put the air fryer basket on the baking pan and slide into Rack Position 2, select Air Fry, set temperature to 390ºF (199ºC), and set time to 5 minutes.
5. Flip the fish halfway through the cooking time.
6. When cooking is complete, the fish should begin to flake. Continue cooking for 1 minute, if necessary. Remove from the oven and serve over hot jasmine rice.

320.Crispy Crab Legs

Servings: 4
Cooking Time: 15 Minutes
Ingredients:
- 3 pounds crab legs
- ½ cup butter, melted

Directions:
1. Preheat on Air Fry function to 380 F. Cover the crab legs with salted water and let them stay for a few minutes. Drain, pat them dry, and place the legs in the basket. Fit in the baking tray and brush with some butter; cook for 10 minutes, flipping once. Drizzle with the remaining butter and serve.

321.Prawn Fried Baked Pastry

Servings:x
Cooking Time:x
Ingredients:
- 2 tbsp. unsalted butter
- 1 ½ cup all-purpose flour
- A pinch of salt to taste
- Add as much water as required to make the dough stiff and firm
- 1 lb. prawn
- ¼ cup boiled peas
- 1 tsp. powdered ginger
- 1 or 2 green chilies that are finely chopped or mashed
- ½ tsp. cumin
- 1 tsp. coarsely crushed coriander

- 1 dry red chili broken into pieces
- A small amount of salt (to taste)
- ½ tsp. dried mango powder
- ½ tsp. red chili power.
- 1-2 tbsp. coriander.

Directions:
1. You will first need to make the outer covering. In a large bowl, add the flour, butter and enough water to knead it into dough that is stiff. Transfer this to a container and leave it to rest for five minutes. Place a pan on medium flame and add the oil. Roast the mustard seeds and once roasted, add the coriander seeds and the chopped dry red chilies. Add all the dry ingredients for the filling and mix the ingredients well.
2. Add a little water and continue to stir the ingredients. Make small balls out of the dough and roll them out. Cut the rolled-out dough into halves and apply a little water on the edges to help you fold the halves into a cone. Add the filling to the cone and close up the samosa. Pre-heat the oven for around 5 to 6 minutes at 300 Fahrenheit. Place all the samosas in the fry basket and close the basket properly.
3. Keep the oven at 200 degrees for another 20 to 25 minutes. Around the halfway point, open the basket and turn the samosas over for uniform cooking. After this, fry at 250 degrees for around 10 minutes in order to give them the desired golden-brown color. Serve hot. Recommended sides are tamarind or mint sauce.

322.Seafood Spring Rolls

Servings:4
Cooking Time: 20 Minutes
Ingredients:
- 1 tablespoon olive oil
- 2 teaspoons minced garlic
- 1 cup matchstick cut carrots
- 2 cups finely sliced cabbage
- 2 (4-ounce / 113-g) cans tiny shrimp, drained
- 4 teaspoons soy sauce
- Salt and freshly ground black pepper, to taste
- 16 square spring roll wrappers
- Cooking spray

Directions:
1. Spray the air fryer basket with cooking spray. Set aside.
2. Heat the olive oil in a medium skillet over medium heat until it shimmers.
3. Add the garlic to the skillet and cook for 30 seconds. Stir in the cabbage and carrots and sauté for about 5 minutes, stirring

occasionally, or until the vegetables are lightly tender.

4. Fold in the shrimp and soy sauce and sprinkle with salt and pepper, then stir to combine. Sauté for another 2 minutes, or until the moisture is evaporated. Remove from the heat and set aside to cool.
5. Put a spring roll wrapper on a work surface and spoon 1 tablespoon of the shrimp mixture onto the lower end of the wrapper.
6. Roll the wrapper away from you halfway, and then fold in the right and left sides, like an envelope. Continue to roll to the very end, using a little water to seal the edge. Repeat with the remaining wrappers and filling.
7. Place the spring rolls in the air fryer basket in a single layer, leaving space between each spring roll. Mist them lightly with cooking spray.
8. Put the air fryer basket on the baking pan and slide into Rack Position 2, select Air Fry, set temperature to 375ºF (190ºC), and set time to 10 minutes.
9. Flip the rolls halfway through the cooking time.
10. When cooking is complete, the spring rolls will be heated through and start to brown. If necessary, continue cooking for 5 minutes more. Remove from the oven and cool for a few minutes before serving.

323.Fish Spicy Lemon Kebab

Servings:x
Cooking Time:x
Ingredients:
- 1 lb. boneless fish roughly chopped
- 3 onions chopped
- 5 green chilies-roughly chopped
- 1 ½ tbsp. ginger paste
- 1 ½ tsp garlic paste
- 1 ½ tsp salt
- 3 tsp lemon juice
- 2 tsp garam masala
- 4 tbsp. chopped coriander
- 3 tbsp. cream
- 2 tbsp. coriander powder
- 4 tbsp. fresh mint chopped
- 3 tbsp. chopped capsicum
- 3 eggs
- 2 ½ tbsp. white sesame seeds

Directions:
1. Take all the ingredients mentioned under the first heading and mix them in a bowl. Grind them thoroughly to make a smooth paste. Take the eggs in a different bowl and beat them. Add a pinch of salt and leave them aside. Take a flat plate and in it mix the sesame seeds and breadcrumbs. Mold the fish mixture into small balls and flatten

them into round and flat kebabs. Dip these kebabs in the egg and salt mixture and then in the mixture of breadcrumbs and sesame seeds. Leave these kebabs in the fridge for an hour or so to set.
2. Pre heat the oven at 160 degrees Fahrenheit for around 5 minutes. Place the kebabs in the basket and let them cook for another 25 minutes at the same temperature. Turn the kebabs over in between the cooking process to get a uniform cook. Serve the kebabs with mint sauce.

324.Flavorful Herb Salmon

Servings: 4
Cooking Time: 15 Minutes
Ingredients:
- 1 lb salmon fillets
- 1/2 tbsp dried rosemary
- 1 tbsp olive oil
- 1/4 tsp dried basil
- 1 tbsp dried chives
- 1/4 tsp dried thyme
- Pepper
- Salt

Directions:
1. Fit the oven with the rack in position 2.
2. Place salmon skin side down in air fryer basket then place an air fryer basket in baking pan.
3. Mix olive oil, thyme, basil, chives, and rosemary in a small bowl.
4. Brush salmon with oil mixture.
5. Place a baking pan on the oven rack. Set to air fry at 400 F for 15 minutes.
6. Serve and enjoy.
- **Nutrition Info:** Calories 182 Fat 10.6 g Carbohydrates 0.4 g Sugar 0 g Protein 22.1 g Cholesterol 50 mg

325.Sweet And Savory Breaded Shrimp

Servings: 2
Cooking Time: 20 Minutes
Ingredients:
- ½ pound of fresh shrimp, peeled from their shells and rinsed
- 2 raw eggs
- ½ cup of breadcrumbs (we like Panko, but any brand or home recipe will do)
- ½ white onion, peeled and rinsed and finely chopped
- 1 teaspoon of ginger-garlic paste
- ½ teaspoon of turmeric powder
- ½ teaspoon of red chili powder
- ½ teaspoon of cumin powder
- ½ teaspoon of black pepper powder
- ½ teaspoon of dry mango powder
- Pinch of salt

Directions:

1. Preparing the Ingredients. Cover the basket of the air fryer oven with a lining of tin foil, leaving the edges uncovered to allow air to circulate through the basket.
2. Preheat the air fryer oven to 350 degrees.
3. In a large mixing bowl, beat the eggs until fluffy and until the yolks and whites are fully combined.
4. Dunk all the shrimp in the egg mixture, fully submerging.
5. In a separate mixing bowl, combine the bread crumbs with all the dry ingredients until evenly blended.
6. One by one, coat the egg-covered shrimp in the mixed dry ingredients so that fully covered, and place on the foil-lined air-fryer basket.
7. Air Frying. Set the air-fryer timer to 20 minutes.
8. Halfway through the cooking time, shake the handle of the air-fryer so that the breaded shrimp jostles inside and fry-coverage is even.
9. After 20 minutes, when the fryer shuts off, the shrimp will be perfectly cooked and their breaded crust golden-brown and delicious! Using tongs, remove from the air fryer oven and set on a serving dish to cool.

326.Roasted Salmon With Asparagus

Servings:4
Cooking Time: 15 Minutes
Ingredients:
- 4 (6-ounce / 170 g) salmon fillets, patted dry
- 1 teaspoon kosher salt, divided
- 1 tablespoon honey
- 2 tablespoons unsalted butter, melted
- 2 teaspoons Dijon mustard
- 2 pounds (907 g) asparagus, trimmed
- Lemon wedges, for serving

Directions:

1. Season both sides of the salmon fillets with ½ teaspoon of kosher salt.
2. Whisk together the honey, 1 tablespoon of butter, and mustard in a small bowl. Set aside.
3. Arrange the asparagus in the baking pan. Drizzle the remaining 1 tablespoon of butter all over and season with the remaining ½ teaspoon of salt, tossing to coat. Move the asparagus to the outside of the pan.
4. Put the salmon fillets in the pan, skin-side down. Brush the fillets generously with the honey mixture.
5. Slide the baking pan into Rack Position 2, select Roast, set temperature to 375ºF (190ºC), and set time to 15 minutes.

6. Toss the asparagus once halfway through the cooking time.
7. When done, transfer the salmon fillets and asparagus to a plate. Serve warm with a squeeze of lemon juice.

327.Garlic-butter Shrimp With Vegetables

Servings:4
Cooking Time: 15 Minutes
Ingredients:
- 1 pound (454 g) small red potatoes, halved
- 2 ears corn, shucked and cut into rounds, 1 to 1½ inches thick
- 2 tablespoons Old Bay or similar seasoning
- ½ cup unsalted butter, melted
- 1 (12- to 13-ounce / 340- to 369-g) package kielbasa or other smoked sausages
- 3 garlic cloves, minced
- 1 pound (454 g) medium shrimp, peeled and deveined

Directions:

1. Place the potatoes and corn in a large bowl.
2. Stir together the butter and Old Bay seasoning in a small bowl. Drizzle half the butter mixture over the potatoes and corn, tossing to coat. Spread out the vegetables in the baking pan.
3. Slide the baking pan into Rack Position 2, select Roast, set temperature to 350ºF (180ºC), and set time to 15 minutes.
4. Meanwhile, cut the sausages into 2-inch lengths, then cut each piece in half lengthwise. Put the sausages and shrimp in a medium bowl and set aside.
5. Add the garlic to the bowl of remaining butter mixture and stir well.
6. After 10 minutes, remove the pan and pour the vegetables into the large bowl. Drizzle with the garlic butter and toss until well coated. Arrange the vegetables, sausages, and shrimp in the pan.
7. Return to the oven and continue cooking. After 5 minutes, check the shrimp for doneness. The shrimp should be pink and opaque. If they are not quite cooked through, roast for an additional 1 minute.
8. When done, remove from the oven and serve on a plate.

328.Greek Cod With Asparagus

Servings: 2
Cooking Time: 20 Minutes
Ingredients:
- 1 lb cod, cut into 4 pieces
- 8 asparagus spears
- 1 leek, sliced
- 1 onion, quartered
- 2 tomatoes, halved
- 1/2 tsp oregano

- 1/2 tsp red chili flakes
- 1/2 cup olives, chopped
- 2 tbsp olive oil
- 1/4 tsp pepper
- 1/4 tsp salt

Directions:
1. Fit the oven with the rack in position
2. Arrange fish pieces, olives, asparagus, leek, onion, and tomatoes in a baking dish.
3. Season with oregano, chili flakes, pepper, and salt and drizzle with olive oil.
4. Set to bake at 400 F for 25 minutes. After 5 minutes place the baking dish in the preheated oven.
5. Serve and enjoy.
- **Nutrition Info:** Calories 489 Fat 20.2 g Carbohydrates 22.5 g Sugar 9.1 g Protein 56.6 g Cholesterol 125 mg

329.Crab Cakes

Servings: 4
Cooking Time: 10 Minutes
Ingredients:
- 8 ounces jumbo lump crabmeat
- 1 tablespoon Old Bay Seasoning
- ⅓ cup bread crumbs
- ¼ cup diced red bell pepper
- ¼ cup diced green bell pepper
- 1 egg
- ¼ cup mayonnaise
- Juice of ½ lemon
- 1 teaspoon flour
- Cooking oil

Directions:
1. Preparing the Ingredients. In a large bowl, combine the crabmeat, Old Bay Seasoning, bread crumbs, red bell pepper, green bell pepper, egg, mayo, and lemon juice. Mix gently to combine.
2. Form the mixture into 4 patties. Sprinkle ¼ teaspoon of flour on top of each patty.
3. Air Frying. Place the crab cakes in the air fryer oven. Spray them with cooking oil. Cook for 10 minutes.
4. Serve.

330.Delicious Fried Seafood

Servings: 4
Cooking Time: 15 Minutes
Ingredients:
- 1 lb fresh scallops, mussels, fish fillets, prawns, shrimp
- 2 eggs, lightly beaten
- Salt and black pepper to taste
- 1 cup breadcrumbs mixed with zest of 1 lemon

Directions:
1. Dip each piece of the seafood into the eggs and season with salt and pepper. Coat in the

crumbs and spray with oil. Arrange into the frying basket and fit in the baking tray; cook for 10 minutes at 400 F on Air Fry function, turning once halfway through. Serve.

331.Baked Spinach Tilapia

Servings: 4
Cooking Time: 10 Minutes
Ingredients:
- 1 lb tilapia fillets
- 1 cup Monterey jack cheese, shredded
- 3 tbsp butter, sliced
- 8 oz spinach

Directions:
1. Fit the oven with the rack in position
2. Add spinach into the baking dish and top with butter slices.
3. Place fish fillets on top of spinach.
4. Sprinkle shredded cheese over fish fillets.
5. Set to bake at 450 F for 15 minutes. After 5 minutes place the baking dish in the preheated oven.
6. Serve and enjoy.
- **Nutrition Info:** Calories 288 Fat 18.4 g Carbohydrates 2.3 g Sugar 0.4 g Protein 29.7 g Cholesterol 103 mg

332.Cheesy Tuna Patties

Servings:4
Cooking Time: 17 To 18 Minutes
Ingredients:
- Tuna Patties:
- 1 pound (454 g) canned tuna, drained
- 1 egg, whisked
- 2 tablespoons shallots, minced
- 1 garlic clove, minced
- 1 cup grated Romano cheese
- Sea salt and ground black pepper, to taste
- 1 tablespoon sesame oil
- Cheese Sauce:
- 1 tablespoon butter
- 1 cup beer
- 2 tablespoons grated Colby cheese

Directions:
1. Mix together the canned tuna, whisked egg, shallots, garlic, cheese, salt, and pepper in a large bowl and stir to incorporate.
2. Divide the tuna mixture into four equal portions and form each portion into a patty with your hands. Refrigerate the patties for 2 hours.
3. When ready, brush both sides of each patty with sesame oil, then place in the baking pan.
4. Slide the baking pan into Rack Position 1, select Convection Bake, set temperature to 360ºF (182ºC), and set time to 14 minutes.
5. Flip the patties halfway through the cooking time.

6. Meanwhile, melt the butter in a saucepan over medium heat.
7. Pour in the beer and whisk constantly, or until it begins to bubble. Add the grated Colby cheese and mix well. Continue cooking for 3 to 4 minutes, or until the cheese melts. Remove from the heat.
8. When cooking is complete, the patties should be lightly browned and cooked through. Remove the patties from the oven to a plate. Drizzle them with the cheese sauce and serve immediately.

333.Piri-piri King Prawns

Servings:2
Cooking Time: 8 Minutes
Ingredients:
- 12 king prawns, rinsed
- 1 tablespoon coconut oil
- Salt and ground black pepper, to taste
- 1 teaspoon onion powder
- 1 teaspoon garlic paste
- 1 teaspoon curry powder
- ½ teaspoon piri piri powder
- ½ teaspoon cumin powder

Directions:
1. Combine all the ingredients in a large bowl and toss until the prawns are completely coated. Place the prawns in the air fryer basket.
2. Put the air fryer basket on the baking pan and slide into Rack Position 2, select Air Fry, set temperature to 360ºF (182ºC), and set time to 8 minutes.
3. Flip the prawns halfway through the cooking time.
4. When cooking is complete, the prawns will turn pink. Remove from the oven and serve hot.

334.Spicy Lemon Cod

Servings: 2
Cooking Time: 10 Minutes
Ingredients:
- 1 lb cod fillets
- 1/4 tsp chili powder
- 1 tbsp fresh parsley, chopped
- 1 1/2 tbsp olive oil
- 1 tbsp fresh lemon juice
- 1/8 tsp cayenne pepper
- 1/4 tsp salt

Directions:
1. Fit the oven with the rack in position
2. Arrange fish fillets in a baking dish. Drizzle with oil and lemon juice.
3. Sprinkle with chili powder, salt, and cayenne pepper.

4. Set to bake at 400 F for 15 minutes. After 5 minutes place the baking dish in the preheated oven.
5. Garnish with parsley and serve.
- **Nutrition Info:** Calories 276 Fat 12.7 g Carbohydrates 0.5 g Sugar 0.2 g Protein 40.7 g Cholesterol 111 mg

335.Fried Cod Nuggets

Servings: 4
Cooking Time: 25 Minutes
Ingredients:
- 1 ¼ lb cod fillets, cut into 4 to 6 chunks each
- ½ cup flour
- 1 egg
- 1 cup cornflakes
- 1 tbsp olive oil
- Salt and black pepper to taste

Directions:
1. Place the olive oil and cornflakes in a food processor and process until crumbed. Season the fish chunks with salt and pepper. In a bowl, beat the egg along with 1 tbsp of water. Dredge the chunks in flour first, then dip in the egg, and finally coat with cornflakes. Arrange the fish pieces on a lined sheet and cook in your on Air Fry at 350 F for 15 minutes until crispy.

336.Bacon Wrapped Shrimp

Servings: 4
Cooking Time: 5 Minutes
Ingredients:
- 1¼ pound tiger shrimp, peeled and deveined
- 1 pound bacon

Directions:
1. Preparing the Ingredients. Wrap each shrimp with a slice of bacon.
2. Refrigerate for about 20 minutes.
3. Preheat the air fryer oven to 390 degrees F.
4. Air Frying. Arrange the shrimp in the Oven rack/basket. Place the Rack on the middle-shelf of the air fryer oven. Cook for about 5-7 minutes.

337.Air Fry Tuna Patties

Servings: 4
Cooking Time: 6 Minutes
Ingredients:
- 1 egg, lightly beaten
- 8 oz can tuna, drained
- 1/4 cup breadcrumbs
- 1 tbsp mustard
- 1/4 tsp garlic powder
- Pepper
- Salt

Directions:
1. Fit the oven with the rack in position 2.

2. Add all ingredients into the large bowl and mix until well combined.
3. Make four equal shapes of patties from the mixture and place in the air fryer basket then place an air fryer basket in the baking pan.
4. Place a baking pan on the oven rack. Set to air fry at 400 F for 6 minutes.
5. Serve and enjoy.
- **Nutrition Info:** Calories 122 Fat 2.7 g Carbohydrates 6.1 g Sugar 0.7 g Protein 17.5 g Cholesterol 58 mg

338.Parmesan Salmon & Asparagus

Servings: 4
Cooking Time: 20 Minutes
Ingredients:
- 4 salmon fillets
- 1 cup parmesan cheese, shredded
- 1 tbsp garlic, minced
- 3 tbsp olive oil
- 1 lb asparagus, ends trimmed
- 1/4 tsp pepper
- 1/4 tsp salt

Directions:
1. Fit the oven with the rack in position
2. Place fish fillets and asparagus in a parchment-lined baking pan.
3. Brush fish fillets with olive oil. Season with pepper and salt.
4. Sprinkle with garlic and shredded parmesan cheese on top.
5. Set to bake at 400 F for 25 minutes. After 5 minutes place the baking pan in the preheated oven.
6. Serve and enjoy.
- **Nutrition Info:** Calories 424 Fat 26.5 g Carbohydrates 6 g Sugar 2.2 g Protein 44.4 g Cholesterol 95 mg

339.Crab Cakes With Bell Peppers

Servings:4
Cooking Time: 10 Minutes
Ingredients:
- 8 ounces (227 g) jumbo lump crab meat
- 1 egg, beaten
- Juice of ½ lemon
- $^1/_3$ cup bread crumbs
- ¼ cup diced green bell pepper
- ¼ cup diced red bell pepper
- ¼ cup mayonnaise
- 1 tablespoon Old Bay seasoning
- 1 teaspoon flour
- Cooking spray

Directions:
1. Make the crab cakes: Place all the ingredients except the flour and oil in a large bowl and stir until well incorporated.

2. Divide the crab mixture into four equal portions and shape each portion into a patty with your hands. Top each patty with a sprinkle of ¼ teaspoon of flour.
3. Arrange the crab cakes in the air fryer basket and spritz them with cooking spray.
4. Put the air fryer basket on the baking pan and slide into Rack Position 2, select Air Fry, set temperature to 375ºF (190ºC), and set time to 10 minutes.
5. Flip the crab cakes halfway through.
6. When cooking is complete, the cakes should be cooked through. Remove from the oven and divide the crab cakes among four plates and serve.

340.Cajun Salmon With Lemon

Servings:1
Cooking Time: 10 Minutes
Ingredients:
- 1 salmon fillet
- ¼ tsp brown sugar
- Juice of ½ lemon
- 1 tbsp cajun seasoning
- 2 lemon wedges
- 1 tbsp fresh parsley, chopped

Directions:
1. Preheat on Bake function to 350 F. Combine sugar and lemon and coat in the salmon. Sprinkle with the Cajun seasoning as well. Place a parchment paper on a baking tray and press Start. Cook for 14-16 minutes. Serve with lemon wedges and chopped parsley.

341.Seafood Pizza

Servings:x
Cooking Time:x
Ingredients:
- One pizza base
- Grated pizza cheese (mozzarella cheese preferably) for topping
- Some pizza topping sauce
- Use cooking oil for brushing and topping purposes
- ingredients for topping:
- 2 onions chopped
- 2 cups mixed seafood
- 2 capsicums chopped
- 2 tomatoes that have been deseeded and chopped
- 1 tbsp. (optional) mushrooms/corns
- 2 tsp. pizza seasoning
- Some cottage cheese that has been cut into small cubes (optional)

Directions:
1. Put the pizza base in a pre-heated oven for around 5 minutes. (Pre heated to 340 Fahrenheit). Take out the base. Pour some

pizza sauce on top of the base at the center. Using a spoon spread the sauce over the base making sure that you leave some gap around the circumference. Grate some mozzarella cheese and sprinkle it over the sauce layer. Take all the vegetables and the seafood and mix them in a bowl. Add some oil and seasoning.

2. Also add some salt and pepper according to taste. Mix them properly. Put this topping over the layer of cheese on the pizza. Now sprinkle some more grated cheese and pizza seasoning on top of this layer. Pre heat the oven at 250 Fahrenheit for around 5 minutes.

3. Open the fry basket and place the pizza inside. Close the basket and keep the fryer at 170 degrees for another 10 minutes. If you feel that it is undercooked you may put it at the same temperature for another 2 minutes or so.

342.Breaded Scallops

Servings:4
Cooking Time: 7 Minutes
Ingredients:
- 1 egg
- 3 tablespoons flour
- 1 cup bread crumbs
- 1 pound (454 g) fresh scallops
- 2 tablespoons olive oil
- Salt and black pepper, to taste

Directions:
1. In a bowl, lightly beat the egg. Place the flour and bread crumbs into separate shallow dishes.
2. Dredge the scallops in the flour and shake off any excess. Dip the flour-coated scallops in the beaten egg and roll in the bread crumbs.
3. Brush the scallops generously with olive oil and season with salt and pepper, to taste. Transfer the scallops to the air fryer basket.
4. Put the air fryer basket on the baking pan and slide into Rack Position 2, select Air Fry, set temperature to 360ºF (182ºC), and set time to 7 minutes.
5. Flip the scallops halfway through the cooking time.
6. When cooking is complete, the scallops should reach an internal temperature of just 145ºF (63ºC) on a meat thermometer. Remove from the oven. Let the scallops cool for 5 minutes and serve.

343.Cheese Carp Fries

Servings:x
Cooking Time:x
Ingredients:
- 1 lb. carp Oregano Fingers

- ingredients for the marinade:
- 1 tbsp. olive oil
- 1 tsp. mixed herbs
- ½ tsp. red chili flakes
- A pinch of salt to taste
- 1 tbsp. lemon juice
- For the garnish:
- 1 cup melted cheddar cheese

Directions:
1. Take all the ingredients mentioned under the heading "For the marinade" and mix them well. Cook the carp Oregano Fingers and soak them in the marinade.
2. Pre heat the oven for around 5 minutes at 300 Fahrenheit. Take out the basket of the fryer and place the carp in them. Close the basket. Now keep the fryer at 220 Fahrenheit for 20 or 25 minutes.
3. In between the process, toss the fries twice or thrice so that they get cooked properly. Towards the end of the cooking process (the last 2 minutes or so), sprinkle the melted cheddar cheese over the fries and serve hot.

344.Baked Buttery Shrimp

Servings: 4
Cooking Time: 15 Minutes
Ingredients:
- 1 lb shrimp, peel & deveined
- 2 tsp garlic powder
- 2 tsp dry mustard
- 2 tsp cumin
- 2 tsp paprika
- 2 tsp black pepper
- 4 tsp cayenne pepper
- 1/2 cup butter, melted
- 2 tsp onion powder
- 1 tsp dried oregano
- 1 tsp dried thyme
- 3 tsp salt

Directions:
1. Fit the oven with the rack in position
2. Add shrimp, butter, and remaining ingredients into the mixing bowl and toss well.
3. Transfer shrimp mixture into the baking pan.
4. Set to bake at 400 F for 20 minutes. After 5 minutes place the baking pan in the preheated oven.
5. Serve and enjoy.
- **Nutrition Info:** Calories 372 Fat 26.2 g Carbohydrates 7.5 g Sugar 1.3 g Protein 27.6 g Cholesterol 300 mg

345.Shrimp And Cherry Tomato Kebabs

Servings:4
Cooking Time: 5 Minutes

Ingredients:

- 1½ pounds (680 g) jumbo shrimp, cleaned, shelled and deveined
- 1 pound (454 g) cherry tomatoes
- 2 tablespoons butter, melted
- 1 tablespoons Sriracha sauce
- Sea salt and ground black pepper, to taste
- 1 teaspoon dried parsley flakes
- ½ teaspoon dried basil
- ½ teaspoon dried oregano
- ½ teaspoon mustard seeds
- ½ teaspoon marjoram
- Special Equipment:
- 4 to 6 wooden skewers, soaked in water for 30 minutes

Directions:

1. Put all the ingredients in a large bowl and toss to coat well.
2. Make the kebabs: Thread, alternating jumbo shrimp and cherry tomatoes, onto the wooden skewers. Place the kebabs in the air fryer basket.
3. Put the air fryer basket on the baking pan and slide into Rack Position 2, select Air Fry, set temperature to 400ºF (205ºC), and set time to 5 minutes.
4. When cooking is complete, the shrimp should be pink and the cherry tomatoes should be softened. Remove from the oven. Let the shrimp and cherry tomato kebabs cool for 5 minutes and serve hot.

346.Baked Lemon Swordfish

Servings: 2
Cooking Time: 10 Minutes
Ingredients:

- 12 oz swordfish fillets
- 1/8 tsp crushed red pepper
- 1 garlic clove, minced
- 2 tsp fresh parsley, chopped
- 3 tbsp olive oil
- 1/2 tsp lemon zest, grated
- 1/2 tsp ginger, grated

Directions:

1. Fit the oven with the rack in position
2. In a small bowl, mix 2 tbsp oil, lemon zest, red pepper, ginger, garlic, and parsley.
3. Season fish fillets with salt.
4. Heat remaining oil in a pan over medium-high heat.
5. Place fish fillets in the pan and cook until browned, about 2-3 minutes.
6. Transfer fish fillets in a baking dish.
7. Set to bake at 400 F for 15 minutes. After 5 minutes place the baking dish in the preheated oven.
8. Pour oil mixture over fish fillets and serve.

- **Nutrition Info:** Calories 449 Fat 29.8 g Carbohydrates 1.1 g Sugar 0.1 g Protein 43.4 g Cholesterol 85 mg

347.Pecan-crusted Catfish Fillets

Servings:4
Cooking Time: 12 Minutes
Ingredients:

- ½ cup pecan meal
- 1 teaspoon fine sea salt
- ¼ teaspoon ground black pepper
- 4 (4-ounce / 113-g) catfish fillets
- Avocado oil spray
- For Garnish (Optional):
- Fresh oregano
- Pecan halves

Directions:

1. Spray the air fryer basket with avocado oil spray.
2. Combine the pecan meal, sea salt, and black pepper in a large bowl. Dredge each catfish fillet in the meal mixture, turning until well coated. Spritz the fillets with avocado oil spray, then transfer to the basket.
3. Put the air fryer basket on the baking pan and slide into Rack Position 2, select Air Fry, set temperature to 375ºF (190ºC), and set time to 12 minutes.
4. Flip the fillets halfway through the cooking time.
5. When cooking is complete, the fish should be cooked through and no longer translucent. Remove from the oven and sprinkle the oregano sprigs and pecan halves on top for garnish, if desired. Serve immediately.

348.Lemony Shrimp

Servings:4
Cooking Time: 8 Minutes
Ingredients:

- 1 pound (454 g) shrimp, deveined
- 4 tablespoons olive oil
- 1½ tablespoons lemon juice
- 1½ tablespoons fresh parsley, roughly chopped
- 2 cloves garlic, finely minced
- 1 teaspoon crushed red pepper flakes, or more to taste
- Garlic pepper, to taste
- Sea salt flakes, to taste

Directions:

1. Toss all the ingredients in a large bowl until the shrimp are coated on all sides.
2. Arrange the shrimp in the air fryer basket.
3. Put the air fryer basket on the baking pan and slide into Rack Position 2, select Air Fry, set temperature to 385ºF (196ºC), and set time to 8 minutes.

4. When cooking is complete, the shrimp should be pink and cooked through. Remove from the oven and serve warm.

349.Basil White Fish

Servings:4
Cooking Time: 20 Minutes
Ingredients:
- 2 tbsp fresh basil, chopped
- 2 garlic cloves, minced
- 1 tbsp Parmesan cheese, grated
- Salt and black pepper to taste
- 2 tbsp pine nuts
- 4 white fish fillets
- 2 tbsp olive oil

Directions:
1. Preheat on AirFry function to 350 F. Season the fillets with salt and pepper and place in the basket. Drizzle with some olive oil and press Start. Cook for 12-14 minutes. In a bowl, mix basil, remaining olive oil, pine nuts, garlic, and Parmesan cheese and spread on the fish. Serve.

350.Herbed Salmon With Roasted Asparagus

Servings:2
Cooking Time: 12 Minutes
Ingredients:
- 2 teaspoons olive oil, plus additional for drizzling
- 2 (5-ounce / 142-g) salmon fillets, with skin
- Salt and freshly ground black pepper, to taste
- 1 bunch asparagus, trimmed
- 1 teaspoon dried tarragon
- 1 teaspoon dried chives
- Fresh lemon wedges, for serving

Directions:
1. Rub the olive oil all over the salmon fillets. Sprinkle with salt and pepper to taste.
2. Put the asparagus on the foil-lined baking pan and place the salmon fillets on top, skin-side down.
3. Slide the baking pan into Rack Position 2, select Roast, set temperature to 425ºF (220ºC), and set time to 12 minutes.
4. When cooked, the fillets should register 145ºF (63ºC) on an instant-read thermometer. Remove from the oven and cut the salmon fillets in half crosswise, then use a metal spatula to lift flesh from skin and transfer to a serving plate. Discard the skin and drizzle the salmon fillets with additional olive oil. Scatter with the herbs.
5. Serve the salmon fillets with roasted asparagus spears and lemon wedges on the side.

351.Tuna Sandwich

Servings:x
Cooking Time:x
Ingredients:
- 2 slices of white bread
- 1 tbsp. softened butter
- 1 tin tuna
- 1 small capsicum
- For Barbeque Sauce:
- ¼ tbsp. Worcestershire sauce
- ½ tsp. olive oil
- ¼ tsp. mustard powder
- ½ flake garlic crushed
- ¼ cup chopped onion
- ½ tbsp. sugar
- 1 tbsp. tomato ketchup
- ½ cup water.
- ¼ tbsp. red chili sauce
- A pinch of salt and black pepper to taste

Directions:
1. Take the slices of bread and remove the edges. Now cut the slices horizontally. Cook the ingredients for the sauce and wait till it thickens. Now, add the lamb to the sauce and stir till it obtains the flavors. Roast the capsicum and peel the skin off. Cut the capsicum into slices. Mix the ingredients together and apply it to the bread slices.
2. Pre-heat the oven for 5 minutes at 300 Fahrenheit. Open the basket of the Fryer and place the prepared Classic Sandwiches in it such that no two Classic Sandwiches are touching each other. Now keep the fryer at 250 degrees for around 15 minutes. Turn the Classic Sandwiches in between the cooking process to cook both slices. Serve the Classic Sandwiches with tomato ketchup or mint sauce.

352.Citrus Cilantro Catfish

Servings:2
Cooking Time: 20 Minutes
Ingredients:
- 2 catfish fillets
- 2 tsp blackening seasoning
- Juice of 1 lime
- 2 tbsp butter, melted
- 1 garlic clove, mashed
- 2 tbsp fresh cilantro, chopped

Directions:
1. In a bowl, blend garlic, lime juice, cilantro, and butter. Pour half of the mixture over the fillets and sprinkle with blackening seasoning. Place the fillets in the basket and press Start. Cook for 15 minutes at 360 F on AirFry function. Serve the fish topped with the remaining sauce.

353.Perfect Baked Cod

Servings: 4
Cooking Time: 15 Minutes
Ingredients:
- 4 cod fillets
- 1 tbsp olive oil
- 1 tsp dried parsley
- 2 tsp paprika
- 3/4 cup parmesan cheese, grated
- 1/4 tsp salt

Directions:
1. Fit the oven with the rack in position
2. In a shallow dish, mix parmesan cheese, paprika, parsley, and salt.
3. Brush fish fillets with oil and coat with parmesan cheese mixture.
4. Place coated fish fillets into the baking dish.
5. Set to bake at 400 F for 20 minutes. After 5 minutes place the baking dish in the preheated oven.
6. Serve and enjoy.
- **Nutrition Info:** Calories 160 Fat 8.1 g Carbohydrates 1.2 g Sugar 0.1 g Protein 21.7 g Cholesterol 56 mg

354.Herb Fish Fillets

Servings: 2
Cooking Time: 5 Minutes
Ingredients:
- 2 salmon fillets
- 1/4 tsp smoked paprika
- 1 tsp herb de Provence
- 1 tbsp butter, melted
- 2 tbsp olive oil
- Pepper
- Salt

Directions:
1. Fit the oven with the rack in position 2.
2. Brush salmon fillets with oil and sprinkle with paprika, herb de Provence, pepper, and salt.
3. Place salmon fillets in the air fryer basket then place an air fryer basket in the baking pan.
4. Place a baking pan on the oven rack. Set to air fry at 390 F for 5 minutes.
5. Drizzle melted butter over salmon and serve.
- **Nutrition Info:** Calories 413 Fat 31.1 g Carbohydrates 0.2 g Sugar 0 g Protein 35.4 g Cholesterol 94 mg

355.Prawn French Cuisine Galette

Servings:x
Cooking Time:x
Ingredients:
- 2 tbsp. garam masala
- 1 lb. minced prawn
- 3 tsp ginger finely chopped
- 1-2 tbsp. fresh coriander leaves
- 2 or 3 green chilies finely chopped
- 1 ½ tbsp. lemon juice
- Salt and pepper to taste

Directions:
1. Mix the ingredients in a clean bowl.
2. Mold this mixture into round and flat French Cuisine Galettes.
3. Wet the French Cuisine Galettes slightly with water.
4. Pre heat the oven at 160 degrees Fahrenheit for 5 minutes. Place the French Cuisine Galettes in the fry basket and let them cook for another 25 minutes at the same temperature. Keep rolling them over to get a uniform cook. Serve either with mint sauce or ketchup.

356.Thyme Rosemary Shrimp

Servings: 4
Cooking Time: 10 Minutes
Ingredients:
- 1 lb shrimp, peeled and deveined
- 1/2 tbsp fresh rosemary, chopped
- 1 tbsp olive oil
- 2 garlic cloves, minced
- 1/2 tbsp fresh thyme, chopped
- Pepper
- Salt

Directions:
1. Fit the oven with the rack in position
2. Add shrimp and remaining ingredients in a large bowl and toss well.
3. Pour shrimp mixture into the baking dish.
4. Set to bake at 400 F for 15 minutes. After 5 minutes place the baking dish in the preheated oven.
5. Serve and enjoy.
- **Nutrition Info:** Calories 169 Fat 5.5 g Carbohydrates 2.7 g Sugar 0 g Protein 26 g Cholesterol 239 mg

357.Orange Fish Fillets

Servings: 2
Cooking Time: 25 Minutes
Ingredients:
- 1 lb salmon fillets
- 1 orange juice
- 1 orange zest, grated
- 2 tbsp honey
- 3 tbsp soy sauce

Directions:
1. Fit the oven with the rack in position
2. In a small bowl, whisk together honey, soy sauce, orange juice, and orange zest.
3. Place salmon fillets in a baking dish and pour honey mixture over salmon fillets.

4. Set to bake at 425 F for 30 minutes. After 5 minutes place the baking dish in the preheated oven.
5. Serve and enjoy.
- **Nutrition Info:** Calories 399 Fat 14.1 g Carbohydrates 24.4 g Sugar 21.3 g Protein 45.9 g Cholesterol 100 mg

358.Parsley Catfish Fillets

Servings:4
Cooking Time: 25 Minutes
Ingredients:
- 4 catfish fillets, rinsed and dried
- ¼ cup seasoned fish fry
- 1 tbsp olive oil
- 1 tbsp fresh parsley, chopped

Directions:
1. Add seasoned fish fry and fillets in a large Ziploc bag; massage well to coat. Place the fillets in the basket and cook for 14-16 minutes at 360 F on AirFry function. Top with parsley.

359.Harissa Shrimp

Servings:4
Cooking Time: 15 Minutes
Ingredients:
- 1 ¼ lb tiger shrimp
- ¼ tsp harissa powder
- ½ tsp old bay seasoning
- Salt to taste
- 1 tbsp olive oil

Directions:
1. Preheat your oven to 390 F on AirFry function. In a bowl, mix the ingredients. Place the mixture in the cooking basket and cook for 5 minutes. Serve with a drizzle of lemon juice.

360.Quick Shrimp Bowl

Servings: 4
Cooking Time: 15 Minutes
Ingredients:
- 1 ¼ pounds tiger shrimp
- ¼ tsp cayenne pepper
- ½ tsp old bay seasoning
- ¼ tsp smoked paprika
- A pinch of salt
- 1 tbsp olive oil

Directions:
1. Preheat your oven to 390 F on Air Fry function. In a bowl, mix all the ingredients. Place the mixture in your the cooking basket and fit in the baking tray; cook for 5 minutes, flipping once. Serve drizzled with lemon juice.

361.Party Cod Nuggets

Servings:4

Cooking Time: 25 Minutes
Ingredients:
- 1 ¼ lb cod fillets, cut into 4 chunks each
- ½ cup flour
- 1 egg
- 1 cup cornflakes
- 1 tbsp olive oil
- Salt and black pepper to taste

Directions:
1. Place the oil and cornflakes in a food processor and process until crumbed. Season the fish chunks with salt and pepper. In a bowl, beat the egg with 1 tbsp of water.
2. Dredge the chunks in flour first, then dip in the egg, and finally coat with cornflakes. Arrange on a lined sheet and press Start. Cook on AirFry function at 350 F for 15 minutes until crispy. Serve.

362.Crispy Cheesy Fish Fingers

Servings: 4
Cooking Time: 20 Minutes
Ingredients:
- Large codfish filet, approximately 6-8 ounces, fresh or frozen and thawed, cut into 1 ½-inch strips
- 2 raw eggs
- ½ cup of breadcrumbs (we like Panko, but any brand or home recipe will do)
- 2 tablespoons of shredded or powdered parmesan cheese
- 1 tablespoons of shredded cheddar cheese
- Pinch of salt and pepper

Directions:
1. Preparing the Ingredients. Cover the basket of the air fryer oven with a lining of tin foil, leaving the edges uncovered to allow air to circulate through the basket.
2. Preheat the air fryer oven to 350 degrees.
3. In a large mixing bowl, beat the eggs until fluffy and until the yolks and whites are fully combined.
4. Dunk all the fish strips in the beaten eggs, fully submerging.
5. In a separate mixing bowl, combine the bread crumbs with the parmesan, cheddar, and salt and pepper, until evenly mixed.
6. One by one, coat the egg-covered fish strips in the mixed dry ingredients so that they're fully covered, and place on the foil-lined Oven rack/basket. Place the Rack on the middle-shelf of the air fryer oven.
7. Air Frying. Set the air-fryer timer to 20 minutes.
8. Halfway through the cooking time, shake the handle of the air-fryer so that the breaded fish jostles inside and fry-coverage is even.

9. After 20 minutes, when the fryer shuts off, the fish strips will be perfectly cooked and their breaded crust golden-brown and delicious! Using tongs, remove from the air fryer oven and set on a serving dish to cool.

363.Old Bay Tilapia Fillets

Servings: 4
Cooking Time: 15 Minutes
Ingredients:
- 1 pound tilapia fillets
- 1 tbsp old bay seasoning
- 2 tbsp canola oil
- 2 tbsp lemon pepper
- Salt to taste
- 2-3 butter buds

Directions:
1. Preheat your oven to 400 F on Bake function. Drizzle tilapia fillets with canola oil. In a bowl, mix salt, lemon pepper, butter buds, and seasoning; spread on the fish. Place the fillet on the basket and fit in the baking tray. Cook for 10 minutes, flipping once until tender and crispy.

364.Parmesan-crusted Hake With Garlic Sauce

Servings:3
Cooking Time: 10 Minutes
Ingredients:
- Fish:
- 6 tablespoons mayonnaise
- 1 tablespoon fresh lime juice
- 1 teaspoon Dijon mustard
- 1 cup grated Parmesan cheese
- Salt, to taste
- ¼ teaspoon ground black pepper, or more to taste
- 3 hake fillets, patted dry
- Nonstick cooking spray
- Garlic Sauce:
- ¼ cup plain Greek yogurt
- 2 tablespoons olive oil
- 2 cloves garlic, minced
- ½ teaspoon minced tarragon leaves

Directions:
1. Mix the mayo, lime juice, and mustard in a shallow bowl and whisk to combine. In another shallow bowl, stir together the grated Parmesan cheese, salt, and pepper.
2. Dredge each fillet in the mayo mixture, then roll them in the cheese mixture until they are evenly coated on both sides.
3. Spray the air fryer basket with nonstick cooking spray. Place the fillets in the pan.
4. Put the air fryer basket on the baking pan and slide into Rack Position 2, select Air Fry, set temperature to 395ºF (202ºC), and set time to 10 minutes.

5. Flip the fillets halfway through the cooking time.
6. Meanwhile, in a small bowl, whisk all the ingredients for the sauce until well incorporated.
7. When cooking is complete, the fish should flake apart with a fork. Remove the fillets from the oven and serve warm alongside the sauce.

365.Tropical Shrimp Skewers

Servings: 4
Cooking Time: 5 Minutes
Ingredients:
- 1 tbsp. lime juice
- 1 tbsp. honey
- ¼ tsp red pepper flakes
- ¼ tsp pepper
- ¼ tsp ginger
- Nonstick cooking spray
- 1 lb. medium shrimp, peel, devein & leave tails on
- 2 cups peaches, drain & chop
- ½ green bell pepper, chopped fine
- ¼ cup scallions, chopped

Directions:
1. Soak 8 small wooden skewers in water for 15 minutes.
2. In a small bowl, whisk together lime juice, honey and spices. Transfer 2 tablespoons of the mixture to a medium bowl.
3. Place the baking pan in position 2 of the oven. Lightly spray fryer basket with cooking spray. Set oven to broil on 400°F for 10 minutes.
4. Thread 5 shrimp on each skewer and brush both sides with marinade. Place in basket and after 5 minutes, place on the baking pan. Cook 4-5 minutes or until shrimp turn pink.
5. Add peaches, bell pepper, and scallions to reserved honey mixture, mix well. Divide salsa evenly between serving plates and top with 2 skewers each. Serve immediately.
- **Nutrition Info:** Calories 181, Total Fat 1g, Saturated Fat 0g, Total Carbs 27g, Net Carbs 25g, Protein 16g, Sugar 21g, Fiber 2g, Sodium 650mg, Potassium 288mg, Phosphorus 297mg

366.Lemon Salmon

Servings:2
Cooking Time: 20 Minutes
Ingredients:
- 2 salmon fillets
- Salt to taste
- Zest of 1 lemon

Directions:
1. Rub the fillets with salt and lemon zest. Place them in the frying basket and spray

with cooking spray. Press Start and cook the salmon in the preheated oven for 14 minutes at 360 F on AirFry function. Serve with steamed asparagus and a drizzle of lemon juice.

367.Roasted Scallops With Snow Peas

Servings:4
Cooking Time: 8 Minutes
Ingredients:
- 1 pound (454 g) sea scallops
- 3 tablespoons hoisin sauce
- ½ cup toasted sesame seeds
- 6 ounces (170 g) snow peas, trimmed
- 3 teaspoons vegetable oil, divided
- 1 teaspoon soy sauce
- 1 teaspoon sesame oil
- 1 cup roasted mushrooms

Directions:
1. Brush the scallops with the hoisin sauce. Put the sesame seeds in a shallow dish. Roll the scallops in the sesame seeds until evenly coated.
2. Combine the snow peas with 1 teaspoon of vegetable oil, the sesame oil, and soy sauce in a medium bowl and toss to coat.
3. Grease the baking pan with the remaining 2 teaspoons of vegetable oil. Put the scallops in the middle of the pan and arrange the snow peas around the scallops in a single layer.
4. Slide the baking pan into Rack Position 2, select Roast, set temperature to 375ºF (190ºC), and set time to 8 minutes.
5. After 5 minutes, remove the pan and flip the scallops. Fold in the mushrooms and stir well. Return the pan to the oven and continue cooking.
6. When done, remove from the oven and cool for 5 minutes. Serve warm.

368.Delightful Catfish Fillets

Servings: 4
Cooking Time: 25 Minutes
Ingredients:
- 4 catfish fillets
- ¼ cup seasoned fish fry
- 1 tbsp olive oil
- 1 tbsp parsley, chopped

Directions:
1. Add seasoned fish fry and catfish fillets in a large Ziploc bag and massage well to coat. Place the fillets in your Air Fryer basket and fit in the baking tray; cook for 10 minutes at 360 F on Air Fry function. Flip the fish and cook for 2-3 more minutes. Top with parsley and serve.

369.Basil Tomato Salmon

Servings: 2
Cooking Time: 20 Minutes
Ingredients:
- 2 salmon fillets
- 1 tomato, sliced
- 1 tbsp dried basil
- 2 tbsp parmesan cheese, grated
- 1 tbsp olive oil

Directions:
1. Fit the oven with the rack in position
2. Place salmon fillets in a baking dish.
3. Sprinkle basil on top of salmon fillets.
4. Arrange tomato slices on top of salmon fillets. Drizzle with oil and top with cheese.
5. Set to bake at 375 F for 25 minutes. After 5 minutes place the baking dish in the preheated oven.
6. Serve and enjoy.
- **Nutrition Info:** Calories 324 Fat 19.6 g Carbohydrates 1.5 g Sugar 0.8 g Protein 37.1 g Cholesterol 83 mg

370.Crispy Crab And Fish Cakes

Servings:4
Cooking Time: 12 Minutes
Ingredients:
- 8 ounces (227 g) imitation crab meat
- 4 ounces (113 g) leftover cooked fish (such as cod, pollock, or haddock)
- 2 tablespoons minced celery
- 2 tablespoons minced green onion
- 2 tablespoons light mayonnaise
- 1 tablespoon plus 2 teaspoons Worcestershire sauce
- ¾ cup crushed saltine cracker crumbs
- 2 teaspoons dried parsley flakes
- 1 teaspoon prepared yellow mustard
- ½ teaspoon garlic powder
- ½ teaspoon dried dill weed, crushed
- ½ teaspoon Old Bay seasoning
- ½ cup panko bread crumbs
- Cooking spray

Directions:
1. Pulse the crab meat and fish in a food processor until finely chopped.
2. Transfer the meat mixture to a large bowl, along with the celery, green onion, mayo, Worcestershire sauce, cracker crumbs, parsley flakes, mustard, garlic powder, dill weed, and Old Bay seasoning. Stir to mix well.
3. Scoop out the meat mixture and form into 8 equal-sized patties with your hands.
4. Place the panko bread crumbs on a plate. Roll the patties in the bread crumbs until they are evenly coated on both sides. Put the patties in the baking pan and spritz them with cooking spray.

5. Slide the baking pan into Rack Position 1, select Convection Bake, set temperature to 390ºF (199ºC), and set time to 12 minutes.
6. Flip the patties halfway through the cooking time.
7. When cooking is complete, they should be golden brown and cooked through. Remove the pan from the oven. Divide the patties among four plates and serve.

371.Baked Tilapia With Garlic Aioli

Servings:4
Cooking Time: 15 Minutes
Ingredients:
- Tilapia:
- 4 tilapia fillets
- 1 tablespoon extra-virgin olive oil
- 1 teaspoon garlic powder
- 1 teaspoon paprika
- 1 teaspoon dried basil
- A pinch of lemon-pepper seasoning
- Garlic Aioli:
- 2 garlic cloves, minced
- 1 tablespoon mayonnaise
- Juice of ½ lemon
- 1 teaspoon extra-virgin olive oil
- Salt and pepper, to taste

Directions:
1. On a clean work surface, brush both sides of each fillet with the olive oil. Sprinkle with the garlic powder, paprika, basil, and lemon-pepper seasoning. Place the fillets in the baking pan.

2. Slide the baking pan into Rack Position 1, select Convection Bake, set temperature to 400ºF (205ºC), and set time to 15 minutes.
3. Flip the fillets halfway through.
4. Meanwhile, make the garlic aioli: Whisk together the garlic, mayo, lemon juice, olive oil, salt, and pepper in a small bowl until smooth.
5. When cooking is complete, the fish should flake apart with a fork and no longer translucent in the center. Remove the fish from the oven and serve with the garlic aioli on the side.

372.Parmesan Fish With Pine Nuts

Servings: 4
Cooking Time: 15 Minutes
Ingredients:
- 2 tbsp fresh basil, chopped
- 2 garlic cloves, minced
- 2 tbsp olive oil
- 1 tbsp Parmesan cheese, grated
- salt and black pepper to taste
- 2 tbsp pine nuts
- 4 white fish fillets
- 2 tbsp olive oil

Directions:
1. Preheat on Air Fry function to 350 F. Season the fish with salt and pepper. Place in the greased basket and fit in the baking tray. Cook the fillets for 8 minutes, flipping once. In a bowl, add basil, olive oil, pine nuts, garlic, and Parmesan cheese; mix well. Serve with the fish.

MEATLESS RECIPES

373.Baked Chickpea Stars

Servings:x
Cooking Time:x
Ingredients:
- 4 tbsp. roasted sesame seeds
- 2 small onion finely chopped
- ½ tsp. coriander powder
- ½ tsp. cumin powder
- Use olive oil for greasing purposes
- 1 cup white chick peas soaked overnight
- 1 tsp. ginger-garlic paste
- 4 tbsp. chopped coriander leaves
- 2 green chilies finely chopped
- 4 tbsp. thick curd
- Pinches of salt and pepper to taste
- 1 tsp. dry mint

Directions:
1. Since the chickpeas have been soaked you will first have to drain them. Add a pinch of salt and pour water until the chickpeas are submerged. Put this container in a pressure cooker and let the chickpeas cook for around 25 minutes until they turn soft. Remove the cooker from the flame. Now mash the chickpeas.
2. Take another container. Into it add the ginger garlic paste, onions, coriander leaves, coriander powder, cumin powder, green chili, salt and pepper, and 1 tbsp. Use your hands to mix these ingredients Pour this mixture into the container with the mashed chickpeas and mix. Spread this mixture over a flat surface to about a half-inch thickness.
3. Cut star shapes out of this layer. Make a mixture of curd and mint leaves and spread this over the surface of the star shaped cutlets. Coat all the sides with sesame seeds. Pre heat the oven at 200-degree Fahrenheit for 5 minutes. Open the basket of the Fryer and put the stars inside. Close the basket properly. Continue to cook the stars for around half an hour. Periodically turn over the stars in the basket in order to prevent overcooking one side. Serve either with mint sauce or tomato ketchup.

374.Cayenne Spicy Green Beans

Servings: 4
Cooking Time: 20 Minutes
Ingredients:
- 1 cup panko breadcrumbs
- 2 whole eggs, beaten
- ½ cup Parmesan cheese, grated
- ½ cup flour
- 1 tsp cayenne pepper
- 1 ½ pounds green beans
- Salt to taste

Directions:
1. In a bowl, mix panko breadcrumbs, Parmesan cheese, cayenne pepper, salt, and pepper. Roll the green beans in flour and dip in eggs. Dredge beans in the parmesan-panko mix. Place the prepared beans in the greased cooking basket and fit in the baking tray; cook for 15 minutes on Air Fry function at 350 F, shaking once. Serve and enjoy!

375.Crispy Veggies With Halloumi

Servings:2
Cooking Time: 14 Minutes
Ingredients:
- 2 zucchinis, cut into even chunks
- 1 large eggplant, peeled, cut into chunks
- 1 large carrot, cut into chunks
- 6 ounces (170 g) halloumi cheese, cubed
- 2 teaspoons olive oil
- Salt and black pepper, to taste
- 1 teaspoon dried mixed herbs

Directions:
1. Combine the zucchinis, eggplant, carrot, cheese, olive oil, salt, and pepper in a large bowl and toss to coat well.
2. Spread the mixture evenly in the air fryer basket.
3. Put the air fryer basket on the baking pan and slide into Rack Position 2, select Air Fry, set temperature to 340ºF (171ºC), and set time to 14 minutes.
4. Stir the mixture once during cooking.
5. When cooking is complete, they should be crispy and golden. Remove from the oven and serve topped with mixed herbs.

376.Onion Rings

Servings: 4
Cooking Time: 10 Minutes
Ingredients:
- 1 large spanish onion
- 1/2 cup buttermilk
- 2 eggs, lightly beaten
- 3/4 cups unbleached all-purpose flour
- 3/4 cups panko bread crumbs
- 1/2 teaspoon baking powder
- 1/2 teaspoon Cayenne pepper, to taste
- Salt

Directions:
1. Preparing the Ingredients. Start by cutting your onion into 1/2 thick rings and separate. Smaller pieces can be discarded or saved for other recipes.
2. Beat the eggs in a large bowl and mix in the buttermilk, then set it aside.
3. In another bowl combine flour, pepper, bread crumbs, and baking powder.

4. Use a large spoon to dip a whole ring in the buttermilk, then pull it through the flour mix on both sides to completely coat the ring.
5. Air Frying. Cook about 8 rings at a time in your air fryer oven for 8-10 minutes at 360 degrees shaking half way through.
- **Nutrition Info:** CALORIES: 225; FAT: 3.8G; PROTEIN:19G; FIBER:2.4G

377.Veggie Gratin

Servings:4
Cooking Time: 30 Minutes
Ingredients:
- 1 cup eggplants, cubed
- ¼ cup red peppers, chopped
- ¼ cup green peppers, chopped
- ¼ cup onions, chopped
- ⅓ cup tomatoes, chopped
- 1 garlic clove, minced
- 4 pimiento-stuffed olives, sliced
- 1 tsp capers
- ¼ tsp dried basil
- ¼ tsp dried marjoram
- Salt and black pepper to taste
- ¼ cup mozzarella cheese, grated
- 1 tbsp breadcrumbs

Directions:
1. In a bowl, add eggplants, green and red peppers, onions, tomatoes, olives, garlic, basil, marjoram, capers, salt, and black pepper. Lightly grease the tray with cooking spray.
2. Ladle the eggplant mixture into the baking tray and level it using the vessel. Sprinkle mozzarella cheese on top and cover with breadcrumbs. Place the dish in the oven and press Start. Cook for 20 minutes on Bake function at 320 F. Serve.

378.Cheese French Fries

Servings:x
Cooking Time:x
Ingredients:
- 2 medium sized potatoes peeled and cut into thick pieces lengthwise
- 1 tsp. mixed herbs
- ½ tsp. red chili flakes
- A pinch of salt to taste
- 1 tbsp. lemon juice
- 1 cup melted cheddar cheese (You could put this into a piping bag and
- 1 tbsp. olive oil
- create a pattern of it on the fries.)

Directions:
1. Take all the ingredients mentioned under the heading "For the marinade" and mix them well. Now pour into a container 3 cups of water.

2. Add a pinch of salt into this water. Bring it to the boil. Now blanch the pieces of potato for around 5 minutes. Drain the water using a sieve. Dry the potato pieces on a towel and then place them on another dry towel. Coat these potato Oregano Fingers with the marinade made in the previous step. Pre heat the oven for around 5 minutes at 300 Fahrenheit. Take out the basket of the fryer and place the potato Oregano Fingers in them.
3. Close the basket. Now keep the fryer at 220 Fahrenheit for 20 or 25 minutes. In between the process, toss the fries twice or thrice so that they get cooked properly. Towards the end of the cooking process (the last 2 minutes or so), sprinkle the cut coriander leaves on the fries. Add the melted cheddar cheese over the fries and serve hot.

379.Cottage Cheese Pops

Servings:x
Cooking Time:x
Ingredients:
- 1 tsp. dry basil
- ½ cup hung curd
- 1 tsp. lemon juice
- 1 cup cottage cheese cut into 2" cubes
- 1 ½ tsp. garlic paste
- Salt and pepper to taste
- 1 tsp. dry oregano
- 1 tsp. red chili flakes

Directions:
1. Cut the cottage cheese into thick and long rectangular pieces.
2. Add the rest of the ingredients into a separate bowl and mix them well to get a consistent mixture.
3. Dip the cottage cheese pieces in the above mixture and leave them aside for some time.
4. Pre heat the oven at 180° C for around 5 minutes. Place the coated cottage cheese pieces in the fry basket and close it properly. Let them cook at the same temperature for 20 more minutes. Keep turning them over in the basket so that they are cooked properly. Serve with tomato ketchup.

380.Nutmeg Broccoli With Eggs & Cheddar Cheese

Servings:4
Cooking Time: 15 Minutes
Ingredients:
- 1 lb broccoli, cut into florets
- 4 eggs
- 1 cup cheddar cheese, shredded
- 1 cup heavy cream
- 1 pinch of nutmeg

- 1 tsp ginger powder

Directions:
1. In boiling water, steam the broccoli for 5 minutes. Drain and place in a bowl. Add in 1 egg, heavy cream, nutmeg, and ginger. Divide the mixture between greased ramekins and sprinkle the cheddar cheese on top. Cook for 10 minutes at 280 F on AirFry function.

381.Carrot & Chickpea Oat Balls With Cashews

Servings:4
Cooking Time: 30 Minutes
Ingredients:
- 2 tbsp olive oil
- 2 tbsp soy sauce
- 1 tbsp flax meal
- 2 cups canned chickpeas, drained
- ½ cup sweet onions, diced
- ½ cup carrots, grated
- ½ cup cashews, toasted
- Juice of 1 lemon
- ½ tsp turmeric
- 1 tsp cumin
- 1 tsp garlic powder
- 1 cup rolled oats

Directions:
1. Preheat on AirFry function to 380 F. Heat olive oil in a skillet and sauté onions and carrots for 5 minutes. Ground the oats and cashews in a food processor. Transfer to a bowl.
2. Place the chickpeas, lemon juice, and soy sauce in the food processor and process until smooth. Add them to the bowl as well. Mix in the onions and carrots.
3. Stir in the remaining ingredients until fully incorporated. Make balls out of the mixture. Place them in the frying basket and press Start. Cook for 12 minutes. Serve warm.

382.Cilantro Roasted Carrots With Cumin Seeds

Servings:4
Cooking Time: 15 Minutes
Ingredients:
- 1 lb carrots, julienned
- 1 tbsp olive oil
- 1 tsp cumin seeds
- 2 tbsp fresh cilantro, chopped

Directions:
1. Preheat on AirFry function to 350 F. In a bowl, mix oil, carrots, and cumin seeds. Gently stir to coat the carrots well. Place the carrots in a baking tray and press Star. Cook for 10 minutes. Scatter fresh coriander over the carrots and serve.

383.Cabbage Flat Cakes

Servings:x
Cooking Time:x
Ingredients:
- 2 or 3 green chilies finely chopped
- 1 ½ tbsp. lemon juice
- Salt and pepper to taste
- 2 tbsp. garam masala
- 2 cups halved cabbage leaves
- 3 tsp. ginger finely chopped
- 1-2 tbsp. fresh coriander leaves

Directions:
1. Mix the ingredients in a clean bowl and add water to it. Make sure that the paste is not too watery but is enough to apply on the cabbage.
2. Pre heat the oven at 160 degrees Fahrenheit for 5 minutes. Place the French Cuisine Galettes in the fry basket and let them cook for another 25 minutes at the same temperature. Keep rolling them over to get a uniform cook. Serve either with mint sauce or ketchup.

384.Bottle Gourd Flat Cakes

Servings:x
Cooking Time:x
Ingredients:
- 2 or 3 green chilies finely chopped
- 1 ½ tbsp. lemon juice
- Salt and pepper to taste
- 2 tbsp. garam masala
- 2 cups sliced bottle gourd
- 3 tsp. ginger finely chopped
- 1-2 tbsp. fresh coriander leaves

Directions:
1. Mix the ingredients in a clean bowl and add water to it. Make sure that the paste is not too watery but is enough to apply on the bottle gourd slices. Pre heat the oven at 160 degrees Fahrenheit for 5 minutes.
2. Place the French Cuisine Galettes in the fry basket and let them cook for another 25 minutes at the same temperature. Keep rolling them over to get a uniform cook. Serve either with mint sauce or ketchup.

385.Sesame-thyme Whole Maitake Mushrooms

Servings:2
Cooking Time: 15 Minutes
Ingredients:
- 1 tablespoon soy sauce
- 2 teaspoons toasted sesame oil
- 3 teaspoons vegetable oil, divided
- 1 garlic clove, minced
- 7 ounces (198 g) maitake (hen of the woods) mushrooms

- ½ teaspoon flaky sea salt
- ½ teaspoon sesame seeds
- ½ teaspoon finely chopped fresh thyme leaves

Directions:
1. Whisk together the soy sauce, sesame oil, 1 teaspoon of vegetable oil, and garlic in a small bowl.
2. Arrange the mushrooms in the air fryer basket in a single layer. Drizzle the soy sauce mixture over the mushrooms.
3. Put the air fryer basket on the baking pan and slide into Rack Position 2, select Roast, set temperature to 300ºF (150ºC), and set time to 15 minutes.
4. After 10 minutes, remove from the oven. Flip the mushrooms and sprinkle the sea salt, sesame seeds, and thyme leaves on top. Drizzle the remaining 2 teaspoons of vegetable oil all over. Return to the oven and continue roasting for an additional 5 minutes.
5. When cooking is complete, remove the mushrooms from the oven to a plate and serve hot.

386.Apricot Spicy Lemon Kebab

Servings:x
Cooking Time:x
Ingredients:
- 3 tsp. lemon juice
- 2 tsp. garam masala
- 3 eggs
- 2 ½ tbsp. white sesame seeds
- 2 cups fresh apricots
- 3 onions chopped
- 5 green chilies-roughly chopped
- 1 ½ tbsp. ginger paste
- 1 ½ tsp. garlic paste
- 1 ½ tsp. salt

Directions:
1. Grind the ingredients except for the egg and form a smooth paste. Coat the apricots in the paste. Now, beat the eggs and add a little salt to it.
2. Dip the coated apricots in the egg mixture and then transfer to the sesame seeds and coat the apricots well. Place the vegetables on a stick.
3. Pre heat the oven at 160 degrees Fahrenheit for around 5 minutes. Place the sticks in the basket and let them cook for another 25 minutes at the same temperature. Turn the sticks over in between the cooking process to get a uniform cook.

387.Bitter Gourd Flat Cakes

Servings:x

Cooking Time:x
Ingredients:
- 2 or 3 green chilies finely chopped
- 1 ½ tbsp. lemon juice
- Salt and pepper to taste
- 2 tbsp. garam masala
- 2 cups sliced bitter gourd
- 3 tsp. ginger finely chopped
- 1-2 tbsp. fresh coriander leaves

Directions:
1. Mix the ingredients in a clean bowl and add water to it. Make sure that the paste is not too watery but is enough to apply on the bitter gourd slices.
2. Pre heat the oven at 160 degrees Fahrenheit for 5 minutes. Place the French Cuisine Galettes in the fry basket and let them cook for another 25 minutes at the same temperature. Keep rolling them over to get a uniform cook. Serve either with mint sauce or ketchup.

388.Chinese Spring Rolls

Servings:4
Cooking Time: 15 Minutes
Ingredients:
- ½ head cabbage, grated
- 2 carrots, grated
- 1 tsp fresh ginger, minced
- 1 garlic clove, minced
- 1 tsp sesame oil
- 1 tsp soy sauce
- 1 tsp sesame seeds
- ½ tsp salt
- 1 tsp olive oil
- 1 package spring roll wrappers

Directions:
1. Combine all ingredients in a bowl. Divide the mixture between the roll sheets and roll them up; arrange on a baking tray. Press Start and cook in the for 5 minutes on Bake function at 370 F.

389.Garlicky Vermouth Mushrooms

Servings: 4
Cooking Time: 20 Minutes
Ingredients:
- 2 lb portobello mushrooms, sliced
- 2 tbsp vermouth
- ½ tsp garlic powder
- 1 tbsp olive oil
- 2 tsp herbs
- 1 tbsp duck fat, softened

Directions:
1. In a bowl, mix the duck fat, garlic powder, and herbs. Rub the mushrooms with the mixture and place them in a baking tray. Drizzle with vermouth and cook in your for 15 minutes on Bake function at 350 F. Serve.

390. Cauliflower Bites

Servings: 4
Cooking Time: 18 Minutes
Ingredients:
- 1 Head Cauliflower, cut into small florets
- Tsps Garlic Powder
- Pinch of Salt and Pepper
- 1 Tbsp Butter, melted
- 1/2 Cup Chili Sauce
- Olive Oil

Directions:
1. Preparing the Ingredients. Place cauliflower into a bowl and pour oil over florets to lightly cover.
2. Season florets with salt, pepper, and the garlic powder and toss well.
3. Air Frying. Place florets into the air fryer oven at 350 degrees for 14 minutes.
4. Remove cauliflower from the Air fryer oven.
5. Combine the melted butter with the chili sauce
6. Pour over the florets so that they are well coated.
7. Return to the air fryer oven and cook for additional 3 to 4 minutes
8. Serve as a side or with ranch or cheese dip as a snack.

391. Mixed Vegetable Patties

Servings: x
Cooking Time: x
Ingredients:
- 1 tbsp. fresh coriander leaves
- ¼ tsp. red chili powder
- ¼ tsp. cumin powder
- 2.55 Cottage cheese Momo's Recipe
- 1 ½ cup all-purpose flour
- ½ tsp. salt
- 1 cup grated mixed vegetables
- A pinch of salt to taste
- ¼ tsp. ginger finely chopped
- 1 green chili finely chopped
- 1 tsp. lemon juice
- 5 tbsp. water
- 2 cups crumbled cottage cheese
- 2 tbsp. oil
- 2 tsp. ginger-garlic paste
- 2 tsp. soya sauce
- 2 tsp. vinegar

Directions:
1. Squeeze the dough and cover it with plastic wrap and set aside. Next, cook the ingredients for the filling and try to ensure that the cottage cheese is covered well with the sauce.
2. Roll the dough and cut it into a square. Place the filling in the center. Now, wrap the dough to cover the filling and pinch the edges together.
3. Pre heat the oven at 200° F for 5 minutes. Place the gnocchi's in the fry basket and close it. Let them cook at the same temperature for another 20 minutes. Recommended sides are chili sauce or ketchup.
4. Mix the ingredients together and ensure that the flavors are right. You will now make round patties with the mixture and roll them out well.
5. Pre heat the oven at 250 Fahrenheit for 5 minutes. Open the basket of the Fryer and arrange the patties in the basket. Close it carefully. Keep the fryer at 150 degrees for around 10 or 12 minutes. In between the cooking process, turn the patties over to get a uniform cook. Serve hot with mint sauce.

392. Stuffed Portobellos With Peppers And Cheese

Servings: 4
Cooking Time: 15 Minutes
Ingredients:
- 4 tablespoons sherry vinegar or white wine vinegar
- 6 garlic cloves, minced, divided
- 1 tablespoon fresh thyme leaves
- 1 teaspoon Dijon mustard
- 1 teaspoon kosher salt, divided
- ¼ cup plus 3¼ teaspoons extra-virgin olive oil, divided
- 8 portobello mushroom caps, each about 3 inches across, patted dry
- 1 small red or yellow bell pepper, thinly sliced
- 1 small green bell pepper, thinly sliced
- 1 small onion, thinly sliced
- ¼ teaspoon red pepper flakes
- Freshly ground black pepper, to taste
- 4 ounces (113 g) shredded Fontina cheese

Directions:
1. Stir together the vinegar, 4 minced garlic cloves, thyme, mustard, and ½ teaspoon of kosher salt in a small bowl. Slowly pour in ¼ cup of olive oil, whisking constantly, or until an emulsion is formed. Reserve 2 tablespoons of the marinade and set aside.
2. Put the mushrooms in a resealable plastic bag and pour in the marinade. Seal and shake the bag, coating the mushrooms in the marinade. Transfer the mushrooms to the baking pan, gill-side down.
3. Put the remaining 2 minced garlic cloves, bell peppers, onion, red pepper flakes, remaining ½ teaspoon of salt, and black pepper in a medium bowl. Drizzle with the remaining 3¼ teaspoons of olive oil and

toss well. Transfer the bell pepper mixture to the pan.

4. Slide the baking pan into Rack Position 2, select Roast, set temperature to 375ºF (190ºC), and set time to 12 minutes.
5. After 7 minutes, remove the pan and stir the peppers and flip the mushrooms. Return the pan to the oven and continue cooking for 5 minutes.
6. Remove from the oven and place the pepper mixture onto a cutting board and coarsely chop.
7. Brush both sides of the mushrooms with the reserved 2 tablespoons marinade. Stuff the caps evenly with the pepper mixture. Scatter the cheese on top.
8. Select Convection Broil, set temperature to High, and set time to 3 minutes.
9. When done, the mushrooms should be tender and the cheese should be melted.
10. Serve warm.

393.Chili Veggie Skewers

Servings: 4
Cooking Time: 20 Minutes
Ingredients:
- 2 tbsp cornflour
- 1 cup canned white beans, drained
- ⅓ cup grated carrots
- 2 boiled and mashed potatoes
- ¼ cup chopped fresh mint leaves
- ½ tsp garam masala powder
- ½ cup paneer
- 1 green chili
- 1-inch piece of fresh ginger
- 3 garlic cloves
- Salt to taste

Directions:
1. Preheat on Air Fry function to 390 F. Place the beans, carrots, garlic, ginger, chili, paneer, and mint in a food processor; process until smooth. Transfer to a bowl. Add in the mashed potatoes, cornflour, salt, and garam masala powder and mix until fully incorporated.
2. Divide the mixture into 12 equal pieces. Shape each of the pieces around a skewer. Cook in your for 10 minutes, turning once. Serve.

394.Parmesan Coated Green Beans

Servings:4
Cooking Time: 20 Minutes
Ingredients:
- 1 cup panko breadcrumbs
- 2 whole eggs, beaten
- ½ cup Parmesan cheese, grated
- ½ cup flour
- 1 tsp cayenne pepper powder

- 1 ½ pounds green beans
- Salt to taste

Directions:
1. Preheat on AirFry function to 380 F. In a bowl, mix breadcrumbs, Parmesan cheese, cayenne pepper powder, salt, and pepper. Flour the green beans and dip them in eggs. Dredge beans in the Parmesan-panko mix. Place in the cooking basket and cook for 15 minutes Serve.

395.Vegetable Spring Rolls

Servings: 4
Cooking Time: 15 Minutes
Ingredients:
- ½ cabbage head, grated
- 2 carrots, grated
- 1 tsp minced ginger
- 1 tsp minced garlic
- 1 tsp sesame oil
- 1 tsp soy sauce
- 1 tsp sesame seeds
- ½ tsp salt
- 1 tsp olive oil
- 1 package spring roll wrappers

Directions:
1. Combine all ingredients except for the wrappers in a large bowl. Divide the mixture between the spring roll wrappers and roll them up. Arrange on a greased baking tray and cook in your for 5 minutes on Bake function at 370 F. Serve.

396.Maple And Pecan Granola

Servings:4
Cooking Time: 20 Minutes
Ingredients:
- 1½ cups rolled oats
- ¼ cup maple syrup
- ¼ cup pecan pieces
- 1 teaspoon vanilla extract
- ½ teaspoon ground cinnamon

Directions:
1. Line a baking sheet with parchment paper.
2. Mix together the oats, maple syrup, pecan pieces, vanilla, and cinnamon in a large bowl and stir until the oats and pecan pieces are completely coated. Spread the mixture evenly in the baking pan.
3. Slide the baking pan into Rack Position 1, select Convection Bake, set temperature to 300ºF (150ºC), and set time to 20 minutes.
4. Stir once halfway through the cooking time.
5. When done, remove from the oven and cool for 30 minutes before serving. The granola may still be a bit soft right after removing, but it will gradually firm up as it cools.

397.Broccoli Momo's Recipe

Servings:x
Cooking Time:x
Ingredients:

- 2 tbsp. oil
- 2 tsp. ginger-garlic paste
- 2 tsp. soya sauce
- 2 tsp. vinegar
- 1 ½ cup all-purpose flour
- ½ tsp. salt
- 5 tbsp. water
- 2 cups grated broccoli

Directions:

1. Squeeze the dough and cover it with plastic wrap and set aside. Next, cook the ingredients for the filling and try to ensure that the broccoli is covered well with the sauce.
2. Roll the dough and cut it into a square. Place the filling in the center. Now, wrap the dough to cover the filling and pinch the edges together.
3. Pre heat the oven at 200° F for 5 minutes. Place the gnocchi's in the fry basket and close it. Let them cook at the same temperature for another 20 minutes. Recommended sides are chili sauce or ketchup.

398.Mexican Burritos

Servings:x
Cooking Time:x
Ingredients:

- 1 tbsp. Olive oil
- 1 medium onion finely sliced
- 3 flakes garlic crushed
- 1 tsp. freshly ground peppercorns
- ½ cup pickled jalapenos (Chop them up finely)
- 2 carrots (Cut in to long thin slices)
- 1-2 lettuce leaves shredded.
- 1 or 2 spring onions chopped finely. Also cut the greens.
- Take one tomato. Remove the seeds and chop it into small pieces.
- ½ cup French beans (Slice them lengthwise into thin and long slices)
- ½ cup mushrooms thinly sliced
- 1 cup cottage cheese cut in too long and slightly thick Oregano Fingers
- ½ cup shredded cabbage
- 1 tbsp. coriander, chopped
- 1 tbsp. vinegar
- 1 tsp. white wine
- ½ cup red kidney beans (soaked overnight)
- ½ small onion chopped
- 1 tbsp. olive oil
- 2 tbsp. tomato puree
- ¼ tsp. red chili powder
- 1 tsp. of salt to taste
- 4-5 flour tortillas
- A pinch of salt to taste
- ½ tsp. red chili flakes
- 1 green chili chopped.
- 1 cup of cheddar cheese grated.

Directions:

1. Cook the beans along with the onion and garlic and mash them finely. Now, make the sauce you will need for the burrito. Ensure that you create a slightly thick sauce.
2. For the filling, you will need to cook the ingredients well in a pan and ensure that the vegetables have browned on the outside.
3. To make the salad, toss the ingredients together.

399.Cottage Cheese Patties

Servings:x
Cooking Time:x
Ingredients:

- 1 tbsp. fresh coriander leaves
- ¼ tsp. red chili powder
- ¼ tsp. cumin powder
- 1 cup grated cottage cheese
- A pinch of salt to taste
- ¼ tsp. ginger finely chopped
- 1 green chili finely chopped
- 1 tsp. lemon juice

Directions:

1. Mix the ingredients together and ensure that the flavors are right. You will now make round patties with the mixture and roll them out well.
2. Pre heat the oven at 250 Fahrenheit for 5 minutes. Open the basket of the Fryer and arrange the patties in the basket. Close it carefully. Keep the
3. fryer at 150 degrees for around 10 or 12 minutes. In between the cooking process, turn the patties over to get a uniform cook. Serve hot with mint sauce.

400.Green Chili Flat Cakes

Servings:x
Cooking Time:x
Ingredients:

- 2 or 3 green chilies finely chopped
- 1 ½ tbsp. lemon juice
- Salt and pepper to taste
- 2 tbsp. garam masala
- 10–12 green chilies
- 3 tsp. ginger finely chopped
- 1-2 tbsp. fresh coriander leaves

Directions:

1. Mix the ingredients in a clean bowl and add water to it. Make sure that the paste is not

too watery but is enough to apply to the green chilies.

2. Pre heat the oven at 160 degrees Fahrenheit for 5 minutes. Place the French Cuisine Galettes in the fry basket and let them cook for another 25 minutes at the same temperature. Keep rolling them over to get a uniform cook. Serve either with mint sauce or ketchup.

401.Cauliflower French Cuisine Galette

Servings:x
Cooking Time:x
Ingredients:
- 3 tsp. ginger finely chopped
- 1-2 tbsp. fresh coriander leaves
- 2 or 3 green chilies finely chopped
- 1 ½ tbsp. lemon juice
- Salt and pepper to taste
- 2 tbsp. garam masala
- 2 cups cauliflower
- 1 ½ cup coarsely crushed peanuts

Directions:
1. Mix the ingredients in a clean bowl.
2. Mold this mixture into round and flat French Cuisine Galettes.
3. Wet the French Cuisine Galettes slightly with water. Coat each French Cuisine Galette with the crushed peanuts.
4. Pre heat the oven at 160 degrees Fahrenheit for 5 minutes. Place the French Cuisine Galettes in the fry basket and let them cook for another 25 minutes at the same temperature. Keep rolling them over to get a uniform cook. Serve either with mint sauce or ketchup.

402.Cheese And Bean Enchiladas

Servings:x
Cooking Time:x
Ingredients:
- A pinch of salt or to taste
- A few red chili flakes to sprinkle
- 1 tsp. of oregano
- 2 tbsp. oil
- 2 tsp. chopped garlic
- 2 onions chopped finely
- 2 capsicums chopped finely
- 2 cups of readymade baked beans
- Flour tortillas (as many as required)
- 4 tbsp. of olive oil
- A pinch of salt
- 1 tsp. oregano
- ½ tsp. pepper
- 1 ½ tsp. red chili flakes or to taste
- 1 tbsp. of finely chopped jalapenos
- 1 cup grated pizza cheese (mix mozzarella and cheddar cheeses)
- 1 ½ tsp. of garlic that has been chopped

- 1 ½ cups of readymade tomato puree
- 3 medium tomatoes. Puree them in a mixer
- 1 tsp. of sugar
- A few drops of Tabasco sauce
- 1 cup crumbled or roughly mashed cottage cheese (cottage cheese)
- 1 cup grated cheddar cheese

Directions:
1. Prepare the flour tortillas. Now move on to making the red sauce. In a pan, pour around 2 tbsp. of oil and heat. Add some garlic. Add the rest of the ingredients mentioned under the heading "For the sauce".
2. Keep stirring. Cook until the sauce reduces and becomes thick. For the filling, heat one tbsp. of oil in another pan. Add onions and garlic and cook until the onions are caramelized or attain a golden-brown color. Add the rest of the ingredients required for the filling and cook for two to three minutes.
3. Take the pan off the flame and grate some cheese over the sauce. Mix it well and let it sit for a while. Let us start assembling the dish. Take a tortilla and spread some of the sauce on the surface. Now place the filling at the center in a line. Roll up the tortilla carefully. Do the same for all the tortillas. Now place all the tortillas in a tray and sprinkle them with grated cheese. Cover this with an aluminum foil. Pre heat the oven at 160° C for 4-5 minutes. Open the basket and place the tray inside.
4. Keep the fryer at the same temperature for another 15 minutes. Turn the tortillas over in between to get a uniform cook.

403.Potato Wedges

Servings:x
Cooking Time:x
Ingredients:
- 1 tsp. mixed herbs
- ½ tsp. red chili flakes
- A pinch of salt to taste
- 1 tbsp. lemon juice
- 2 medium sized potatoes (Cut into wedges)
- ingredients for the marinade:
- 1 tbsp. olive oil

Directions:
1. Boil the potatoes and blanch them. Mix the ingredients for the marinade and add the potato Oregano Fingers to it making sure that they are coated well.
2. Pre heat the oven for around 5 minutes at 300 Fahrenheit. Take out the basket of the fryer and place the potato Oregano Fingers in them. Close the basket.
3. Now keep the fryer at 200 Fahrenheit for 20 or 25 minutes. In between the process, toss

the fries twice or thrice so that they get cooked properly.

404.Simple Ricotta & Spinach Balls

Servings: 4
Cooking Time: 20 Minutes
Ingredients:
- 14 oz store-bought crescent dough
- 1 cup steamed spinach
- 1 cup crumbled ricotta cheese
- ¼ tsp garlic powder
- 1 tsp chopped oregano
- ¼ tsp salt

Directions:
1. Preheat on Air Fry function to 350 F. Roll the dough onto a lightly floured flat surface. Combine the ricotta cheese, spinach, oregano, salt, and garlic powder together in a bowl. Cut the dough into 4 equal pieces.
2. Divide the spinach/feta mixture between the dough pieces. Make sure to place the filling in the center. Fold the dough and secure with a fork. Place onto a lined baking dish and then in your oven. Cook for 12 minutes until lightly browned. Serve.

405.Garlic Toast With Cheese

Servings:x
Cooking Time:x
Ingredients:
- ¾ cup grated cheese
- 2 tsp. of oregano seasoning
- Some red chili flakes to sprinkle on top
- Take some French bread and cut it into slices
- 1 tbsp. olive oil (Optional)
- 2 tbsp. softened butter
- 4-5 flakes crushed garlic
- A pinch of salt to taste
- ½ tsp. black pepper powder

Directions:
1. Take a clean and dry container. Place all the ingredients mentioned under the heading "Garlic Butter" into it and mix properly to obtain garlic butter. On each slice of the French bread, spread some of this garlic butter. Sprinkle some cheese on top of the layer of butter. Pour some oil if wanted.
2. Sprinkle some chili flakes and some oregano.
3. Pre heat the oven at 240 Fahrenheit for around 5 minutes. Open the fry basket and place the bread in it making sure that no two slices touch each other. Close the basket and continue to cook the bread at 160 degrees for another 10 minutes to toast the bread well.

406.Mushroom French Cuisine Galette

Servings:x
Cooking Time:x
Ingredients:
- 2 or 3 green chilies finely chopped
- 1 ½ tbsp. lemon juice
- Salt and pepper to taste
- 2 tbsp. garam masala
- 2 cups sliced mushrooms
- 1 ½ cup coarsely crushed peanuts
- 3 tsp. ginger finely chopped
- 1-2 tbsp. fresh coriander leaves

Directions:
1. Mix the ingredients in a clean bowl.
2. Mold this mixture into round and flat French Cuisine Galettes.
3. Wet the French Cuisine Galettes slightly with water. Coat each French Cuisine Galette with the crushed peanuts.
4. Pre heat the oven at 160 degrees Fahrenheit for 5 minutes. Place the French Cuisine Galettes in the fry basket and let them cook for another 25 minutes at the same temperature. Keep rolling them over to get a uniform cook. Serve either with mint sauce or ketchup.

407.Potato Flat Cakes

Servings:x
Cooking Time:x
Ingredients:
- 2 or 3 green chilies finely chopped
- 1 ½ tbsp. lemon juice
- Salt and pepper to taste
- 2 tbsp. garam masala
- 2 cups sliced potato
- 3 tsp. ginger finely chopped
- 1-2 tbsp. fresh coriander leaves

Directions:
1. Mix the ingredients in a clean bowl and add water to it. Make sure that the paste is not too watery but is enough to apply on the potato slices.
2. Pre heat the oven at 160 degrees Fahrenheit for 5 minutes. Place the French Cuisine Galettes in the fry basket and let them cook for another 25 minutes at the same temperature. Keep rolling them over to get a uniform cook. Serve either with mint sauce or ketchup.

408.Stuffed Eggplant Baskets

Servings:x
Cooking Time:x
Ingredients:
- 1 tsp. cumin powder
- Salt and pepper to taste
- 3 tbsp. grated cheese
- 1 tsp. red chili flakes

- ½ tsp. oregano
- 6 eggplants
- ½ tsp. salt
- ½ tsp. pepper powder
- 1 medium onion finely chopped
- 1 green chili finely chopped
- 1 ½ tbsp. chopped coriander leaves
- 1 tsp. fenugreek
- 1 tsp. dried mango powder
- ½ tsp. basil
- ½ tsp. parsley

Directions:
1. Take all the ingredients under the heading "Filling" and mix them together in a bowl.
2. Remove the stem of the eggplant. Cut off the caps. Remove a little of the flesh as well. Sprinkle some salt and pepper on the inside of the capsicums.
3. Leave them aside for some time.
4. Now fill the eggplant with the filling prepared but leave a small space at the top. Sprinkle grated cheese and also add the seasoning.
5. Pre heat the oven at 140 degrees Fahrenheit for 5 minutes. Put the capsicums in the fry basket and close it. Let them cook at the same temperature for another 20 minutes. Turn them over in between to prevent over cooking.

409.Onion French Cuisine Galette

Servings:x
Cooking Time:x
Ingredients:
- 2 or 3 green chilies finely chopped
- 1 ½ tbsp. lemon juice
- Salt and pepper to taste
- 2 tbsp. garam masala
- 2 medium onions (Cut long)
- 1 ½ cup coarsely crushed peanuts
- 3 tsp. ginger finely chopped
- 1-2 tbsp. fresh coriander leaves

Directions:
1. Mix the ingredients in a clean bowl.
2. Mold this mixture into round and flat French Cuisine Galettes.
3. Wet the French Cuisine Galettes slightly with water. Coat each French Cuisine Galette with the crushed peanuts.
4. Pre heat the oven at 160 degrees Fahrenheit for 5 minutes. Place the French Cuisine Galettes in the fry basket and let them cook for another 25 minutes at the same temperature. Keep rolling them over to get a uniform cook. Serve either with mint sauce or ketchup.

410.Radish Flat Cakes

Servings:x

Cooking Time:x
Ingredients:
- 1-2 tbsp. fresh coriander leaves
- 2 or 3 green chilies finely chopped
- 1 ½ tbsp. lemon juice
- Salt and pepper to taste
- 2 tbsp. garam masala
- 2 cups sliced radish
- 3 tsp. ginger finely chopped

Directions:
1. Mix the ingredients in a clean bowl and add water to it. Make sure that the paste is not too watery but is enough to apply on the radish.
2. Pre heat the oven at 160 degrees Fahrenheit for 5 minutes. Place the French Cuisine Galettes in the fry basket and let them cook for another 25 minutes at the same temperature. Keep rolling them over to get a uniform cook. Serve either with mint sauce or ketchup.

411.Cottage Cheese Flat Cakes

Servings:x
Cooking Time:x
Ingredients:
- 2 or 3 green chilies finely chopped
- 1 ½ tbsp. lemon juice
- Salt and pepper to taste
- 2 tbsp. garam masala
- 2 cups sliced cottage cheese
- 3 tsp. ginger finely chopped
- 1-2 tbsp. fresh coriander leaves

Directions:
1. Mix the ingredients in a clean bowl and add water to it. Make sure that the paste is not too watery but is enough to apply on the cottage cheese slices.
2. Pre heat the oven at 160 degrees Fahrenheit for 5 minutes. Place the French Cuisine Galettes in the fry basket and let them cook for another 25 minutes at the same temperature. Keep rolling them over to get a uniform cook. Serve either with mint sauce or ketchup.

412.Parsley Feta Triangles

Servings: 4
Cooking Time: 20 Minutes
Ingredients:
- 4 oz feta cheese
- 2 sheets filo pastry
- 1 egg yolk
- 2 tbsp parsley, finely chopped
- 1 scallion, finely chopped
- 2 tbsp olive oil
- salt and black pepper

Directions:

1. In a bowl, beat the yolk and mix with feta cheese, parsley, scallion, salt, and black pepper. Cut each filo sheet in three parts or strips. Put a teaspoon of the feta mixture on the bottom. Roll the strip in a spinning spiral way until the filling of the inside mixture is wrapped in a triangle.
2. Preheat on Bake function to 360 F. Brush the surface of filo with olive oil. Arrange the triangles on a greased baking tray and cook for 5 minutes. Lower the temperature to 330 F and cook for 3 more minutes or until golden brown. Serve chilled.

413. Crispy Eggplant Slices With Parsley

Servings:4
Cooking Time: 12 Minutes
Ingredients:
- 1 cup flour
- 4 eggs
- Salt, to taste
- 2 cups bread crumbs
- 1 teaspoon Italian seasoning
- 2 eggplants, sliced
- 2 garlic cloves, sliced
- 2 tablespoons chopped parsley
- Cooking spray

Directions:
1. Spritz the air fryer basket with cooking spray. Set aside.
2. On a plate, place the flour. In a shallow bowl, whisk the eggs with salt. In another shallow bowl, combine the bread crumbs and Italian seasoning.
3. Dredge the eggplant slices, one at a time, in the flour, then in the whisked eggs, finally in the bread crumb mixture to coat well.
4. Lay the coated eggplant slices in the basket.
5. Put the air fryer basket on the baking pan and slide into Rack Position 2, select Air Fry, set temperature to 390ºF (199ºC), and set time to 12 minutes.
6. Flip the eggplant slices halfway through the cooking time.
7. When cooking is complete, the eggplant slices should be golden brown and crispy. Transfer the eggplant slices to a plate and sprinkle the garlic and parsley on top before serving.

414. Honey-glazed Baby Carrots

Servings:4
Cooking Time: 12 Minutes
Ingredients:
- 1 pound (454 g) baby carrots
- 2 tablespoons olive oil
- 1 tablespoon honey
- 1 teaspoon dried dill
- Salt and black pepper, to taste

Directions:
1. Place the carrots in a large bowl. Add the olive oil, honey, dill, salt, and pepper and toss to coat well.
2. Transfer the carrots to the air fryer basket.
3. Put the air fryer basket on the baking pan and slide into Rack Position 2, select Roast, set temperature to 350ºF (180ºC), and set time to 12 minutes.
4. Stir the carrots once during cooking.
5. When cooking is complete, the carrots should be crisp-tender. Remove from the oven and serve warm.

415. Mom's Blooming Buttery Onion

Servings: 4
Cooking Time: 40 Minutes
Ingredients:
- 4 onions
- 2 tbsp butter, melted
- 1 tbsp olive oil

Directions:
1. Preheat on Air Fry function to 350 F. Peel the onions and slice off the root bottom so it can sit well. Cut slices into the onion to make it look like a blooming flower, make sure not to go all the way through; four cuts will do.
2. Place the onions in a greased baking tray. Drizzle with olive oil and butter and cook for about 30 minutes. Serve with garlic mayo dip.

416. Asparagus Flat Cakes

Servings:x
Cooking Time:x
Ingredients:
- 2 or 3 green chilies finely chopped
- 1 ½ tbsp. lemon juice
- Salt and pepper to taste
- 2 tbsp. garam masala
- 2 cups sliced asparagus
- 3 tsp. ginger finely chopped
- 1-2 tbsp. fresh coriander leaves

Directions:
1. Mix the ingredients in a clean bowl and add water to it. Make sure that the paste is not too watery but is enough to apply on the asparagus.
2. Pre heat the oven at 160 degrees Fahrenheit for 5 minutes. Place the French Cuisine Galettes in the fry basket and let them cook for another 25 minutes at the same temperature. Keep rolling them over to get a uniform cook. Serve either with mint sauce or ketchup.

417. Cheese And Mushroom Spicy Lemon Kebab

Servings:x
Cooking Time:x
Ingredients:

- 1-2 tbsp. all-purpose flour for coating purposes
- 1-2 tbsp. mint
- 1 cup molten cheese
- 1 onion that has been finely chopped
- ½ cup milk
- 2 cups sliced mushrooms
- 1-2 green chilies chopped finely
- ¼ tsp. red chili powder
- A pinch of salt to taste
- ½ tsp. dried mango powder
- ¼ tsp. black salt

Directions:

1. Take the mushroom slices and add the grated ginger and the cut green chilies. Grind this mixture until it becomes a thick paste.
2. Keep adding water as and when required. Now add the onions, mint, the breadcrumbs and all the various masalas required. Mix this well until you get a soft dough. Now take small balls of this mixture (about the size of a lemon) and mold them into the shape of flat and round kebabs. Here is where the milk comes into play.
3. Pour a very small amount of milk onto each kebab to wet it. Now roll the kebab in the dry breadcrumbs. Pre heat the oven for 5 minutes at 300 Fahrenheit. Take out the basket. Arrange the kebabs in the basket leaving gaps between them so that no two kebabs are touching each other. Keep the fryer at 340 Fahrenheit for around half an hour.
4. Half way through the cooking process, turn the kebabs over so that they can be cooked properly. Recommended sides for this dish are mint sauce, tomato ketchup or yoghurt sauce.

418. Portobello Steaks

Servings: 4
Cooking Time: 20 Minutes
Ingredients:

- Nonstick cooking spray
- ¼ cup olive oil
- 2 tbsp. steak seasoning, unsalted
- 1 rosemary stem
- 4 Portobello mushrooms, large caps with stems removed

Directions:

1. Place baking pan in position 2 and spray with cooking spray.
2. In a large bowl, stir together oil, steak seasoning, and rosemary.
3. Add mushrooms and toss to coat all sides thoroughly.
4. Set oven to bake on 400°F for 25 minutes. After 5 minutes, place the mushrooms on the pan and bake 20 minutes, or until mushrooms are tender. Serve immediately.
- **Nutrition Info:** Calories 142, Total Fat 14g, Saturated Fat 2g, Total Carbs 3g, Net Carbs 2g, Protein 1g, Sugar 1g, Fiber 1g, Sodium 309mg, Potassium 118mg, Phosphorus 20mg

419. Mushroom Marinade Cutlet

Servings:x
Cooking Time:x
Ingredients:

- 2 cup fresh green coriander
- ½ cup mint leaves
- 4 tsp. fennel
- 2 tbsp. ginger-garlic paste
- 1 small onion
- 6-7 flakes garlic (optional)
- Salt to taste
- 2 cups sliced mushrooms
- 1 big capsicum (Cut this capsicum into big cubes)
- 1 onion (Cut it into quarters. Now separate the layers carefully.)
- 5 tbsp. gram flour
- A pinch of salt to taste
- 3 tbsp. lemon juice

Directions:

1. Take a clean and dry container. Put into it the coriander, mint, fennel, and ginger, onion/garlic, salt and lemon juice. Mix them.
2. Pour the mixture into a grinder and blend until you get a thick paste. Slit the mushroom almost till the end and leave them aside. Now stuff all the pieces with the paste and set aside. Take the sauce and add to it the gram flour and some salt. Mix them together properly. Rub this mixture all over the stuffed mushroom.
3. Now, to the leftover sauce, add the capsicum and onions. Apply the sauce generously on each of the pieces of capsicum and onion. Now take satay sticks and arrange the cottage cheese pieces and vegetables on separate sticks.
4. Pre heat the oven at 290 Fahrenheit for around 5 minutes. Open the basket. Arrange the satay sticks properly. Close the basket. Keep the sticks with the mushroom at 180 degrees for around half an hour while the sticks with the vegetables are to be kept at the same temperature for only 7 minutes. Turn the sticks in between so that one side

does not get burnt and also to provide a uniform cook.

420.Zucchini Crisps

Servings:4
Cooking Time: 25 Minutes
Ingredients:
- 4 small zucchinis, cut lengthwise
- ½ cup Parmesan cheese, grated
- ½ cup breadcrumbs
- ¼ cup butter, melted
- ¼ cup fresh parsley, chopped
- 4 garlic cloves, minced
- Salt and black pepper to taste

Directions:
1. Preheat on AirFry function to 350 F. In a bowl, mix breadcrumbs, Parmesan cheese, garlic, and parsley. Season with salt and pepper and stir in the butter.
2. Arrange the zucchinis with the cut side up. Spread the cheese mixture onto the zucchini and place them in the basket. Press Start and cook for 14-16 minutes. Serve hot.

421.Masala Potato Wedges

Servings:x
Cooking Time:x
Ingredients:
- 1 tsp. mixed herbs
- ½ tsp. red chili flakes
- A pinch of salt to taste
- 1 tbsp. lemon juice
- 2 medium sized potatoes (Cut into wedges)
- ingredients for the marinade:
- 1 tbsp. olive oil
- 1 tsp. garam masala

Directions:
1. Boil the potatoes and blanch them. Mix the ingredients for the marinade and add the potato Oregano Fingers to it making sure that they are coated well.
2. Pre heat the oven for around 5 minutes at 300 Fahrenheit. Take out the basket of the fryer and place the potato Oregano Fingers in them. Close the basket.
3. Now keep the fryer at 200 Fahrenheit for 20 or 25 minutes. In between the process, toss the fries twice or thrice so that they get cooked properly.

422.Cottage Cheese Fried Baked Pastry

Servings:x
Cooking Time:x
Ingredients:
- 1 or 2 green chilies that are finely chopped or mashed
- ½ tsp. cumin
- 1 tsp. coarsely crushed coriander
- 1 dry red chili broken into pieces

- A small amount of salt (to taste)
- ½ tsp. dried mango powder
- ½ tsp. red chili power
- 1-2 tbsp. coriander
- 2 tbsp. unsalted butter
- 1 ½ cup all-purpose flour
- A pinch of salt to taste
- Water
- 2 cups mashed cottage cheese
- ¼ cup boiled peas
- 1 tsp. powdered ginger

Directions:
1. Mix the dough for the outer covering and make it stiff and smooth. Leave it to rest in a container while making the filling.
2. Cook the ingredients in a pan and stir them well to make a thick paste. Roll the paste out.
3. Roll the dough into balls and flatten them. Cut them in halves and add the filling. Use water to help you fold the edges to create the shape of a cone.
4. Pre-heat the oven for around 5 to 6 minutes at 300 Fahrenheit. Place all the samosas in the fry basket and close the basket properly. Keep the oven at 200 degrees for another 20 to 25 minutes. Around the halfway point, open the basket and turn the samosas over for uniform cooking. After this, fry at 250 degrees for around 10 minutes in order to give them the desired golden-brown color. Serve hot. Recommended sides are tamarind or mint sauce.

423.Zucchini Fried Baked Pastry

Servings:x
Cooking Time:x
Ingredients:
- 1 or 2 green chilies that are finely chopped or mashed
- ½ tsp. cumin
- 1 tsp. coarsely crushed coriander
- 1 dry red chili broken into pieces
- A small amount of salt (to taste)
- ½ tsp. dried mango powder
- ½ tsp. red chili power.
- 2 tbsp. unsalted butter
- 1 ½ cup all-purpose flour
- A pinch of salt to taste
- Add as much water as required to make the dough stiff and firm
- 3 medium zucchinis (mashed)
- ¼ cup boiled peas
- 1 tsp. powdered ginger
- 1-2 tbsp. coriander.

Directions:

1. Mix the dough for the outer covering and make it stiff and smooth. Leave it to rest in a container while making the filling.
2. Cook the ingredients in a pan and stir them well to make a thick paste. Roll the paste out.
3. Roll the dough into balls and flatten them. Cut them in halves and add the
4. filling. Use water to help you fold the edges to create the shape of a cone.
5. Pre-heat the oven for around 5 to 6 minutes at 300 Fahrenheit. Place all the samosas in the fry basket and close the basket properly. Keep the oven at 200 degrees for another 20 to 25 minutes. Around the halfway point, open the basket and turn the samosas over for uniform cooking. After this, fry at 250 degrees for around 10 minutes in order to give them the desired golden-brown color. Serve hot. Recommended sides are tamarind or mint sauce.

424.Potato Fries With Ketchup

Servings:2
Cooking Time: 20 Minutes
Ingredients:
- 2 potatoes
- 1 tbsp ketchup
- 2 tbsp olive oil
- Salt and black pepper to taste

Directions:
1. Use a spiralizer to spiralize the potatoes. In a bowl, mix olive oil, salt, and pepper. Drizzle the potatoes with the oil mixture. Place them in the basket and press Start. Cook for 15 minutes on AirFry function at 360 F. Serve with ketchup or mayonnaise.

425.Mushroom Fried Baked Pastry

Servings:x
Cooking Time:x
Ingredients:
- 2 capsicum sliced
- 2 carrot sliced
- 2 cabbage sliced
- 2 tbsp. soya sauce
- 2 tsp. vinegar
- 1 cup all-purpose flour
- 2 tbsp. unsalted butter
- A pinch of salt to taste
- Take the amount of water sufficient enough to make a stiff dough
- 3 cups whole mushrooms
- 2 onion sliced
- 2 tbsp. green chilies finely chopped
- 2 tbsp. ginger-garlic paste
- Some salt and pepper to taste

Directions:

1. Mix the dough for the outer covering and make it stiff and smooth. Leave it to rest in a container while making the filling.
2. Cook the ingredients in a pan and stir them well to make a thick paste. Roll the paste out.
3. Roll the dough into balls and flatten them. Cut them in halves and add the filling. Use water to help you fold the edges to create the shape of a cone.
4. Pre-heat the oven for around 5 to 6 minutes at 300 Fahrenheit. Place all the samosas in the fry basket and close the basket properly. Keep the oven at 200 degrees for another 20 to 25 minutes. Around the halfway point, open the basket and turn the samosas over for uniform cooking. After this, fry at 250 degrees for around 10 minutes in order to give them the desired golden-brown color. Serve hot. Recommended sides are tamarind or mint sauce.

426.Simple Polenta Crisps

Servings:4
Cooking Time: 25 Minutes + Chilling Time
Ingredients:
- 2 cups milk
- 1 cup instant polenta
- Salt and black pepper
- Fresh thyme, chopped

Directions:
1. Line a tray with parchment paper. Pour milk and 2 cups of water into a saucepan and simmer. Keep whisking as you pour in the polenta. Continue to whisk until polenta thickens and bubbles; season to taste. Add polenta to the lined tray and spread out. Refrigerate for 45 minutes.
2. Slice the polenta into batons and spray with oil. Arrange the polenta chips on the basket and press Start. Cook for 16 minutes at 380 F on AirFry function until golden and crispy.

427.Snake Gourd French Cuisine Galette

Servings:x
Cooking Time:x
Ingredients:
- 1-2 tbsp. fresh coriander leaves
- 2 or 3 green chilies finely chopped
- 1 ½ tbsp. lemon juice
- Salt and pepper to taste
- 2 tbsp. garam masala
- 1 cup sliced snake gourd
- 1 ½ cup coarsely crushed peanuts
- 3 tsp. ginger finely chopped

Directions:
1. Mix the ingredients in a clean bowl.

2. Mold this mixture into round and flat French Cuisine Galettes.
3. Wet the French Cuisine Galettes slightly with water. Coat each French Cuisine Galette with the crushed peanuts.
4. Pre heat the oven at 160 degrees Fahrenheit for 5 minutes. Place the French Cuisine Galettes in the fry basket and let them cook for another 25 minutes at the same temperature. Keep rolling them over to get a uniform cook. Serve either with mint sauce or ketchup.

428.Sweet And Spicy Broccoli

Servings:4
Cooking Time: 15 To 20 Minutes
Ingredients:
- ½ teaspoon olive oil, plus more for greasing
- 1 pound (454 g) fresh broccoli, cut into florets
- ½ tablespoon minced garlic
- Salt, to taste
- Sauce:
- 1½ tablespoons soy sauce
- 2 teaspoons hot sauce or sriracha
- 1½ teaspoons honey
- 1 teaspoon white vinegar
- Freshly ground black pepper, to taste

Directions:
1. Grease the air fryer basket with olive oil.
2. Add the broccoli florets, ½ teaspoon of olive oil, and garlic to a large bowl and toss well. Season with salt to taste.
3. Put the broccoli in the basket in a single layer.
4. Put the air fryer basket on the baking pan and slide into Rack Position 2, select Air Fry, set temperature to 400ºF (205ºC), and set time to 15 minutes.
5. Stir the broccoli florets three times during cooking.
6. Meanwhile, whisk together all the ingredients for the sauce in a small bowl until well incorporated. If the honey doesn't incorporate well, microwave the sauce for 10 to 20 seconds until the honey is melted.
7. When cooking is complete, the broccoli should be lightly browned and crispy. Continue cooking for 5 minutes, if desired. Remove from the oven to a serving bowl. Pour over the sauce and toss to combine. Add more salt and pepper, if needed. Serve warm.

429.Cottage Cheese And Mushroom Mexican Burritos

Servings:x
Cooking Time:x
Ingredients:
- ½ cup mushrooms thinly sliced
- 1 cup cottage cheese cut in too long and slightly thick Oregano Fingers
- A pinch of salt to taste
- ½ tsp. red chili flakes
- 1 tsp. freshly ground peppercorns
- ½ cup pickled jalapenos
- 1-2 lettuce leaves shredded.
- ½ cup red kidney beans (soaked overnight)
- ½ small onion chopped
- 1 tbsp. olive oil
- 2 tbsp. tomato puree
- ¼ tsp. red chili powder
- 1 tsp. of salt to taste
- 4-5 flour tortillas
- 1 or 2 spring onions chopped finely. Also cut the greens.
- Take one tomato. Remove the seeds and chop it into small pieces.
- 1 green chili chopped.
- 1 cup of cheddar cheese grated.
- 1 cup boiled rice (not necessary).
- A few flour tortillas to put the filing in.

Directions:
1. Cook the beans along with the onion and garlic and mash them finely.
2. Now, make the sauce you will need for the burrito. Ensure that you create a slightly thick sauce.
3. For the filling, you will need to cook the ingredients well in a pan and ensure that the vegetables have browned on the outside.
4. To make the salad, toss the ingredients together. Place the tortilla and add a layer of sauce, followed by the beans and the filling at the center. Before you roll it, you will need to place the salad on top of the filling.
5. Pre-heat the oven for around 5 minutes at 200 Fahrenheit. Open the fry basket and keep the burritos inside. Close the basket properly. Let the Air
6. Fryer remain at 200 Fahrenheit for another 15 minutes or so. Halfway through, remove the basket and turn all the burritos over in order to get a uniform cook.

430.Mushroom Homemade Fried Sticks

Servings:x
Cooking Time:x
Ingredients:
- One or two poppadums'
- 4 or 5 tbsp. corn flour
- 1 cup of water
- 2 cups whole mushrooms
- 1 big lemon-juiced
- 1 tbsp. ginger-garlic paste
- For seasoning, use salt and red chili powder in small amounts
- ½ tsp. carom

Directions:
1. Make a mixture of lemon juice, red chili powder, salt, ginger garlic paste and carom to use as a marinade. Let the cottage cheese pieces marinate in the mixture for some time and then roll them in dry corn flour. Leave them aside for around 20 minutes.
2. Take the poppadum into a pan and roast them. Once they are cooked, crush them into very small pieces. Now take another container and pour around 100 ml of water into it. Dissolve 2 tbsp. of corn flour in this water. Dip the cottage cheese pieces in this solution of corn flour and roll them on to the pieces of crushed poppadum so that the poppadum sticks to the cottage cheese.
3. Pre heat the oven for 10 minutes at 290 Fahrenheit. Then open the basket of the fryer and place the cottage cheese pieces inside it. Close the basket properly. Let the fryer stay at 160 degrees for another 20 minutes. Halfway through, open the basket and toss the cottage cheese around a bit to allow for uniform cooking. Once they are done, you can serve it either with ketchup or mint sauce. Another recommended side is mint sauce.

431.Vegetable Skewer

Servings:x
Cooking Time:x
Ingredients:
- 3 tbsp. cream
- 3 eggs
- 2 cups mixed vegetables
- 3 onions chopped
- 5 green chilies
- 1 ½ tbsp. ginger paste
- 1 ½ tsp. garlic paste
- 1 ½ tsp. salt
- 2 ½ tbsp. white sesame seeds

Directions:
1. Grind the ingredients except for the egg and form a smooth paste. Coat the vegetables in the paste. Now, beat the eggs and add a little salt to it.
2. Dip the coated vegetables in the egg mixture and then transfer to the sesame seeds and coat the vegetables well. Place the vegetables on a stick.
3. Pre heat the oven at 160 degrees Fahrenheit for around 5 minutes. Place the sticks in the basket and let them cook for another 25 minutes at the same temperature. Turn the sticks over in between the cooking process to get a uniform cook.

432.Mushroom Pops

Servings:x

Cooking Time:x
Ingredients:
- 1 tsp. dry basil
- 1 tsp. lemon juice
- 1 tsp. red chili flakes
- 1 cup whole mushrooms
- 1 ½ tsp. garlic paste
- Salt and pepper to taste
- 1 tsp. dry oregano

Directions:
1. Add the ingredients into a separate bowl and mix them well to get a consistent mixture.
2. Dip the mushrooms in the above mixture and leave them aside for some time.
3. Pre heat the oven at 180° C for around 5 minutes. Place the coated cottage cheese pieces in the fry basket and close it properly. Let them cook at the same temperature for 20 more minutes. Keep turning them over in the basket so that they are cooked properly. Serve with tomato ketchup.

433.Asparagus Spicy Lemon Kebab

Servings:x
Cooking Time:x
Ingredients:
- 3 tsp. lemon juice
- 2 tsp. garam masala
- 3 eggs
- 2 ½ tbsp. white sesame seeds
- 2 cups sliced asparagus
- 3 onions chopped
- 5 green chilies-roughly chopped
- 1 ½ tbsp. ginger paste
- 1 ½ tsp. garlic paste
- 1 ½ tsp. salt

Directions:
1. Grind the ingredients except for the egg and form a smooth paste. Coat the asparagus in the paste. Now, beat the eggs and add a little salt to it.
2. Dip the coated apricots in the egg mixture and then transfer to the sesame seeds and coat the asparagus. Place the vegetables on a stick.
3. Pre heat the oven at 160 degrees Fahrenheit for around 5 minutes. Place the sticks in the basket and let them cook for another 25 minutes at the same temperature. Turn the sticks over in between the cooking process to get a uniform cook.

434.Cauliflower Spicy Lemon Kebab

Servings:x
Cooking Time:x
Ingredients:
- 3 tsp. lemon juice

- 2 tsp. garam masala
- 3 eggs
- 2 ½ tbsp. white sesame seeds
- 2 cups cauliflower florets
- 3 onions chopped
- 5 green chilies-roughly chopped
- 1 ½ tbsp. ginger paste
- 1 ½ tsp. garlic paste
- 1 ½ tsp. salt

Directions:

1. Grind the ingredients except for the egg and form a smooth paste. Coat the florets in the paste. Now, beat the eggs and add a little salt to it.

2. Dip the coated florets in the egg mixture and then transfer to the sesame seeds and coat the florets well. Place the vegetables on a stick.

3. Pre heat the oven at 160 degrees Fahrenheit for around 5 minutes. Place the sticks in the basket and let them cook for another 25 minutes at the same temperature. Turn the sticks over in between the cooking process to get a uniform cook.

SNACKS AND DESSERTS RECIPES

435.Walnut Carrot Cake

Servings: 4
Cooking Time: 25 Minutes
Ingredients:
- 1 egg
- 1/2 cup sugar
- 1/4 cup canola oil
- 1/4 cup walnuts, chopped
- 1/2 tsp baking powder
- 1/2 cup flour
- 1/4 cup grated carrot
- 1/2 tsp vanilla
- 1/2 tsp cinnamon

Directions:
1. Fit the oven with the rack in position
2. In a medium bowl, beat sugar and oil for 1 minute. Add vanilla, cinnamon, and egg and beat for 30 seconds.
3. Add remaining ingredients and stir everything well until just combined.
4. Pour batter into the greased baking dish.
5. Set to bake at 350 F for 30 minutes. After 5 minutes place the baking dish in the preheated oven.
6. Serve and enjoy.
- **Nutrition Info:** Calories 340 Fat 20 g Carbohydrates 40 g Sugar 25 g Protein 5 g Cholesterol 41 mg

436.Cinnamon Apple Wedges

Servings:4
Cooking Time: 12 Minutes
Ingredients:
- 2 medium apples, cored and sliced into ¼-inch wedges
- 1 teaspoon canola oil
- 2 teaspoons peeled and grated fresh ginger
- ½ teaspoon ground cinnamon
- ½ cup low-fat Greek vanilla yogurt, for serving

Directions:
1. In a large bowl, toss the apple wedges with the canola oil, ginger, and cinnamon until evenly coated. Put the apple wedges in the air fryer basket.
2. Put the air fryer basket on the baking pan and slide into Rack Position 2, select Air Fry, set temperature to 360ºF (182ºC), and set time to 12 minutes.
3. When cooking is complete, the apple wedges should be crisp-tender. Remove the apple wedges from the oven and serve drizzled with the yogurt.

437.Baked Apple

Servings: 4
Cooking Time: 20 Minutes

Ingredients:
- ¼ C. water
- ¼ tsp. nutmeg
- ¼ tsp. cinnamon
- 1 ½ tsp. melted ghee
- 2 tbsp. raisins
- 2 tbsp. chopped walnuts
- 1 medium apple

Directions:
1. Preparing the Ingredients. Preheat your air fryer oven to 350 degrees.
2. Slice an apple in half and discard some of the flesh from the center.
3. Place into frying pan.
4. Mix remaining ingredients together except water. Spoon mixture to the middle of apple halves.
5. Pour water overfilled apples.
6. Air Frying. Place pan with apple halves into the air fryer oven, bake 20 minutes.
- **Nutrition Info:** CALORIES: 199; FAT:9G; PROTEIN:1G; SUGAR:3G

438.Cheesy Zucchini Tots

Servings:8
Cooking Time: 6 Minutes
Ingredients:
- 2 medium zucchini (about 12 ounces / 340 g), shredded
- 1 large egg, whisked
- ½ cup grated pecorino romano cheese
- ½ cup panko bread crumbs
- ¼ teaspoon black pepper
- 1 clove garlic, minced
- Cooking spray

Directions:
1. Using your hands, squeeze out as much liquid from the zucchini as possible. In a large bowl, mix the zucchini with the remaining ingredients except the oil until well incorporated.
2. Make the zucchini tots: Use a spoon or cookie scoop to place tablespoonfuls of the zucchini mixture onto a lightly floured cutting board and form into 1-inch logs.
3. Spritz the air fryer basket with cooking spray. Place the zucchini tots in the pan.
4. Put the air fryer basket on the baking pan and slide into Rack Position 2, select Air Fry, set temperature to 375ºF (190ºC), and set time to 6 minutes.
5. When cooking is complete, the tots should be golden brown. Remove from the oven to a serving plate and serve warm.

439.Air Fryer Biscuit Donuts

Servings: 4
Cooking Time: 5 Minutes

Ingredients:
- Coconut oil
- 1 can of biscuit dough, premade
- 1/2 cup of white sugar
- 1/2 cup of powdered sugar
- 2 tablespoons of melted butter
- 2 teaspoons of cinnamon

Directions:
1. Set the Instant Vortex on Air fryer to 350 degrees F for 5 minutes. Cut the dough with the biscuit cutter. Brush the coconut oil on the cooking tray and place the biscuits on it. Insert the cooking tray in the Vortex when it displays "Add Food". Flip the sides when it displays "Turn Food". Remove from the oven when cooking time is complete. Drizzle the melted butter over the donuts and coat with either the cinnamon-sugar mixture or the powdered sugar. Serve warm.
- **Nutrition Info:** Calories: 301 Cal Total Fat: 32.2 g Saturated Fat: 0 g Cholesterol: 0 mg Sodium: 0 mg Total Carbs: 25 g Fiber: 0 g Sugar: 0 g Protein: 8.8 g

440.Roasted Mixed Nuts

Servings:6
Cooking Time: 20 Minutes
Ingredients:
- 2 cups mixed nuts (walnuts, pecans, and almonds)
- 2 tablespoons egg white
- 2 tablespoons sugar
- 1 teaspoon paprika
- 1 teaspoon ground cinnamon
- Cooking spray

Directions:
1. Line the air fryer basket with parchment paper and spray with cooking spray.
2. Stir together the mixed nuts, egg white, sugar, paprika, and cinnamon in a small bowl until the nuts are fully coated. Place the nuts in the basket.
3. Put the air fryer basket on the baking pan and slide into Rack Position 2, select Roast, set temperature to 300ºF (150ºC), and set time to 20 minutes.
4. Stir the nuts halfway through the cooking time.
5. When cooking is complete, remove from the oven. Transfer the nuts to a bowl and serve warm.

441.Shrimp And Artichoke Puffs

Servings:x
Cooking Time:x
Ingredients:
- 1 (10-ounce) package frozen artichoke hearts, thawed
- 1 (3-ounce) package cream cheese, softened

- 1 cup shredded Coda cheese
- ½ cup mayonnaise
- 1 tablespoon lemon juice
- 1 teaspoon dried basil leaves
- 6 slices whole wheat bread
- 2 shallots, chopped
- 1 tablespoon olive oil
- ½ pound cooked shrimp

Directions:
1. Preheat oven to 300ºF. Using a 2-inch cookie cutter, cut rounds from bread slices. Place rounds on a baking sheet and bake at 300ºF for 7 to 9 minutes, or until crisp, turning once. Remove from oven and cool on wire racks.
2. In a heavy skillet, cook shallots in olive oil over medium heat until tender. Remove from heat. Chop shrimp and add to skillet along with thawed, drained, and chopped artichoke hearts. Add both cheeses, mayonnaise, lemon juice, and basil; stir well to blend.
3. Spoon 1 tablespoon shrimp mixture onto each bread round, covering the top and mounding the filling. Flash freeze on baking sheets. When frozen solid, pack in rigid containers, with waxed paper between layers. Label puffs and freeze.
4. To reheat: Place frozen puffs on a baking sheet and bake at 400ºF for 10 to 12 minutes or until topping is hot and bubbling.

442.Salsa Cheese Dip

Servings: 10
Cooking Time: 30 Minutes
Ingredients:
- 16 oz cream cheese, softened
- 3 cups cheddar cheese, shredded
- 1 cup sour cream
- 1/2 cup hot salsa

Directions:
1. Fit the oven with the rack in position
2. In a bowl, mix all ingredients until just combined and pour into the baking dish.
3. Set to bake at 350 F for 35 minutes. After 5 minutes place the baking dish in the preheated oven.
4. Serve and enjoy.
- **Nutrition Info:** Calories 348 Fat 31.9 g Carbohydrates 3.4 g Sugar 0.7 g Protein 12.8 g Cholesterol 96 mg

443.Gooey Chocolate Fudge Cake

Servings:x
Cooking Time:x
Ingredients:
- 3 Tbsp cocoa powder
- ½ cup water
- ¼ cup whole milk

- 1 egg
- 1 tsp vanilla extract
- 1 cup flour
- ½ tsp baking soda
- 1 cup sugar
- Pinch of salt
- ½ cup vegetable oil

Directions:
1. Preheat the oven to 350°F.
2. In a large bowl, whisk flour, baking soda, sugar and salt.
3. Combine oil, cocoa powder and water in another bowl.
4. Whisk in flour mixture and pour into oven.
5. Incorporate milk, egg and vanilla into the batter.
6. Bake for 25 minutes, or until edges are set and center is only slightly jiggly.

444.Air Fryer Mixed Nuts

Servings: 2
Cooking Time: 4 Minutes
Ingredients:
- 2 cup mixed nuts
- 1 tbsp olive oil
- 1 tsp ground cumin
- 1 tsp pepper
- 1/4 tsp cayenne
- 1 tsp salt

Directions:
1. Fit the oven with the rack in position 2.
2. In a bowl, add all ingredients and toss well.
3. Add the nuts mixture to the air fryer basket then place an air fryer basket in the baking pan.
4. Place a baking pan on the oven rack. Set to air fry at 350 F for 4 minutes.
5. Serve and enjoy.
- **Nutrition Info:** Calories 953 Fat 88.2 g Carbohydrates 33.3 g Sugar 6.4 g Protein 22.7 g Cholesterol 0 mg

445.Choco-peanut Mug Cake

Servings: 1
Cooking Time: 20 Minutes
Ingredients:
- Softened butter, 1 tsp.
- Egg, 1.
- Peanut butter, 1 tbsp.
- Vanilla extract, ½ tsp.
- Erythritol, 2 tbsps.
- Unsweetened cocoa powder, 2 tbsps.
- Baking powder, ¼ tsp.
- Heavy cream, 1 tbsp.

Directions:
1. Preheat the air fryer for 5 minutes.
2. Combine all ingredients in a mixing bowl.
3. Pour into a greased mug.

4. Set in the air fryer basket and cook for 20 minutes at 400 ºF
- **Nutrition Info:** Calories: 293 Protein: 12.4g Fat: 23.3g Carbs: 8.5g

446.Air Fryer Paprika Almonds

Servings: 6
Cooking Time: 6 Minutes
Ingredients:
- 1 cup almonds
- 1/4 tsp smoked paprika
- 2 tsp olive oil
- 1/4 tsp cumin
- 1 tsp chili powder

Directions:
1. Fit the oven with the rack in position 2.
2. Add almond into the bowl and remaining ingredients and toss to coat.
3. Transfer almonds in the air fryer basket then place an air fryer basket in the baking pan.
4. Place a baking pan on the oven rack. Set to air fry at 320 F for 6 minutes.
5. Serve and enjoy.
- **Nutrition Info:** Calories 107 Fat 9.6 g Carbohydrates 3.7 g Sugar 0.7 g Protein 3.4 g Cholesterol 0 mg

447.Sesame Banana Dessert

Servings: 5
Cooking Time: 15 Minutes
Ingredients:
- 1 ½ cups flour
- 5 bananas, sliced
- 1 tsp salt
- 3 tbsp sesame seeds
- 1 cup water
- 2 eggs, beaten
- 1 tsp baking powder
- ½ tbsp sugar

Directions:
1. Preheat on Bake function to 340 F. In a bowl, mix salt, sesame seeds, flour, baking powder, eggs, sugar, and water. Coat sliced bananas with the flour mixture. Place the prepared slices in the Air Fryer basket and fit in the baking tray; cook for 8-10 minutes. Serve chilled.

448.Berry Crumble With Lemon

Servings:6
Cooking Time: 30 Minutes
Ingredients:
- 12 oz fresh strawberries
- 7 oz fresh raspberries
- 5 oz fresh blueberries
- 5 tbsp cold butter
- 2 tbsp lemon juice
- 1 cup flour

- ½ cup sugar
- 1 tbsp water
- A pinch of salt

Directions:
1. Preheat on Bake function to 360 F. Gently mash the berries, but make sure there are chunks left. Mix with the lemon juice and 2 tbsp of sugar. Place the berry mixture at the bottom of a greased cake pan. Combine the flour with salt and sugar in a bowl. Mix well.
2. Add the water and rub the butter with your fingers until the mixture becomes crumbled. Pour the batter over the berries. Press Start and cook for 20 minutes. Serve chilled.

449. Banana S'mores

Servings: 4
Cooking Time: 4 Minutes
Ingredients:
- 4 bananas
- 3 tablespoons of mini semi-sweet chocolate chips
- 3 tablespoons of mini marshmallows
- 3 tablespoons of graham cracker cereal
- Aluminum foil
- Cooking oil spray

Directions:
1. Set the Instant Vortex on Air fryer to 350 degrees F for 4 minutes. Place the bananas on the aluminum foil sheet greased with cooking oil spray. Tear open the banana from one side to form a pocket. Top with the chocolate chips, marshmallows, and graham cracker cereal. Cover completely with foil and place on the cooking tray. Insert the cooking tray in the Vortex when it displays "Add Food". Remove from the oven when cooking time is complete. Serve warm.
- **Nutrition Info:** Calories: 249 Cal Total Fat: 11.9 g Saturated Fat: 0 g Cholesterol: 0 mg Sodium: 0 mg Total Carbs: 14.8 g Fiber: 0 g Sugar: 0 g Protein: 5 g

450. Italian Rice Balls

Servings: 8 Rice Balls
Cooking Time: 10 Minutes
Ingredients:
- 1½ cups cooked sticky rice
- ½ teaspoon Italian seasoning blend
- ¾ teaspoon salt, divided
- 8 black olives, pitted
- 1 ounce (28 g) Mozzarella cheese, cut into tiny pieces (small enough to stuff into olives)
- 2 eggs
- $^1/_3$ cup Italian bread crumbs
- ¾ cup panko bread crumbs
- Cooking spray

Directions:

1. Stuff each black olive with a piece of Mozzarella cheese.
2. In a bowl, combine the cooked sticky rice, Italian seasoning blend, and ½ teaspoon of salt and stir to mix well. Form the rice mixture into a log with your hands and divide it into 8 equal portions. Mold each portion around a black olive and roll into a ball.
3. Transfer to the freezer to chill for 10 to 15 minutes until firm.
4. In a shallow dish, place the Italian bread crumbs. In a separate shallow dish, whisk the eggs. In a third shallow dish, combine the panko bread crumbs and remaining salt.
5. One by one, roll the rice balls in the Italian bread crumbs, then dip in the whisked eggs, finally coat them with the panko bread crumbs.
6. Arrange the rice balls in the air fryer basket and spritz both sides with cooking spray.
7. Put the air fryer basket on the baking pan and slide into Rack Position 2, select Air Fry, set temperature to 390ºF (199ºC), and set time to 10 minutes.
8. Flip the balls halfway through the cooking time.
9. When cooking is complete, the rice balls should be golden brown. Remove from the oven and serve warm.

451. Air Fryer Walnuts

Servings: 6
Cooking Time: 5 Minutes
Ingredients:
- 2 cups walnuts
- 1 tsp olive oil
- Pepper
- Salt

Directions:
1. Fit the oven with the rack in position 2.
2. Add walnuts, oil, pepper, and salt into the bowl and toss well.
3. Add walnuts to the air fryer basket then place an air fryer basket in baking pan.
4. Place a baking pan on the oven rack. Set to air fry at 350 F for 5 minutes.
5. Serve and enjoy.
- **Nutrition Info:** Calories 264 Fat 25.4 g Carbohydrates 4.1 g Sugar 0.5 g Protein 10 g Cholesterol 0 mg

452. Strawberry Tart

Servings:x
Cooking Time:x
Ingredients:
- 2 cups sliced strawberries
- 1 cup fresh cream
- 3 tbsp. butter
- 1 ½ cup plain flour

- 3 tbsp. unsalted butter
- 2 tbsp. powdered sugar
- 2 cups cold water

Directions:
1. In a large bowl, mix the flour, cocoa powder, butter and sugar with your Oregano Fingers. The mixture should resemble breadcrumbs. Squeeze the dough using the cold milk and wrap it and leave it to cool for ten minutes. Roll the dough out into the pie and prick the sides of the pie.
2. Mix the ingredients for the filling in a bowl. Make sure that it is a little
3. thick. Preheat the fryer to 300 Fahrenheit for five minutes. You will need to place the tin in the basket and cover it. When the pastry has turned golden brown, you will need to remove the tin and let it cool. Cut into slices and serve with a dollop of cream.

453.Mixed Berries With Pecan Streusel

Servings: 3
Cooking Time: 15 Minutes
Ingredients:
- 3 tablespoons pecans, chopped
- 3 tablespoons almonds, slivered
- 2 tablespoons walnuts, chopped
- 3 tablespoons granulated swerve
- 1/2 teaspoon ground cinnamon
- 1 egg
- 2 tablespoons cold salted butter, cut into pieces
- 1/2 cup mixed berries

Directions:
1. Mix your nuts, swerve, cinnamon, egg, and butter until well combined.
2. Place mixed berries on the bottom of a lightly greased Air Fryer-safe dish. Top with the prepared topping.
3. Bake at 340 degrees F for 17 minutes. Serve at room temperature.
- **Nutrition Info:** 255 Calories; 28g Fat; 1g Carbs; 3g Protein; 6g Sugars; 4g FiberEasy Fluffy Pancakes

454.Bruschetta With Tomato And Basil

Servings:6
Cooking Time: 3 Minutes
Ingredients:
- 4 tomatoes, diced
- $^1/_3$ cup shredded fresh basil
- ¼ cup shredded Parmesan cheese
- 1 tablespoon balsamic vinegar
- 1 tablespoon minced garlic
- 1 teaspoon olive oil
- 1 teaspoon salt
- 1 teaspoon freshly ground black pepper
- 1 loaf French bread, cut into 1-inch-thick slices

- Cooking spray

Directions:
1. Mix together the tomatoes and basil in a medium bowl. Add the cheese, vinegar, garlic, olive oil, salt, and pepper and stir until well incorporated. Set aside.
2. Spritz the baking pan with cooking spray and lay the bread slices in the pan in a single layer. Spray the slices with cooking spray.
3. Slide the baking pan into Rack Position 1, select Convection Bake, set temperature to 250ºF (121ºC), and set time to 3 minutes.
4. When cooking is complete, remove from the oven to a plate. Top each slice with a generous spoonful of the tomato mixture and serve.

455.Pumpkin Pudding And Vanilla Wafers

Servings:4
Cooking Time: 15 Minutes
Ingredients:
- 1 cup canned no-salt-added pumpkin purée (not pumpkin pie filling)
- ¼ cup packed brown sugar
- 3 tablespoons all-purpose flour
- 1 egg, whisked
- 2 tablespoons milk
- 1 tablespoon unsalted butter, melted
- 1 teaspoon pure vanilla extract
- 4 low-fat vanilla wafers, crumbled
- Cooking spray

Directions:
1. Coat the baking pan with cooking spray. Set aside.
2. Mix the pumpkin purée, brown sugar, flour, whisked egg, milk, melted butter, and vanilla in a medium bowl and whisk to combine. Transfer the mixture to the baking pan.
3. Slide the baking pan into Rack Position 1, select Convection Bake, set temperature to 350ºF (180ºC), and set time to 15 minutes.
4. When cooking is complete, the pudding should be set.
5. Remove the pudding from the oven to a wire rack to cool.
6. Divide the pudding into four bowls and serve with the vanilla wafers sprinkled on top.

456.Perfectly Puffy Coconut Cookies

Servings: 12
Cooking Time: 15 Minutes
Ingredients:
- 1 cup butter, melted
- 1 ¾ cups granulated swerve
- 3 eggs
- 2 tablespoons coconut milk

- 1 teaspoon coconut extract
- 1 teaspoon vanilla extract
- 1 cup coconut flour
- 1 ¼ cups almond flour
- 1/2 teaspoon baking powder
- 1/2 teaspoon baking soda
- 1/2 teaspoon fine table salt
- 1/2 cups coconut chips, unsweetened

Directions:
1. Begin by preheating your Air Fryer to 350 degrees F.
2. In the bowl of an electric mixer, beat the butter and swerve until well combined. Now, add the eggs one at a time, and mix well; add the coconut milk, coconut extract, and vanilla; beat until creamy and uniform.
3. Mix the flour with baking powder, baking soda, and salt. Then, stir the flour mixture into the butter mixture and stir until everything is well incorporated.
4. Finally, fold in the coconut chips and mix again. Scoop out 1 tablespoon size balls of the batter on a cookie pan, leaving 2 inches between each cookie.
5. Bake for 10 minutes or until golden brown, rotating the pan once or twice through the cooking time. Let your cookies cool on wire racks.
- **Nutrition Info:** 304 Calories; 17g Fat; 32g Carbs; 3g Protein; 16g Sugars; 2g Fiber

457. Jalapeno Spinach Dip

Servings: 6
Cooking Time: 30 Minutes
Ingredients:
- 10 oz frozen spinach, thawed and drained
- 2 tsp jalapeno pepper, minced
- 1/2 cup cheddar cheese, shredded
- 8 oz cream cheese
- 1/2 cup onion, diced
- 2 tsp garlic, minced
- 1/2 cup mozzarella cheese, shredded
- 1/2 cup Monterey jack cheese, shredded
- 1/2 tsp salt

Directions:
1. Fit the oven with the rack in position
2. Add all ingredients into the mixing bowl and mix until well combined.
3. Pour mixture into the 1-quart casserole dish.
4. Set to bake at 350 F for 35 minutes. After 5 minutes place the casserole dish in the preheated oven.
5. Serve and enjoy.
- **Nutrition Info:** Calories 228 Fat 19.8 g Carbohydrates 4.2 g Sugar 0.8 g Protein 9.7 g Cholesterol 61 mg

458. Air Fryer Spicy Chickpeas

Servings: 4

Cooking Time: 12 Minutes
Ingredients:
- 14 oz can chickpeas, rinsed, drained and pat dry
- 1/2 tsp smoked paprika
- 1/4 tsp cayenne
- 1/2 tsp chili powder
- 1 tbsp olive oil
- Pepper
- Salt

Directions:
1. Fit the oven with the rack in position 2.
2. Add chickpeas, chili powder, cayenne, paprika, oil, pepper, and salt into the bowl and toss well.
3. Spread chickpeas in the air fryer basket then place the air fryer basket in the baking pan.
4. Place a baking pan on the oven rack. Set to air fry at 375 F for 12 minutes.
5. Serve and enjoy.
- **Nutrition Info:** Calories 150 Fat 4.7 g Carbohydrates 22.8 g Sugar 0.1 g Protein 5 g Cholesterol 0 mg

459. Carrot Bread

Servings: 6
Cooking Time: 30 Minutes
Ingredients:
- 1 cup all-purpose flour
- 1 teaspoon baking soda
- ½ teaspoon ground cinnamon
- ¼ teaspoon ground cloves
- ¼ teaspoon ground nutmeg ½ teaspoon salt
- 2 large eggs
- ¾ cup vegetable oil
- 1/3 cup white sugar
- 1/3 cup light brown sugar
- ½ teaspoon vanilla extract
- 1½ cups carrots, peeled and grated

Directions:
1. In a bowl, mix together the flour, baking soda, spices and salt.
2. In a large bowl, add the eggs, oil, sugars and vanilla extract and beat until well combined.
3. Add the flour mixture and mix until just combined.
4. Fold in the carrots.
5. Place the mixture into a lightly greased baking pan.
6. Press "Power Button" of Air Fry Oven and turn the dial to select the "Air Crisp" mode.
7. Press the Time button and again turn the dial to set the cooking time to 30 minutes.
8. Now push the Temp button and rotate the dial to set the temperature at 320 degrees F.
9. Press "Start/Pause" button to start.
10. When the unit beeps to show that it is preheated, open the lid.

11. Arrange the pan in "Air Fry Basket" and insert in the oven.
12. Place the pan onto a wire rack to cool for about 10 minutes.
13. Carefully, invert the bread onto wire rack to cool completely before slicing.
14. Cut the bread into desired-sized slices and serve.
- **Nutrition Info:** Calories 426 Total Fat 29.2 g Saturated Fat 5.9 g Cholesterol 62 mg Sodium 450 mg Total Carbs 38 g Fiber 1.4 g Sugar 20.5 g Protein 4.5 g

460.Air Fry Olives

Servings: 4
Cooking Time: 5 Minutes
Ingredients:
- 2 cups olives
- 2 tsp garlic, minced
- 2 tbsp olive oil
- 1/2 tsp dried oregano
- Pepper
- Salt

Directions:
1. Fit the oven with the rack in position 2.
2. Add olives and remaining ingredients into the large bowl and toss well.
3. Add olives to the air fryer basket then place an air fryer basket in baking pan.
4. Place a baking pan on the oven rack. Set to air fry at 300 F for 5 minutes.
5. Serve and enjoy.
- **Nutrition Info:** Calories 140 Fat 14.2 g Carbohydrates 4.8 g Sugar 0 g Protein 0.7 g Cholesterol 0 mg

461.Authentic Raisin Apple Treat

Servings: 4
Cooking Time: 15 Minutes
Ingredients:
- 4 apples, cored
- 1 ½ oz almonds
- ¾ oz raisins
- 2 tbsp sugar

Directions:
1. Preheat on Bake function to 360 F. In a bowl, mix sugar, almonds, and raisins. Blend the mixture using a hand mixer. Fill cored apples with the almond mixture. Place the apples in a baking tray and cook for 10 minutes. Serve with a sprinkle of powdered sugar.

462.Sago Payada

Servings:x
Cooking Time:x
Ingredients:
- 3 tbsp. powdered sugar
- 3 tbsp. unsalted butter
- 2 cups milk
- 2 cups-soaked sago
- 2 tbsp. custard powder

Directions:
1. Boil the milk and the sugar in a pan and add the custard powder followed by the sago and stir till you get a thick mixture.
2. Preheat the fryer to 300 Fahrenheit for five minutes. Place the dish in the basket and reduce the temperature to 250 Fahrenheit. Cook for ten minutes and set aside to cool.

463.Strawberries Stew

Servings: 4
Cooking Time: 20 Minutes
Ingredients:
- 1-pound strawberries, halved
- 4 tablespoons stevia
- 1 tablespoon lemon juice
- 1 and ½ cups water

Directions:
1. In a pan that fits your air fryer, mix all the ingredients, toss, put it in the fryer and cook at 340 degrees F for 20 minutes.
2. Divide the stew into cups and serve cold.
- **Nutrition Info:** calories 176, fat 2, fiber 1, carbs 3, protein 5

464.Chocolate Donuts

Servings: 8-10
Cooking Time: 20 Minutes
Ingredients:
- (8-ounce) can jumbo biscuits
- Cooking oil
- Chocolate sauce, such as Hershey's

Directions:
1. Preparing the Ingredients. Separate the biscuit dough into 8 biscuits and place them on a flat work surface. Use a small circle cookie cutter or a biscuit cutter to cut a hole in the center of each biscuit. You can also cut the holes using a knife.
2. Spray the Oven rack/basket with cooking oil. Place the Rack on the middle-shelf of the air fryer oven.
3. Air Frying. Place 4 donuts in the air fryer oven. Do not stack. Spray with cooking oil. Cook for 4 minutes.
4. Open the air fryer oven and flip the donuts. Cook for an additional 4 minutes.
5. Remove the cooked donuts from the air fryer, then repeat steps 3 and 4 for the remaining 4 donuts.
6. Drizzle chocolate sauce over the donuts and enjoy while warm.
- **Nutrition Info:** CALORIES: 181; FAT:98G; PROTEIN:3G; FIBER:1G

465.Lemon Blackberries Cake(1)

Servings: 4
Cooking Time: 25 Minutes
Ingredients:

- 2 eggs, whisked
- 4 tablespoons swerve
- 2 tablespoons ghee, melted
- ¼ cup almond milk
- 1 and ½ cups almond flour
- 1 cup blackberries, chopped
- ½ teaspoon baking powder
- 1 teaspoon lemon zest, grated
- 1 teaspoon lemon juice

Directions:
1. In a bowl, mix all the ingredients and whisk well.
2. Pour this into a cake pan that fits the air fryer lined with parchment paper, put the pan in your air fryer and cook at 340 degrees F for 25 minutes.
3. Cool the cake down, slice and serve.
- **Nutrition Info:** calories 193, fat 5, fiber 1, carbs 4, protein 4

466.Easy Sweet Potato Fries

Servings: 2
Cooking Time: 16 Minutes
Ingredients:

- 2 sweet potatoes, peeled and cut into fries shape
- 1 tbsp olive oil
- Salt

Directions:
1. Fit the oven with the rack in position 2.
2. Toss sweet potato fries with oil and salt and place in the air fryer basket then place the air fryer basket in the baking pan.
3. Place a baking pan on the oven rack. Set to air fry at 375 F for 16 minutes.
4. Serve and enjoy.
- **Nutrition Info:** Calories 178 Fat 7.2 g Carbohydrates 27.9 g Sugar 0.5 g Protein 1.5 g Cholesterol 0 mg

467.Cappuccino Blondies

Servings: 16
Cooking Time: 30 Minutes
Ingredients:

- Nonstick cooking spray
- 1 cup butter, soft
- 2 cups brown sugar
- 2 eggs
- 2 tsp baking powder
- 1 tsp salt
- 4 tsp espresso powder
- 2 2/3 cups flour

Directions:

1. Place rack in position Lightly spray an 8x11-inch baking pan with cooking spray.
2. In a large bowl, beat together butter and sugar. Add eggs and beat until light and fluffy.
3. Add baking powder, salt, and espresso and mix well. Stir in flour until combined.
4. Set oven to bake on 350°F for 35 minutes.
5. Spread batter in prepared pan. Once oven has preheated, place brownies in oven and bake 25-30 minutes.
6. Remove from oven and let cool before cutting.
- **Nutrition Info:** Calories 296, Total Fat 12g, Saturated Fat 7g, Total Carbs 44g, Net Carbs 43g, Protein 3g, Sugar 28g, Fiber 1g, Sodium 254mg, Potassium 137mg, Phosphorus 82mg

468.Moist Baked Donuts

Servings: 12
Cooking Time: 15 Minutes
Ingredients:

- 2 eggs
- 3/4 cup sugar
- 1/2 cup buttermilk
- 1/4 cup vegetable oil
- 1 cup all-purpose flour
- 1/2 tsp vanilla
- 1 tsp baking powder
- 1/2 tsp salt

Directions:
1. Fit the oven with the rack in position
2. Spray donut pan with cooking spray and set aside.
3. In a bowl, mix together oil, vanilla, baking powder, sugar, eggs, buttermilk, and salt until well combined.
4. Stir in flour and mix until smooth.
5. Pour batter into the prepared donut pan.
6. Set to bake at 350 F for 20 minutes. After 5 minutes place the donut pan in the preheated oven.
7. Serve and enjoy.
- **Nutrition Info:** Calories 140 Fat 5.5 g Carbohydrates 21.2 g Sugar 13.1 g Protein 2.3 g Cholesterol 28 mg

469.Mini Pecan Pies

Servings: 8
Cooking Time: 10 Minutes
Ingredients:

- Nonstick cooking spray
- 1 sheet puff pastry, thawed
- 4 tbsp. brown sugar
- ½ stick butter, melted
- 2 tbsp. maple syrup
- ½ cup pecans, chopped fine

Directions:

1. Place baking pan in position 2. Lightly spray fryer basket with cooking spray.
2. In a plastic bowl, stir together butter, syrup and pecans. Freeze 10 minutes.
3. Unfold pastry on a lightly floured surface. Gently roll it out. Cut in 8 equal triangles.
4. Spoon 2 teaspoons of pecan mixture onto the right side of rectangles, leaving a border. Fold left side over filling and seal edges with a fork. Pierce the tops of each pie.
5. Place half the pies in the fryer basket and put it on the baking pan. Set oven to air fryer on 375°F for 10 minutes. Cook pies 7 minutes or until puffed and golden brown. Repeat with remaining pies. Serve warm.

- **Nutrition Info:** Calories 161, Total Fat 13g, Saturated Fat 4g, Total Carbs 10g, Net Carbs 9g, Protein 1g, Sugar 7g, Fiber 1g, Sodium 62mg, Potassium 48mg, Phosphorus 24mg

470.Vanilla-lemon Cupcakes With Lemon Glaze

Servings:6
Cooking Time: 30 Minutes
Ingredients:
- 1 cup flour
- ½ cup sugar
- 1 small egg
- 1 tsp lemon zest
- ¾ tsp baking powder
- ¼ tsp baking soda
- ½ tsp salt
- 2 tbsp vegetable oil
- ½ cup milk
- ½ tsp vanilla extract
- Glaze:
- ½ cup powdered sugar
- 2 tsp lemon juice

Directions:
1. Preheat on Bake function to 350 F. In a bowl, combine all dry muffin ingredients. In another bowl, whisk together the wet ingredients. Gently combine the two mixtures.
2. Divide the batter between 6 greased muffin tins. Place the tins in the oven and cook for 13 to 16 minutes. Whisk the powdered sugar with the lemon juice. Spread the glaze over the muffins.

471.Roasted Veggie Bowl

Servings: 2
Cooking Time: 35 Minutes
Ingredients:
- ¼ medium white onion; peeled.and sliced ¼-inch thick
- ½ medium green bell pepper; seeded and sliced ¼-inch thick
- 1 cup broccoli florets
- 1 cup quartered Brussels sprouts
- ½ cup cauliflower florets
- 1 tbsp. coconut oil
- ½ tsp. garlic powder.
- ½ tsp. cumin
- 2 tsp. chili powder

Directions:
1. Toss all ingredients together in a large bowl until vegetables are fully coated with oil and seasoning. Pour vegetables into the air fryer basket.
2. Adjust the temperature to 360 Degrees F and set the timer for 15 minutes. Shake two- or three-times during cooking. Serve warm.

- **Nutrition Info:** Calories: 121; Protein: 4.3g; Fiber: 5.2g; Fat: 7.1g; Carbs: 13.1g

472.Apple Wedges With Apricots

Servings:4
Cooking Time: 15 To 18 Minutes
Ingredients:
- 4 large apples, peeled and sliced into 8 wedges
- 2 tablespoons olive oil
- ½ cup dried apricots, chopped
- 1 to 2 tablespoons sugar
- ½ teaspoon ground cinnamon

Directions:
1. Toss the apple wedges with the olive oil in a mixing bowl until well coated.
2. Place the apple wedges in the air fryer basket.
3. Put the air fryer basket on the baking pan and slide into Rack Position 2, select Air Fry, set temperature to 350ºF (180ºC), and set time to 15 minutes.
4. After about 12 minutes, remove from the oven. Sprinkle with the dried apricots and air fry for another 3 minutes.
5. Meanwhile, thoroughly combine the sugar and cinnamon in a small bowl.
6. Remove the apple wedges from the oven to a plate. Serve sprinkled with the sugar mixture.

473.Pumpkin Bread

Servings: 10
Cooking Time: 40 Minutes
Ingredients:
- 1 1/3 cups all-purpose flour
- 1 cup sugar
- ¾ teaspoon baking soda
- 1 teaspoon pumpkin pie spice
- 1/3 teaspoon ground cinnamon
- ¼ teaspoon salt
- 2 eggs
- ½ cup pumpkin puree
- 1/3 cup vegetable oil

- ¼ cup water

Directions:
1. In a bowl, mix together the flour, sugar, baking soda, spices and salt
2. In another large bowl, add the eggs, pumpkin, oil and water and beat until well combined.
3. In a large mixing bowl or stand mixer.
4. Add the flour mixture and mix until just combined.
5. Place the mixture into a lightly greased loaf pan.
6. With a piece of foil, cover the pan loosely.
7. Press "Power Button" of Air Fry Oven and turn the dial to select the "Air Bake" mode.
8. Press the Time button and again turn the dial to set the cooking time to 40 minutes.
9. Now push the Temp button and rotate the dial to set the temperature at 325 degrees F.
10. Press "Start/Pause" button to start.
11. When the unit beeps to show that it is preheated, open the lid.
12. Arrange the pan in "Air Fry Basket" and insert in the oven.
13. After 25 minutes of cooking, remove the foil.
14. Place the pan onto a wire rack to cool for about 10 minutes.
15. Carefully, invert the bread onto wire rack to cool completely before slicing.
16. Cut the bread into desired-sized slices and serve.
- **Nutrition Info:** Calories 217 Total Fat 8.4 g Saturated Fat 1.4 g Cholesterol 33 mg Sodium 167 mg Total Carbs 34 g Fiber 0.9 g Sugar 20.5g Protein 3 g

474.Sweet And Salty Snack Mix

Servings: About 10 Cups
Cooking Time: 10 Minutes
Ingredients:
- 3 tablespoons butter, melted
- ½ cup honey
- 1 teaspoon salt
- 2 cups granola
- 2 cups sesame sticks
- 2 cups crispy corn puff cereal
- 2 cups mini pretzel crisps
- 1 cup cashews
- 1 cup pepitas
- 1 cup dried cherries

Directions:
1. In a small mixing bowl, mix together the butter, honey, and salt until well incorporated.
2. In a large bowl, combine the granola, sesame sticks, corn puff cereal and pretzel crisps, cashews, and pepitas. Drizzle with the butter mixture and toss until evenly coated. Transfer the snack mix to the air fryer basket.
3. Put the air fryer basket on the baking pan and slide into Rack Position 2, select Air Fry, set temperature to 370ºF (188ºC), and set time to 10 minutes.
4. Stir the snack mix halfway through the cooking time.
5. When cooking is complete, they should be lightly toasted. Remove from the oven and allow to cool completely. Scatter with the dried cherries and mix well. Serve immediately.

475.Air Fried Chicken Wings

Servings:4
Cooking Time: 18 Minutes
Ingredients:
- 2 pounds (907 g) chicken wings
- Cooking spray

Directions:
1. Marinade:
2. cup buttermilk
3. ½ teaspoon salt
4. ½ teaspoon black pepper
5. Coating:
6. cup flour
7. cup panko bread crumbs
8. tablespoons poultry seasoning
9. teaspoons salt
10. Whisk together all the ingredients for the marinade in a large bowl.
11. Add the chicken wings to the marinade and toss well. Transfer to the refrigerator to marinate for at least an hour.
12. Spritz the air fryer basket with cooking spray. Set aside.
13. Thoroughly combine all the ingredients for the coating in a shallow bowl.
14. Remove the chicken wings from the marinade and shake off any excess. Roll them in the coating mixture.
15. Place the chicken wings in the basket in a single layer. Mist the wings with cooking spray.
16. Put the air fryer basket on the baking pan and slide into Rack Position 2, select Air Fry, set temperature to 360ºF (182ºC), and set time to 18 minutes.
17. Flip the wings halfway through the cooking time.
18. When cooking is complete, the wings should be crisp and golden brown on the outside. Remove from the oven to a plate and serve hot.

476.Mushroom And Spinach calzones

Servings:4
Cooking Time: 26 To 27 Minutes
Ingredients:

- 2 tablespoons olive oil
- 1 onion, chopped
- 2 garlic cloves, minced
- ¼ cup chopped mushrooms
- 1 pound (454 g) spinach, chopped
- 1 tablespoon Italian seasoning
- ½ teaspoon oregano
- Salt and black pepper, to taste
- 1½ cups marinara sauce
- 1 cup ricotta cheese, crumbled
- 1 (13-ounce / 369-g) pizza crust
- Cooking spray

Directions:
1. Make the Filling:
2. Heat the olive oil in a pan over medium heat until shimmering.
3. Add the onion, garlic, and mushrooms and sauté for 4 minutes, or until softened.
4. Stir in the spinach and sauté for 2 to 3 minutes, or until the spinach is wilted. Sprinkle with the Italian seasoning, oregano, salt, and pepper and mix well.
5. Add the marinara sauce and cook for about 5 minutes, stirring occasionally, or until the sauce is thickened.
6. Remove the pan from the heat and stir in the ricotta cheese. Set aside.
7. Make the Calzones:
8. Spritz the air fryer basket with cooking spray. Set aside.
9. Roll the pizza crust out with a rolling pin on a lightly floured work surface, then cut it into 4 rectangles.
10. Spoon ¼ of the filling into each rectangle and fold in half. Crimp the edges with a fork to seal. Mist them with cooking spray. Transfer the calzones to the basket.
11. Put the air fryer basket on the baking pan and slide into Rack Position 2, select Air Fry, set temperature to 375ºF (190ºC), and set time to 15 minutes.
12. Flip the calzones halfway through the cooking time.
13. When cooking is complete, the calzones should be golden brown and crisp. Transfer the calzones to a paper towel-lined plate and serve.

477.Air Fryer Pepperoni Chips

Servings: 6
Cooking Time: 8 Minutes
Ingredients:
- 6 oz pepperoni slices

Directions:
1. Fit the oven with the rack in position 2.
2. Place pepperoni slices in an air fryer basket then place an air fryer basket in baking pan.
3. Place a baking pan on the oven rack. Set to air fry at 360 F for 8 minutes.

4. Serve and enjoy.
- **Nutrition Info:** Calories 51 Fat 1 g Carbohydrates 2 g Sugar 0 g Protein 9.1 g Cholesterol 0 mg

478.Currant Cookies

Servings: 6
Cooking Time: 15 Minutes
Ingredients:
- ½ cup currants
- ½ cup swerve
- 2 cups almond flour
- ½ cup ghee; melted
- 1 tsp. vanilla extract
- 2 tsp. baking soda

Directions:
1. Take a bowl and mix all the ingredients and whisk well.
2. Spread this on a baking sheet lined with parchment paper, put the pan in the air fryer and cook at 350°F for 30 minutes
3. Cool down; cut into rectangles and serve.
- **Nutrition Info:** Calories: 172; Fat: 5g; Fiber: 2g; Carbs: 3g; Protein: 5g

479.Lemon Butter Cake

Servings: 10
Cooking Time: 55 Minutes
Ingredients:
- 4 eggs
- 1/2 cup butter softened
- 2 tsp baking powder
- 1/4 cup coconut flour
- 2 cups almond flour
- 2 tbsp lemon zest
- 1/2 cup fresh lemon juice
- 1/4 cup erythritol
- 1 tbsp vanilla

Directions:
1. Fit the oven with the rack in position
2. In a large bowl, whisk all ingredients until a smooth batter is formed.
3. Pour batter into the loaf pan.
4. Set to bake at 300 F for 60 minutes. After 5 minutes place the loaf pan in the preheated oven.
5. Slice and serve.
- **Nutrition Info:** Calories 85 Fat 5.7 g Carbohydrates 5 g Sugar 0.9 g Protein 3.8 g Cholesterol 65 mg

480.Peanut Butter-chocolate Bread Pudding

Servings:8
Cooking Time: 10 Minutes
Ingredients:
- 1 egg
- 1 egg yolk
- ¾ cup chocolate milk

- 3 tablespoons brown sugar
- 3 tablespoons peanut butter
- 2 tablespoons cocoa powder
- 1 teaspoon vanilla
- 5 slices firm white bread, cubed
- Nonstick cooking spray

Directions:
1. Spritz the baking pan with nonstick cooking spray.
2. Whisk together the egg, egg yolk, chocolate milk, brown sugar, peanut butter, cocoa powder, and vanilla until well combined.
3. Fold in the bread cubes and stir to mix well. Allow the bread soak for 10 minutes.
4. When ready, transfer the egg mixture to the prepared baking pan.
5. Slide the baking pan into Rack Position 1, select Convection Bake, set temperature to 330ºF (166ºC), and set time to 10 minutes.
6. When done, the pudding should be just firm to the touch.
7. Serve at room temperature.

481.Crunchy Chickpeas

Servings:4
Cooking Time: 18 Minutes
Ingredients:
- ½ teaspoon chili powder
- ½ teaspoon ground cumin
- ¼ teaspoon cayenne pepper
- ¼ teaspoon salt
- 1 (19-ounce / 539-g) can chickpeas, drained and rinsed
- Cooking spray

Directions:
1. Lina the air fryer basket with parchment paper and lightly spritz with cooking spray.
2. Mix the chili powder, cumin, cayenne pepper, and salt in a small bowl.
3. Place the chickpeas in a medium bowl and lightly mist with cooking spray.
4. Add the spice mixture to the chickpeas and toss until evenly coated. Transfer the chickpeas to the parchment.
5. Put the air fryer basket on the baking pan and slide into Rack Position 2, select Air Fry, set temperature to 390ºF (199ºC), and set time to 18 minutes.
6. Stir the chickpeas twice during cooking.
7. When cooking is complete, the chickpeas should be crunchy. Remove from the oven and let the chickpeas cool for 5 minutes before serving.

482.Apple Pastries

Servings: 6
Cooking Time: 10 Minutes
Ingredients:
- ½ of large apple, peeled, cored and chopped

- 1 teaspoon fresh orange zest, grated finely
- ½ tablespoon white sugar
- ½ teaspoon ground cinnamon
- 7.05 oz. prepared frozen puff pastry

Directions:
1. In a bowl, mix together all ingredients except puff pastry.
2. Cut the pastry in 16 squares.
3. Place about a teaspoon of the apple mixture in the center of each square.
4. Fold each square into a triangle and press the edges slightly with wet fingers.
5. Then with a fork, press the edges firmly.
6. Press "Power Button" of Air Fry Oven and turn the dial to select the "Air Fry" mode.
7. Press the Time button and again turn the dial to set the cooking time to 10 minutes.
8. Now push the Temp button and rotate the dial to set the temperature at 390 degrees F.
9. Press "Start/Pause" button to start.
10. When the unit beeps to show that it is preheated, open the lid.
11. Arrange the pastries in greased "Air Fry Basket" and insert in the oven.
12. Serve warm.
- **Nutrition Info:** Calories 198 Total Fat 12.7 g Saturated Fat 3.2 g Cholesterol 0 mg Sodium 83 mg Total Carbs 18.8 g Fiber 1.1 g Sugar 3.2 g Protein 2.5 g

483.Chocolate And Coconut Cake

Servings:6
Cooking Time: 15 Minutes
Ingredients:
- ½ cup unsweetened chocolate, chopped
- ½ stick butter, at room temperature
- 1 tablespoon liquid stevia
- 1½ cups coconut flour
- 2 eggs, whisked
- ½ teaspoon vanilla extract
- A pinch of fine sea salt
- Cooking spray

Directions:
1. Place the chocolate, butter, and stevia in a microwave-safe bowl. Microwave for about 30 seconds until melted.
2. Let the chocolate mixture cool for 5 to 10 minutes.
3. Add the remaining ingredients to the bowl of chocolate mixture and whisk to incorporate.
4. Lightly spray the baking pan with cooking spray.
5. Scrape the chocolate mixture into the prepared baking pan.
6. Slide the baking pan into Rack Position 1, select Convection Bake, set temperature to 330ºF (166ºC), and set time to 15 minutes.

7. When cooking is complete, the top should spring back lightly when gently pressed with your fingers.
8. Let the cake cool for 5 minutes and serve.

484.Chocolate Chip Pan Cookie

Servings: 4
Cooking Time: 15 Minutes
Ingredients:
- ½ cup blanched finely ground almond flour.
- 1 large egg.
- ¼ cup powdered erythritol
- 2 tbsp. unsalted butter; softened.
- 2 tbsp. low-carb, sugar-free chocolate chips
- ½ tsp. unflavored gelatin
- ½ tsp. baking powder.
- ½ tsp. vanilla extract.

Directions:
1. Take a large bowl, mix almond flour and erythritol. Stir in butter, egg and gelatin until combined.
2. Stir in baking powder and vanilla and then fold in chocolate chips
3. Pour batter into 6-inch round baking pan. Place pan into the air fryer basket.
4. Adjust the temperature to 300 Degrees F and set the timer for 7 minutes
5. When fully cooked, the top will be golden brown and a toothpick inserted in center will come out clean. Let cool at least 10 minutes.
- **Nutrition Info:** Calories: 188; Protein: 5.6g; Fiber: 2.0g; Fat: 15.7g; Carbs: 16.8g

485.Roasted Chickpeas

Servings: 4
Cooking Time: 10 Minutes
Ingredients:
- 3 cup boiled chickpeas
- ¼ tsp. rosemary
- ¼ tsp. dry mango powder
- 1 tsp. olive oil
- ½ tsp. cinnamon powder
- ¼ tsp. cumin powder
- 1 tsp. salt
- ½ tsp. chili powder
- ¼ tsp. dry coriander powder

Directions:
1. Preheat your Air Fryer to a temperature of 370°F (190°C).
2. Transfer chickpeas with olive oil in fryer basket and cook for 8 minutes.
3. Shake fryer basket after every 2 minutes.
4. In a bowl add chickpeas with all spices and toss to combine.
5. Serve!
- **Nutrition Info:** Calories: 214 Protein: 10.98 g Fat: 4.4 g Carbs: 34.27 g

486.Crispy Shrimps

Servings: 2
Cooking Time: 8 Minutes
Ingredients:
- 1 egg
- ¼ pound nacho chips, crushed
- 10 shrimps, peeled and deveined
- 1 tablespoon olive oil
- Salt and black pepper, to taste

Directions:
1. Preheat the Air fryer to 365 ºF and grease an Air fryer basket.
2. Crack egg in a shallow dish and beat well.
3. Place the nacho chips in another shallow dish.
4. Season the shrimps with salt and black pepper, coat into egg and then roll into nacho chips.
5. Place the coated shrimps into the Air fryer basket and cook for about 8 minutes.
6. Dish out and serve warm.
- **Nutrition Info:** Calories: 514, Fat: 25.8g, Carbohydrates: 36.9g, Sugar: 2.3g, Protein: 32.5g, Sodium: 648mg

487.Berry Crumble

Servings:6
Cooking Time: 35 Minutes
Ingredients:
- 2 ounces (57 g) unsweetened mixed berries
- ½ cup granulated Swerve
- 2 tablespoons golden flaxseed meal
- 1 teaspoon xanthan gum
- ½ teaspoon ground cinnamon
- ¼ teaspoon ground star anise
- Topping:
- ½ stick butter, cut into small pieces
- 1 cup powdered Swerve
- $2/3$ cup almond flour
- $1/3$ cup unsweetened coconut, finely shredded
- ½ teaspoon baking powder
- Cooking spray

Directions:
1. Coat 6 ramekins with cooking spray.
2. In a mixing dish, stir together the mixed berries, granulated Swerve, flaxseed meal, xanthan gum, cinnamon, star anise. Divide the berry mixture evenly among the prepared ramekins.
3. Combine the remaining ingredients in a separate mixing dish and stir well. Scatter the topping over the berry mixture.
4. Put the ramekins into Rack Position 1, select Convection Bake, set temperature to 330ºF (166ºC), and set time to 35 minutes.
5. When done, the topping should be golden brown.
6. Serve warm.

488.Muffins And Jam

Servings:x
Cooking Time:x
Ingredients:

- 1 tbsp. unsalted butter
- 2 cups buttermilk
- Parchment paper
- 1 cup + 2 tbsp. powdered sugar
- 1 ½ cups + 2 tbsp. all-purpose flour
- 1 tsp. baking powder
- ½ tsp. baking soda
- 2 tbsp. jam

Directions:

1. In a bowl, add the flour and the buttermilk. Fold the mixture using a spatula. Add the jam and whisk the ingredients to ensure that the jam has thinned. Add the remaining ingredients to the bowl and continue to mix the ingredients. Do not mix too much.
2. Grease the muffin cups and line them with the parchment paper. Transfer the mixture into the cups and set them aside. Preheat the fryer to 300 Fahrenheit for five minutes. Place the muffin cups in the basket and reduce the temperature to 250 Fahrenheit. Cool in the basket and serve warm.

489.Mini Crab Cakes

Servings:x
Cooking Time:x
Ingredients:

- ½ cup dried bread crumbs
- ½ cup mayonnaise
- ¼ cup minced green onions
- 3 tablespoons olive oil
- 1-pound canned lump crabmeat
- 1 cup fresh cilantro leaves
- ½ cup chopped walnuts
- ½ cup grated Romano cheese
- 2 tablespoons olive oil

Directions:

1. Drain crabmeat well and pick over to remove any cartilage. Set aside in large bowl. In food processor or blender, combine cilantro, walnuts, cheese, and 2 tablespoons olive oil (6 tablespoons for triple batch). Process or blend until mixture forms a paste. Stir into crabmeat.
2. Add bread crumbs, mayonnaise, and green onions to crab mixture. Stir to combine. Form into 2- inch patties about ½-inch thick. Flash freeze on baking sheet. When frozen solid, pack crab cakes in rigid containers, with waxed paper between the layers. Label crab cakes and freeze. Reserve remaining olive oil in pantry.
3. To thaw and reheat: Thaw crab cakes in refrigerator overnight. Heat 3 tablespoons olive oil (9 for triple batch) in large, heavy skillet over medium heat. Fry crab cakes until golden and hot, turning once, about 3 to 5 minutes on each side.

490.Baked Sardines With Tomato Sauce

Servings:4
Cooking Time: 20 Minutes
Ingredients:

- 2 pounds (907 g) fresh sardines
- 3 tablespoons olive oil, divided
- 4 Roma tomatoes, peeled and chopped
- 1 small onion, sliced thinly
- Zest of 1 orange
- Sea salt and freshly ground pepper, to taste
- 2 tablespoons whole-wheat bread crumbs
- ½ cup white wine

Directions:

1. Grease the baking pan with a little olive oil. Set aside.
2. Rinse the sardines under running water. Slit the belly, remove the spine and butterfly the fish. Set aside.
3. Heat the remaining olive oil in a large skillet. Add the tomatoes, onion, orange zest, salt and pepper to the skillet and simmer for 20 minutes, or until the mixture thickens and softens.
4. Place half the sauce in the bottom of the greased pan. Arrange the sardines on top and spread the remaining half the sauce over the fish. Sprinkle with the bread crumbs and drizzle with the white wine.
5. Slide the baking pan into Rack Position 1, select Convection Bake, set temperature to 425ºF (220ºC) and set time to 20 minutes.
6. When cooking is complete, remove the pan from the oven. Serve immediately.

491.Air Fried Chicken Tenders

Servings: 4
Cooking Time: 10 Minutes
Ingredients:

- 12 oz chicken breasts, cut into tenders
- 1 egg white
- 1/8 cup flour
- ½ cup panko bread crumbs
- Salt and black pepper, to taste

Directions:

1. Preheat the Air fryer to 350 degree F and grease an Air fryer basket.
2. Season the chicken tenders with salt and black pepper.
3. Coat the chicken tenders with flour, then dip in egg whites and then dredge in the panko bread crumbs.
4. Arrange in the Air fryer basket and cook for about 10 minutes.
5. Dish out in a platter and serve warm.

- **Nutrition Info:** Calories: 220, Fat: 17.1g, Carbohydrates: 6g, Sugar: 3.5g, Protein: 12.8g, Sodium: 332mg

492.Cherry Apple Risotto

Servings: 4
Cooking Time: 12 Minutes
Ingredients:
- 1 tablespoon of butter
- ¼ cup of brown sugar
- ½ cup of apple juice
- 1½ cups of milk
- ¾ cup of Arborio rice, boiled
- 1 apple, diced
- 2 pinches salt
- ¾ teaspoon of cinnamon powder
- ¼ cup of dried cherries
- 1½ tablespoons of almonds, roasted and sliced
- ¼ cup of whipped cream

Directions:
1. Set the Instant Vortex on Air fryer to 375 degrees F for 12 minutes. Combine rice with butter, sugar, apple juice, milk, apple, salt, and cinnamon in a bowl. Pour the rice mixture into the cooking tray. Insert the cooking tray in the Vortex when it displays "Add Food". Toss the food when it displays "Turn Food". Remove from the oven when cooking time is complete. Top with the dried cherries, almonds, and whipped cream to serve.
- **Nutrition Info:** Calories: 317 Cal Total Fat: 8.5 g Saturated Fat: 0 g Cholesterol: 0 mg Sodium: 0 mg Total Carbs: 54.8 g Fiber: 0 g Sugar: 0 g Protein: 6.2 g

493.Blackberry Chocolate Cake

Servings:8
Cooking Time: 22 Minutes
Ingredients:
- ½ cup butter, at room temperature
- 2 ounces (57 g) Swerve
- 4 eggs
- 1 cup almond flour
- 1 teaspoon baking soda
- $^1/_3$ teaspoon baking powder
- ½ cup cocoa powder
- 1 teaspoon orange zest
- $^1/_3$ cup fresh blackberries

Directions:
1. With an electric mixer or hand mixer, beat the butter and Swerve until creamy.
2. One at a time, mix in the eggs and beat again until fluffy.
3. Add the almond flour, baking soda, baking powder, cocoa powder, orange zest and mix well. Add the butter mixture to the almond

flour mixture and stir until well blended. Fold in the blackberries.
4. Scrape the batter into the baking pan.
5. Slide the baking pan into Rack Position 1, select Convection Bake, set temperature to 335ºF (168ºC), and set time to 22 minutes.
6. When cooking is complete, a toothpick inserted into the center of the cake should come out clean.
7. Allow the cake cool on a wire rack to room temperature. Serve immediately.

494.Vanilla Banana Brownies

Servings: 12
Cooking Time: 20 Minutes
Ingredients:
- 1 egg
- 1 cup all-purpose flour
- 4 oz white chocolate
- 1/4 cup butter
- 1 tsp vanilla extract
- 1/2 cup granulated sugar
- 2 medium bananas, mashed
- 1/4 tsp salt

Directions:
1. Fit the oven with the rack in position
2. Add white chocolate and butter in a microwave-safe bowl and microwave for 30 seconds. Stir until melted.
3. Stir in sugar. Add mashed bananas, eggs, vanilla, and salt and mix until combined.
4. Add flour and mix until just combined.
5. Pour batter into the greased baking dish.
6. Set to bake at 350 F for 25 minutes. After 5 minutes place the baking dish in the preheated oven.
7. Slice and serve.
- **Nutrition Info:** Calories 178 Fat 7.4 g Carbohydrates 26.4 g Sugar 16.4 g Protein 2.3 g Cholesterol 26 mg

495.Shrimp Toasts With Sesame Seeds

Servings:4 To 6
Cooking Time: 8 Minutes
Ingredients:
- ½ pound (227 g) raw shrimp, peeled and deveined
- 1 egg, beaten
- 2 scallions, chopped, plus more for garnish
- 2 tablespoons chopped fresh cilantro
- 2 teaspoons grated fresh ginger
- 1 to 2 teaspoons sriracha sauce
- 1 teaspoon soy sauce
- ½ teaspoon toasted sesame oil
- 6 slices thinly sliced white sandwich bread
- ½ cup sesame seeds
- Cooking spray
- Thai chili sauce, for serving

Directions:

1. In a food processor, add the shrimp, egg, scallions, cilantro, ginger, sriracha sauce, soy sauce and sesame oil, and pulse until chopped finely. You'll need to stop the food processor occasionally to scrape down the sides. Transfer the shrimp mixture to a bowl.
2. On a clean work surface, cut the crusts off the sandwich bread. Using a brush, generously brush one side of each slice of bread with shrimp mixture.
3. Place the sesame seeds on a plate. Press bread slices, shrimp-side down, into sesame seeds to coat evenly. Cut each slice diagonally into quarters.
4. Spritz the air fryer basket with cooking spray. Spread the coated slices in a single layer in the basket.
5. Put the air fryer basket on the baking pan and slide into Rack Position 2, select Air Fry, set temperature to 400ºF (205ºC), and set time to 8 minutes.
6. Flip the bread slices halfway through.
7. When cooking is complete, they should be golden and crispy. Remove from the oven to a plate and let cool for 5 minutes. Top with the chopped scallions and serve warm with Thai chili sauce.

496.Parmesan Zucchini Fries

Servings: 4
Cooking Time: 10 Minutes
Ingredients:
- 2 medium zucchini, cut into fries shape
- 1/2 cup breadcrumbs
- 1 egg, lightly beaten
- 1/2 tsp garlic powder
- 1 tsp Italian seasoning
- 1/2 cup parmesan cheese, grated
- Pepper
- Salt

Directions:
1. Fit the oven with the rack in position 2.
2. Add egg in a bowl and whisk well.
3. In a shallow bowl, mix together breadcrumbs, spices, parmesan cheese, pepper, and salt.
4. Dip zucchini in egg then coat with breadcrumb mixture and place in air fryer basket then place air fryer basket in baking pan.
5. Place a baking pan on the oven rack. Set to air fry at 400 F for 10 minutes.
6. Serve and enjoy.
- **Nutrition Info:** Calories 126 Fat 4.8 g Carbohydrates 13.9 g Sugar 2.8 g Protein 8.1 g Cholesterol 50 mg

OTHER FAVORITE RECIPES

497.Asian Dipping Sauce

Servings: About 1 Cup
Cooking Time: 0 Minutes
Ingredients:
- ¼ cup rice vinegar
- ¼ cup hoisin sauce
- ¼ cup low-sodium chicken or vegetable stock
- 3 tablespoons soy sauce
- 1 tablespoon minced or grated ginger
- 1 tablespoon minced or pressed garlic
- 1 teaspoon chili-garlic sauce or sriracha (or more to taste)

Directions:
1. Stir together all the ingredients in a small bowl, or place in a jar with a tight-fitting lid and shake until well mixed.
2. Use immediately.

498.Spinach And Chickpea Casserole

Servings:4
Cooking Time: 21 To 22 Minutes
Ingredients:
- 2 tablespoons olive oil
- 2 garlic cloves, minced
- 1 tablespoon ginger, minced
- 1 onion, chopped
- 1 chili pepper, minced
- Salt and ground black pepper, to taste
- 1 pound (454 g) spinach
- 1 can coconut milk
- ½ cup dried tomatoes, chopped
- 1 (14-ounce / 397-g) can chickpeas, drained

Directions:
1. Heat the olive oil in a saucepan over medium heat. Sauté the garlic and ginger in the olive oil for 1 minute, or until fragrant.
2. Add the onion, chili pepper, salt and pepper to the saucepan. Sauté for 3 minutes.
3. Mix in the spinach and sauté for 3 to 4 minutes or until the vegetables become soft. Remove from heat.
4. Pour the vegetable mixture into the baking pan. Stir in coconut milk, dried tomatoes and chickpeas until well blended.
5. Slide the baking pan into Rack Position 1, select Convection Bake, set temperature to 370ºF (188ºC) and set time to 15 minutes.
6. When cooking is complete, transfer the casserole to a serving dish. Let cool for 5 minutes before serving.

499.South Carolina Shrimp And Corn Bake

Servings:2
Cooking Time: 18 Minutes
Ingredients:
- 1 ear corn, husk and silk removed, cut into 2-inch rounds
- 8 ounces (227 g) red potatoes, unpeeled, cut into 1-inch pieces
- 2 teaspoons Old Bay Seasoning, divided
- 2 teaspoons vegetable oil, divided
- ¼ teaspoon ground black pepper
- 8 ounces (227 g) large shrimps (about 12 shrimps), deveined
- 6 ounces (170 g) andouille or chorizo sausage, cut into 1-inch pieces
- 2 garlic cloves, minced
- 1 tablespoon chopped fresh parsley

Directions:
1. Put the corn rounds and potatoes in a large bowl. Sprinkle with 1 teaspoon of Old Bay seasoning and drizzle with vegetable oil. Toss to coat well.
2. Transfer the corn rounds and potatoes into the baking pan.
3. Slide the baking pan into Rack Position 1, select Convection Bake, set temperature to 400ºF (205ºC) and set time to 18 minutes.
4. After 6 minutes, remove from the oven. Stir the corn rounds and potatoes. Return the pan to the oven and continue cooking.
5. Meanwhile, cut slits into the shrimps but be careful not to cut them through. Combine the shrimps, sausage, remaining Old Bay seasoning, and remaining vegetable oil in the large bowl. Toss to coat well.
6. After 6 minutes, remove the pan from the oven. Add the shrimps and sausage to the pan. Return the pan to the oven and continue cooking for 6 minutes. Stir the shrimp mixture halfway through the cooking time.
7. When done, the shrimps should be opaque. Transfer the dish to a plate and spread with parsley before serving.

500.Air Fried Blistered Tomatoes

Servings:4 To 6
Cooking Time: 10 Minutes
Ingredients:
- 2 pounds (907 g) cherry tomatoes
- 2 tablespoons olive oil
- 2 teaspoons balsamic vinegar
- ½ teaspoon salt
- ½ teaspoon ground black pepper

Directions:
1. Toss the cherry tomatoes with olive oil in a large bowl to coat well. Pour the tomatoes in the baking pan.
2. Put the air fryer basket on the baking pan and slide into Rack Position 2, select Air Fry, set temperature to 400ºF (205ºC) and set time to 10 minutes.

3. Stir the tomatoes halfway through the cooking time.
4. When cooking is complete, the tomatoes will be blistered and lightly wilted.
5. Transfer the blistered tomatoes to a large bowl and toss with balsamic vinegar, salt, and black pepper before serving.

501.Golden Salmon And Carrot Croquettes

Servings:6
Cooking Time: 10 Minutes
Ingredients:
- 2 egg whites
- 1 cup almond flour
- 1 cup panko bread crumbs
- 1 pound (454 g) chopped salmon fillet
- $^2/_3$ cup grated carrots
- 2 tablespoons minced garlic cloves
- ½ cup chopped onion
- 2 tablespoons chopped chives
- Cooking spray

Directions:
1. Spritz the air fryer basket with cooking spray.
2. Whisk the egg whites in a bowl. Put the flour in a second bowl. Pour the bread crumbs in a third bowl. Set aside.
3. Combine the salmon, carrots, garlic, onion, and chives in a large bowl. Stir to mix well.
4. Form the mixture into balls with your hands. Dredge the balls into the flour, then egg, and then bread crumbs to coat well.
5. Arrange the salmon balls on the basket and spritz with cooking spray.
6. Put the air fryer basket on the baking pan and slide into Rack Position 2, select Air Fry, set temperature to 350ºF (180ºC) and set time to 10 minutes.
7. Flip the salmon balls halfway through cooking.
8. When cooking is complete, the salmon balls will be crispy and browned. Remove from the oven and serve immediately.

502.Supplì Al Telefono (risotto Croquettes)

Servings:6
Cooking Time: 54 Minutes
Ingredients:
- Risotto Croquettes:
- 4 tablespoons unsalted butter
- 1 small yellow onion, minced
- 1 cup Arborio rice
- 3½ cups chicken stock
- ½ cup dry white wine
- 3 eggs
- Zest of 1 lemon
- ½ cup grated Parmesan cheese
- 2 ounces (57 g) fresh Mozzarella cheese
- ¼ cup peas
- 2 tablespoons water
- ½ cup all-purpose flour
- 1½ cups panko bread crumbs
- Kosher salt and ground black pepper, to taste
- Cooking spray
- Tomato Sauce:
- 2 tablespoons extra-virgin olive oil
- 4 cloves garlic, minced
- ¼ teaspoon red pepper flakes
- 1 (28-ounce / 794-g) can crushed tomatoes
- 2 teaspoons granulated sugar
- Kosher salt and ground black pepper, to taste

Directions:
1. Melt the butter in a pot over medium heat, then add the onion and salt to taste. Sauté for 5 minutes or until the onion in translucent.
2. Add the rice and stir to coat well. Cook for 3 minutes or until the rice is lightly browned. Pour in the chicken stock and wine.
3. Bring to a boil. Then cook for 20 minutes or until the rice is tender and liquid is almost absorbed.
4. Make the risotto: When the rice is cooked, break the egg into the pot. Add the lemon zest and Parmesan cheese. Sprinkle with salt and ground black pepper. Stir to mix well.
5. Pour the risotto in a baking sheet, then level with a spatula to spread the risotto evenly. Wrap the baking sheet in plastic and refrigerate for1 hour.
6. Meanwhile, heat the olive oil in a saucepan over medium heat until shimmering.
7. Add the garlic and sprinkle with red pepper flakes. Sauté for a minute or until fragrant.
8. Add the crushed tomatoes and sprinkle with sugar. Stir to mix well. Bring to a boil. Reduce the heat to low and simmer for 15 minutes or until lightly thickened. Sprinkle with salt and pepper to taste. Set aside until ready to serve.
9. Remove the risotto from the refrigerator. Scoop the risotto into twelve 2-inch balls, then flatten the balls with your hands.
10. Arrange a about ½-inch piece of Mozzarella and 5 peas in the center of each flattened ball, then wrap them back into balls.
11. Transfer the balls to a baking sheet lined with parchment paper, then refrigerate for 15 minutes or until firm.
12. Whisk the remaining 2 eggs with 2 tablespoons of water in a bowl. Pour the flour in a second bowl and pour the panko in a third bowl.

13. Dredge the risotto balls in the bowl of flour first, then into the eggs, and then into the panko. Shake the excess off.
14. Transfer the balls to the baking pan and spritz with cooking spray.
15. Slide the baking pan into Rack Position 1, select Convection Bake, set temperature to 400ºF (205ºC) and set time to 10 minutes.
16. Flip the balls halfway through the cooking time.
17. When cooking is complete, the balls should be until golden brown.
18. Serve the risotto balls with the tomato sauce.

503. Cinnamon Rolls With Cream Glaze

Servings:8
Cooking Time: 5 Minutes
Ingredients:
- 1 pound (454 g) frozen bread dough, thawed
- 2 tablespoons melted butter
- 1½ tablespoons cinnamon
- ¾ cup brown sugar
- Cooking spray
- Cream Glaze:
- 4 ounces (113 g) softened cream cheese
- ½ teaspoon vanilla extract
- 2 tablespoons melted butter
- 1¼ cups powdered erythritol

Directions:
1. Place the bread dough on a clean work surface, then roll the dough out into a rectangle with a rolling pin.
2. Brush the top of the dough with melted butter and leave 1-inch edges uncovered.
3. Combine the cinnamon and sugar in a small bowl, then sprinkle the dough with the cinnamon mixture.
4. Roll the dough over tightly, then cut the dough log into 8 portions. Wrap the portions in plastic, better separately, and let sit to rise for 1 or 2 hours.
5. Meanwhile, combine the ingredients for the glaze in a separate small bowl. Stir to mix well.
6. Spritz the air fryer basket with cooking spray. Transfer the risen rolls to the basket.
7. Put the air fryer basket on the baking pan and slide into Rack Position 2, select Air Fry, set temperature to 350ºF (180ºC) and set time to 5 minutes.
8. Flip the rolls halfway through the cooking time.
9. When cooking is complete, the rolls will be golden brown.
10. Serve the rolls with the glaze.

504. Apple Fritters With Sugary Glaze

Servings: 15 Fritters

Cooking Time: 8 Minutes
Ingredients:
- Apple Fritters:
- 2 firm apples, peeled, cored, and diced
- ½ teaspoon cinnamon
- Juice of 1 lemon
- 1 cup all-purpose flour
- 1½ teaspoons baking powder
- ½ teaspoon kosher salt
- 2 eggs
- ¼ cup milk
- 2 tablespoons unsalted butter, melted
- 2 tablespoons granulated sugar
- Cooking spray
- Glaze:
- ½ teaspoon vanilla extract
- 1¼ cups powdered sugar, sifted
- ¼ cup water

Directions:
1. Line the air fryer basket with parchment paper.
2. Combine the apples with cinnamon and lemon juice in a small bowl. Toss to coat well.
3. Combine the flour, baking powder, and salt in a large bowl. Stir to mix well.
4. Whisk the egg, milk, butter, and sugar in a medium bowl. Stir to mix well.
5. Make a well in the center of the flour mixture, then pour the egg mixture into the well and stir to mix well. Mix in the apple until a dough forms.
6. Use an ice cream scoop to scoop 15 balls from the dough onto the pan. Spritz with cooking spray.
7. Put the air fryer basket on the baking pan and slide into Rack Position 2, select Air Fry, set temperature to 360ºF (182ºC) and set time to 8 minutes.
8. Flip the apple fritters halfway through the cooking time.
9. Meanwhile, combine the ingredients for the glaze in a separate small bowl. Stir to mix well.
10. When cooking is complete, the apple fritters will be golden brown. Serve the fritters with the glaze on top or use the glaze for dipping.

505. Air Fried Crispy Brussels Sprouts

Servings:4
Cooking Time: 20 Minutes
Ingredients:
- ¼ teaspoon salt
- ⅛ teaspoon ground black pepper
- 1 tablespoon extra-virgin olive oil
- 1 pound (454 g) Brussels sprouts, trimmed and halved
- Lemon wedges, for garnish

Directions:

1. Combine the salt, black pepper, and olive oil in a large bowl. Stir to mix well.
2. Add the Brussels sprouts to the bowl of mixture and toss to coat well. Arrange the Brussels sprouts in the air fryer basket.
3. Put the air fryer basket on the baking pan and slide into Rack Position 2, select Air Fry, set temperature to 350ºF (180ºC) and set time to 20 minutes.
4. Stir the Brussels sprouts two times during cooking.
5. When cooked, the Brussels sprouts will be lightly browned and wilted. Transfer the cooked Brussels sprouts to a large plate and squeeze the lemon wedges on top to serve.

506.Potato Chips With Lemony Cream Dip

Servings:2 To 4
Cooking Time: 15 Minutes
Ingredients:
- 2 large russet potatoes, sliced into ⅛-inch slices, rinsed
- Sea salt and freshly ground black pepper, to taste
- Cooking spray
- Lemony Cream Dip:
- ½ cup sour cream
- ¼ teaspoon lemon juice
- 2 scallions, white part only, minced
- 1 tablespoon olive oil
- ¼ teaspoon salt
- Freshly ground black pepper, to taste

Directions:
1. Soak the potato slices in water for 10 minutes, then pat dry with paper towels.
2. Transfer the potato slices in the air fryer basket. Spritz the slices with cooking spray.
3. Put the air fryer basket on the baking pan and slide into Rack Position 2, select Air Fry, set temperature to 300ºF (150ºC) and set time to 15 minutes.
4. Stir the potato slices three times during cooking. Sprinkle with salt and ground black pepper in the last minute.
5. Meanwhile, combine the ingredients for the dip in a small bowl. Stir to mix well.
6. When cooking is complete, the potato slices will be crispy and golden brown. Remove from the oven and serve the potato chips immediately with the dip.

507.Arancini

Servings: 10 Arancini
Cooking Time: 30 Minutes
Ingredients:
- ²/₃ cup raw white Arborio rice
- 2 teaspoons butter
- ½ teaspoon salt
- 1¹/₃ cups water

- 2 large eggs, well beaten
- 1¼ cups seasoned Italian-style dried bread crumbs
- 10 ¾-inch semi-firm Mozzarella cubes
- Cooking spray

Directions:
1. Pour the rice, butter, salt, and water in a pot. Stir to mix well and bring a boil over medium-high heat. Keep stirring.
2. Reduce the heat to low and cover the pot. Simmer for 20 minutes or until the rice is tender.
3. Turn off the heat and let sit, covered, for 10 minutes, then open the lid and fluffy the rice with a fork. Allow to cool for 10 more minutes.
4. Pour the beaten eggs in a bowl, then pour the bread crumbs in a separate bowl.
5. Scoop 2 tablespoons of the cooked rice up and form it into a ball, then press the Mozzarella into the ball and wrap.
6. Dredge the ball in the eggs first, then shake the excess off the dunk the ball in the bread crumbs. Roll to coat evenly. Repeat to make 10 balls in total with remaining rice.
7. Transfer the balls in the air fryer basket and spritz with cooking spray.
8. Put the air fryer basket on the baking pan and slide into Rack Position 2, select Air Fry, set temperature to 375ºF (190ºC) and set time to 10 minutes.
9. When cooking is complete, the balls should be lightly browned and crispy.
10. Remove the balls from the oven and allow to cool before serving.

508.Simple Cheesy Shrimps

Servings:4 To 6
Cooking Time: 8 Minutes
Ingredients:
- ²/₃ cup grated Parmesan cheese
- 4 minced garlic cloves
- 1 teaspoon onion powder
- ½ teaspoon oregano
- 1 teaspoon basil
- 1 teaspoon ground black pepper
- 2 tablespoons olive oil
- 2 pounds (907 g) cooked large shrimps, peeled and deveined
- Lemon wedges, for topping
- Cooking spray

Directions:
1. Spritz the air fryer basket with cooking spray.
2. Combine all the ingredients, except for the shrimps, in a large bowl. Stir to mix well.
3. Dunk the shrimps in the mixture and toss to coat well. Shake the excess off. Arrange the shrimps in the basket.

4. Put the air fryer basket on the baking pan and slide into Rack Position 2, select Air Fry, set temperature to 350ºF (180ºC) and set time to 8 minutes.
5. Flip the shrimps halfway through the cooking time.
6. When cooking is complete, the shrimps should be opaque. Transfer the cooked shrimps onto a large plate and squeeze the lemon wedges over before serving.

509.Herbed Cheddar Frittata

Servings:4
Cooking Time: 20 Minutes
Ingredients:
- ½ cup shredded Cheddar cheese
- ½ cup half-and-half
- 4 large eggs
- 2 tablespoons chopped scallion greens
- 2 tablespoons chopped fresh parsley
- ½ teaspoon kosher salt
- ½ teaspoon ground black pepper
- Cooking spray

Directions:
1. Spritz the baking pan with cooking spray.
2. Whisk together all the ingredients in a large bowl, then pour the mixture into the prepared baking pan.
3. Slide the baking pan into Rack Position 1, select Convection Bake, set temperature to 300ºF (150ºC) and set time to 20 minutes.
4. Stir the mixture halfway through.
5. When cooking is complete, the eggs should be set.
6. Serve immediately.

510.Southwest Corn And Bell Pepper Roast

Servings:4
Cooking Time: 10 Minutes
Ingredients:
- Corn:
- 1½ cups thawed frozen corn kernels
- 1 cup mixed diced bell peppers
- 1 jalapeño, diced
- 1 cup diced yellow onion
- ½ teaspoon ancho chile powder
- 1 tablespoon fresh lemon juice
- 1 teaspoon ground cumin
- ½ teaspoon kosher salt
- Cooking spray
- For Serving:
- ¼ cup feta cheese
- ¼ cup chopped fresh cilantro
- 1 tablespoon fresh lemon juice

Directions:
1. Spritz the air fryer basket with cooking spray.

2. Combine the ingredients for the corn in a large bowl. Stir to mix well.
3. Pour the mixture into the basket.
4. Put the air fryer basket on the baking pan and slide into Rack Position 2, select Air Fry, set temperature to 375ºF (190ºC) and set time to 10 minutes.
5. Stir the mixture halfway through the cooking time.
6. When done, the corn and bell peppers should be soft.
7. Transfer them onto a large plate, then spread with feta cheese and cilantro. Drizzle with lemon juice and serve.

511.Hot Wings

Servings: 16 Wings
Cooking Time: 15 Minutes
Ingredients:
- 16 chicken wings
- 3 tablespoons hot sauce
- Cooking spray

Directions:
1. Spritz the air fryer basket with cooking spray.
2. Arrange the chicken wings in the basket.
3. Put the air fryer basket on the baking pan and slide into Rack Position 2, select Air Fry, set temperature to 360ºF (182ºC) and set time to 15 minutes.
4. Flip the wings at lease three times during cooking.
5. When cooking is complete, the chicken wings will be well browned. Remove from the oven.
6. Transfer the air fried wings to a plate and serve with hot sauce.

512.Parmesan Cauliflower Fritters

Servings:6
Cooking Time: 8 Minutes
Ingredients:
- 2 cups cooked cauliflower
- 1 cup panko bread crumbs
- 1 large egg, beaten
- ½ cup grated Parmesan cheese
- 1 tablespoon chopped fresh chives Spritz the air fryer basket with cooking spray
- Cooking spray.

Directions:
1. Put the cauliflower, panko bread crumbs, egg, Parmesan, and chives in a food processor, then pulse to lightly mash and combine the mixture until chunky and thick.
2. Shape the mixture into 6 flat patties, then arrange them in the basket and spritz with cooking spray.
3. Put the air fryer basket on the baking pan and slide into Rack Position 2, select Air Fry,

set temperature to 390ºF (199ºC) and set time to 8 minutes.

4. Flip the patties halfway through the cooking time.
5. When done, the patties should be crispy and golden brown. Remove from the oven and serve immediately.

513. Oven Baked Rice

Servings: About 4 Cups
Cooking Time: 35 Minutes
Ingredients:
- 1 cup long-grain white rice, rinsed and drained
- 1 tablespoon unsalted butter, melted, or 1 tablespoon extra-virgin olive oil
- 2 cups water
- 1 teaspoon kosher salt or ½ teaspoon fine salt

Directions:
1. Add the butter and rice to the baking pan and stir to coat. Pour in the water and sprinkle with the salt. Stir until the salt is dissolved.
2. Select Bake, set the temperature to 325ºF (163ºC), and set the time for 35 minutes. Select Start to begin preheating.
3. Once the unit has preheated, place the pan in the oven.
4. After 20 minutes, remove the pan from the oven. Stir the rice. Transfer the pan back to the oven and continue cooking for 10 to 15 minutes, or until the rice is mostly cooked through and the water is absorbed.
5. When done, remove the pan from the oven and cover with aluminum foil. Let stand for 10 minutes. Using a fork, gently fluff the rice.
6. Serve immediately.

514. Fried Dill Pickles With Buttermilk Dressing

Servings: 6 To 8
Cooking Time: 8 Minutes
Ingredients:
- Buttermilk Dressing:
- ¼ cup buttermilk
- ¼ cup chopped scallions
- ¾ cup mayonnaise
- ½ cup sour cream
- ½ teaspoon cayenne pepper
- ½ teaspoon onion powder
- ½ teaspoon garlic powder
- 1 tablespoon chopped chives
- 2 tablespoons chopped fresh dill
- Kosher salt and ground black pepper, to taste
- Fried Dill Pickles:
- ¾ cup all-purpose flour

- 1 (2-pound / 907-g) jar kosher dill pickles, cut into 4 spears, drained
- 2½ cups panko bread crumbs
- 2 eggs, beaten with 2 tablespoons water
- Kosher salt and ground black pepper, to taste
- Cooking spray

Directions:
1. Combine the ingredients for the dressing in a bowl. Stir to mix well.
2. Wrap the bowl in plastic and refrigerate for 30 minutes or until ready to serve.
3. Pour the flour in a bowl and sprinkle with salt and ground black pepper. Stir to mix well. Put the bread crumbs in a separate bowl. Pour the beaten eggs in a third bowl.
4. Dredge the pickle spears in the flour, then into the eggs, and then into the panko to coat well. Shake the excess off.
5. Arrange the pickle spears in a single layer in the air fryer basket and spritz with cooking spray.
6. Put the air fryer basket on the baking pan and slide into Rack Position 2, select Air Fry, set temperature to 400ºF (205ºC) and set time to 8 minutes.
7. Flip the pickle spears halfway through the cooking time.
8. When cooking is complete, remove from the oven.
9. Serve the pickle spears with buttermilk dressing.

515. Dehydrated Vegetable Black Pepper Chips

Servings: x
Cooking Time: x
Ingredients:
- Spice mix for parsnip chips
- ½ teaspoon ground turmeric
- 1 teaspoon kosher salt
- ½ teaspoon ground white or black pepper
- Red wine vinegar glaze for beet chips
- 2 tablespoons red wine vinegar
- 1 medium sweet potato
- 2 medium parsnips
- 2 medium beets
- Spice mix for sweet potato chips
- ½ teaspoon dried thyme
- ½ teaspoon onion powder
- ½ teaspoon garlic powder
- ¼ teaspoon ground white pepper
- 1 teaspoon kosher salt
- ½ teaspoon kosher salt
- ½ teaspoon ground white or black pepper

Directions:
1. For the sweet potato chips, combine spice mix in a little bowl and set aside. Peel sweet curry then slice using a mandolin.

2. Arrange slices in One coating on the dehydrate baskets. Gently and evenly sprinkle with the spice mixture. Place dehydrate baskets in rack positions 5 and 3 and press START. Assess on crispiness and rotate trays occasionally, every 4--5 hours.
3. Chips should sense paper-dry and snap in half easily. For the parsnip chips, combine spice mix in a little bowl and set aside. Arrange pieces in a single layer on the dehydrate baskets. Lightly and evenly sprinkle with the spice mixture.
4. Dehydrate chips as per step 3, altering the dehydrate period to 6 hours. For the beet chips, peel beets then thinly slice using a mandolin. Arrange slices in a single layer on the dehydrate baskets. Lightly brush with red wine vinegar then lightly and evenly sprinkle with pepper and salt. Dehydrate chips According to step 3.

516.Fast Cinnamon Toast

Servings:6
Cooking Time: 5 Minutes
Ingredients:
- 1½ teaspoons cinnamon
- 1½ teaspoons vanilla extract
- ½ cup sugar
- 2 teaspoons ground black pepper
- 2 tablespoons melted coconut oil
- 12 slices whole wheat bread

Directions:
1. Combine all the ingredients, except for the bread, in a large bowl. Stir to mix well.
2. Dunk the bread in the bowl of mixture gently to coat and infuse well. Shake the excess off. Arrange the bread slices in the air fryer basket.
3. Put the air fryer basket on the baking pan and slide into Rack Position 2, select Air Fry, set temperature to 400ºF (205ºC) and set time to 5 minutes.
4. Flip the bread halfway through.
5. When cooking is complete, the bread should be golden brown.
6. Remove the bread slices from the oven and slice to serve.

517.Shrimp With Sriracha And Worcestershire Sauce

Servings:4
Cooking Time: 10 Minutes
Ingredients:
- 1 tablespoon Sriracha sauce
- 1 teaspoon Worcestershire sauce
- 2 tablespoons sweet chili sauce
- ¾ cup mayonnaise
- 1 egg, beaten
- 1 cup panko bread crumbs
- 1 pound (454 g) raw shrimp, shelled and deveined, rinsed and drained
- Lime wedges, for serving
- Cooking spray

Directions:
1. Spritz the air fryer basket with cooking spray.
2. Combine the Sriracha sauce, Worcestershire sauce, chili sauce, and mayo in a bowl. Stir to mix well. Reserve $1/3$ cup of the mixture as the dipping sauce.
3. Combine the remaining sauce mixture with the beaten egg. Stir to mix well. Put the panko in a separate bowl.
4. Dredge the shrimp in the sauce mixture first, then into the panko. Roll the shrimp to coat well. Shake the excess off.
5. Place the shrimp in the basket, then spritz with cooking spray.
6. Put the air fryer basket on the baking pan and slide into Rack Position 2, select Air Fry, set temperature to 360ºF (182ºC) and set time to 10 minutes.
7. Flip the shrimp halfway through the cooking time.
8. When cooking is complete, the shrimp should be opaque.
9. Remove the shrimp from the oven and serve with reserve sauce mixture and squeeze the lime wedges over.

518.Teriyaki Shrimp Skewers

Servings: 12 Skewered Shrimp
Cooking Time: 6 Minutes
Ingredients:
- 1½ tablespoons mirin
- 1½ teaspoons ginger juice
- 1½ tablespoons soy sauce
- 12 large shrimp (about 20 shrimps per pound), peeled and deveined
- 1 large egg
- ¾ cup panko bread crumbs
- Cooking spray

Directions:
1. Combine the mirin, ginger juice, and soy sauce in a large bowl. Stir to mix well.
2. Dunk the shrimp in the bowl of mirin mixture, then wrap the bowl in plastic and refrigerate for 1 hour to marinate.
3. Spritz the air fryer basket with cooking spray.
4. Run twelve 4-inch skewers through each shrimp.
5. Whisk the egg in the bowl of marinade to combine well. Pour the bread crumbs on a plate.
6. Dredge the shrimp skewers in the egg mixture, then shake the excess off and roll over the bread crumbs to coat well.

7. Arrange the shrimp skewers in the basket and spritz with cooking spray.
8. Put the air fryer basket on the baking pan and slide into Rack Position 2, select Air Fry, set temperature to 400ºF (205ºC) and set time to 6 minutes.
9. Flip the shrimp skewers halfway through the cooking time.
10. When done, the shrimp will be opaque and firm.
11. Serve immediately.

519.Smoked Trout And Crème Fraiche Frittata

Servings:4
Cooking Time: 17 Minutes
Ingredients:
- 2 tablespoons olive oil
- 1 onion, sliced
- 1 egg, beaten
- ½ tablespoon horseradish sauce
- 6 tablespoons crème fraiche
- 1 cup diced smoked trout
- 2 tablespoons chopped fresh dill
- Cooking spray

Directions:
1. Spritz the baking pan with cooking spray.
2. Heat the olive oil in a nonstick skillet over medium heat until shimmering.
3. Add the onion and sauté for 3 minutes or until translucent.
4. Combine the egg, horseradish sauce, and crème fraiche in a large bowl. Stir to mix well, then mix in the sautéed onion, smoked trout, and dill.
5. Pour the mixture in the prepared baking pan.
6. Slide the baking pan into Rack Position 1, select Convection Bake, set temperature to 350ºF (180ºC) and set time to 14 minutes.
7. Stir the mixture halfway through.
8. When cooking is complete, the egg should be set and the edges should be lightly browned.
9. Serve immediately.

520.Simple Baked Green Beans

Servings: 2 Cups
Cooking Time: 10 Minutes
Ingredients:
- ½ teaspoon lemon pepper
- 2 teaspoons granulated garlic
- ½ teaspoon salt
- 1 tablespoon olive oil
- 2 cups fresh green beans, trimmed and snapped in half

Directions:
1. Combine the lemon pepper, garlic, salt, and olive oil in a bowl. Stir to mix well.

2. Add the green beans to the bowl of mixture and toss to coat well.
3. Arrange the green beans in the the baking pan.
4. Slide the baking pan into Rack Position 1, select Convection Bake, set temperature to 370ºF (188ºC) and set time to 10 minutes.
5. Stir the green beans halfway through the cooking time.
6. When cooking is complete, the green beans will be tender and crispy. Remove from the oven and serve immediately.

521.Goat Cheese And Asparagus Frittata

Servings:2 To 4
Cooking Time: 25 Minutes
Ingredients:
- 1 cup asparagus spears, cut into 1-inch pieces
- 1 teaspoon vegetable oil
- 1 tablespoon milk
- 6 eggs, beaten
- 2 ounces (57 g) goat cheese, crumbled
- 1 tablespoon minced chives, optional
- Kosher salt and pepper, to taste
- Add the asparagus spears to a small bowl and drizzle with the vegetable oil. Toss until well coated and transfer to the air fryer basket.

Directions:
1. Put the air fryer basket on the baking pan and slide into Rack Position 2, select Air Fry, set temperature to 400ºF (205ºC) and set time to 5 minutes.
2. Flip the asparagus halfway through.
3. When cooking is complete, the asparagus should be tender and slightly wilted.
4. Remove from the oven to the baking pan.
5. Stir together the milk and eggs in a medium bowl. Pour the mixture over the asparagus in the pan. Sprinkle with the goat cheese and the chives (if using) over the eggs. Season with salt and pepper.
6. Slide the baking pan into Rack Position 1, select Convection Bake, set temperature to 320ºF (160ºC) and set time to 20 minutes.
7. When cooking is complete, the top should be golden and the eggs should be set.
8. Transfer to a serving dish. Slice and serve.

522.Pão De Queijo

Servings: 12 Balls
Cooking Time: 12 Minutes
Ingredients:
- 2 tablespoons butter, plus more for greasing
- ½ cup milk
- 1½ cups tapioca flour
- ½ teaspoon salt

- 1 large egg
- $^2/_3$ cup finely grated aged Asiago cheese

Directions:
1. Put the butter in a saucepan and pour in the milk, heat over medium heat until the liquid boils. Keep stirring.
2. Turn off the heat and mix in the tapioca flour and salt to form a soft dough. Transfer the dough in a large bowl, then wrap the bowl in plastic and let sit for 15 minutes.
3. Break the egg in the bowl of dough and whisk with a hand mixer for 2 minutes or until a sanity dough forms. Fold the cheese in the dough. Cover the bowl in plastic again and let sit for 10 more minutes.
4. Grease the baking pan with butter.
5. Scoop 2 tablespoons of the dough into the baking pan. Repeat with the remaining dough to make dough 12 balls. Keep a little distance between each two balls.
6. Slide the baking pan into Rack Position 1, select Convection Bake, set temperature to 375ºF (190ºC) and set time to 12 minutes.
7. Flip the balls halfway through the cooking time.
8. When cooking is complete, the balls should be golden brown and fluffy.
9. Remove the balls from the oven and allow to cool for 5 minutes before serving.

523.Lush Seafood Casserole

Servings:2
Cooking Time: 22 Minutes
Ingredients:
- 1 tablespoon olive oil
- 1 small yellow onion, chopped
- 2 garlic cloves, minced
- 4 ounces (113 g) tilapia pieces
- 4 ounces (113 g) rockfish pieces
- ½ teaspoon dried basil
- Salt and ground white pepper, to taste
- 4 eggs, lightly beaten
- 1 tablespoon dry sherry
- 4 tablespoons cheese, shredded

Directions:
1. Heat the olive oil in a nonstick skillet over medium-high heat until shimmering.
2. Add the onion and garlic and sauté for 2 minutes or until fragrant.
3. Add the tilapia, rockfish, basil, salt, and white pepper to the skillet. Sauté to combine well and transfer them into the baking pan.
4. Combine the eggs, sherry and cheese in a large bowl. Stir to mix well. Pour the mixture in the baking pan over the fish mixture.

5. Slide the baking pan into Rack Position 1, select Convection Bake, set temperature to 360ºF (182ºC) and set time to 20 minutes.
6. When cooking is complete, the eggs should be set and the casserole edges should be lightly browned.
7. Serve immediately.

524.Easy Corn And Bell Pepper Casserole

Servings:4
Cooking Time: 20 Minutes
Ingredients:
- 1 cup corn kernels
- ¼ cup bell pepper, finely chopped
- ½ cup low-fat milk
- 1 large egg, beaten
- ½ cup yellow cornmeal
- ½ cup all-purpose flour
- ½ teaspoon baking powder
- 2 tablespoons melted unsalted butter
- 1 tablespoon granulated sugar
- Pinch of cayenne pepper
- ¼ teaspoon kosher salt
- Cooking spray

Directions:
1. Spritz the baking pan with cooking spray.
2. Combine all the ingredients in a large bowl. Stir to mix well. Pour the mixture into the baking pan.
3. Slide the baking pan into Rack Position 1, select Convection Bake, set temperature to 330ºF (166ºC) and set time to 20 minutes.
4. When cooking is complete, the casserole should be lightly browned and set.
5. Remove from the oven and serve immediately.

525.Ritzy Chicken And Vegetable Casserole

Servings:4
Cooking Time: 15 Minutes
Ingredients:
- 4 boneless and skinless chicken breasts, cut into cubes
- 2 carrots, sliced
- 1 yellow bell pepper, cut into strips
- 1 red bell pepper, cut into strips
- 15 ounces (425 g) broccoli florets
- 1 cup snow peas
- 1 scallion, sliced
- Cooking spray
- Sauce:
- 1 teaspoon Sriracha
- 3 tablespoons soy sauce
- 2 tablespoons oyster sauce
- 1 tablespoon rice wine vinegar
- 1 teaspoon cornstarch
- 1 tablespoon grated ginger

- 2 garlic cloves, minced
- 1 teaspoon sesame oil
- 1 tablespoon brown sugar

Directions:
1. Spritz the baking pan with cooking spray.
2. Combine the chicken, carrot, and bell peppers in a large bowl. Stir to mix well.
3. Combine the ingredients for the sauce in a separate bowl. Stir to mix well.
4. Pour the chicken mixture into the baking pan, then pour the sauce over. Stir to coat well.
5. Slide the baking pan into Rack Position 1, select Convection Bake, set temperature to 370ºF (188ºC) and set time to 13 minutes.
6. Add the broccoli and snow peas to the pan halfway through.
7. When cooking is complete, the vegetables should be tender.
8. Remove from the oven and sprinkle with sliced scallion before serving.

526.Spanakopita

Servings:6
Cooking Time: 8 Minutes
Ingredients:
- ½ (10-ounce / 284-g) package frozen spinach, thawed and squeezed dry
- 1 egg, lightly beaten
- ¼ cup pine nuts, toasted
- ¼ cup grated Parmesan cheese
- ¾ cup crumbled feta cheese
- ⅛ teaspoon ground nutmeg
- ½ teaspoon salt
- Freshly ground black pepper, to taste
- 6 sheets phyllo dough
- ½ cup butter, melted

Directions:
1. Combine all the ingredients, except for the phyllo dough and butter, in a large bowl. Whisk to combine well. Set aside.
2. Place a sheet of phyllo dough on a clean work surface. Brush with butter then top with another layer sheet of phyllo. Brush with butter, then cut the layered sheets into six 3-inch-wide strips.
3. Top each strip with 1 tablespoon of the spinach mixture, then fold the bottom left corner over the mixture towards the right strip edge to make a triangle. Keep folding triangles until each strip is folded over.
4. Brush the triangles with butter and repeat with remaining strips and phyllo dough.
5. Place the triangles in the baking pan.
6. Put the air fryer basket on the baking pan and slide into Rack Position 2, select Air Fry, set temperature to 350ºF (180ºC) and set time to 8 minutes.

7. Flip the triangles halfway through the cooking time.
8. When cooking is complete, the triangles should be golden brown. Remove from the oven and serve immediately.

527.Crispy Cheese Wafer

Servings:2
Cooking Time: 5 Minutes
Ingredients:
- 1 cup shredded aged Manchego cheese
- 1 teaspoon all-purpose flour
- ½ teaspoon cumin seeds
- ¼ teaspoon cracked black pepper

Directions:
1. Line the air fryer basket with parchment paper.
2. Combine the cheese and flour in a bowl. Stir to mix well. Spread the mixture in the pan into a 4-inch round.
3. Combine the cumin and black pepper in a small bowl. Stir to mix well. Sprinkle the cumin mixture over the cheese round.
4. Put the air fryer basket on the baking pan and slide into Rack Position 2, select Air Fry, set temperature to 375ºF (190ºC) and set time to 5 minutes.
5. When cooked, the cheese will be lightly browned and frothy.
6. Use tongs to transfer the cheese wafer onto a plate and slice to serve.

528.Kale Salad Sushi Rolls With Sriracha Mayonnaise

Servings:12
Cooking Time: 10 Minutes
Ingredients:
- Kale Salad:
- 1½ cups chopped kale
- 1 tablespoon sesame seeds
- ¾ teaspoon soy sauce
- ¾ teaspoon toasted sesame oil
- ½ teaspoon rice vinegar
- ¼ teaspoon ginger
- ⅛ teaspoon garlic powder
- Sushi Rolls:
- 3 sheets sushi nori
- 1 batch cauliflower rice
- ½ avocado, sliced
- Sriracha Mayonnaise:
- ¼ cup Sriracha sauce
- ¼ cup vegan mayonnaise
- Coating:
- ½ cup panko bread crumbs

Directions:
1. In a medium bowl, toss all the ingredients for the salad together until well coated and set aside.

2. Place a sheet of nori on a clean work surface and spread the cauliflower rice in an even layer on the nori. Scoop 2 to 3 tablespoon of kale salad on the rice and spread over. Place 1 or 2 avocado slices on top. Roll up the sushi, pressing gently to get a nice, tight roll. Repeat to make the remaining 2 rolls.
3. In a bowl, stir together the Sriracha sauce and mayonnaise until smooth. Add bread crumbs to a separate bowl.
4. Dredge the sushi rolls in Sriracha Mayonnaise, then roll in bread crumbs till well coated.
5. Place the coated sushi rolls in the air fryer basket.
6. Put the air fryer basket on the baking pan and slide into Rack Position 2, select Air Fry, set temperature to 390ºF (199ºC) and set time to 10 minutes.
7. Flip the sushi rolls halfway through the cooking time.
8. When cooking is complete, the sushi rolls will be golden brown and crispy. .
9. Transfer to a platter and rest for 5 minutes before slicing each roll into 8 pieces. Serve warm.

529.Broccoli, Carrot, And Tomato Quiche

Servings:4
Cooking Time: 14 Minutes
Ingredients:
- 4 eggs
- 1 teaspoon dried thyme
- 1 cup whole milk
- 1 steamed carrots, diced
- 2 cups steamed broccoli florets
- 2 medium tomatoes, diced
- ¼ cup crumbled feta cheese
- 1 cup grated Cheddar cheese
- 1 teaspoon chopped parsley
- Salt and ground black pepper, to taste
- Cooking spray

Directions:
1. Spritz the baking pan with cooking spray.
2. Whisk together the eggs, thyme, salt, and ground black pepper in a bowl and fold in the milk while mixing.
3. Put the carrots, broccoli, and tomatoes in the prepared baking pan, then spread with feta cheese and ½ cup Cheddar cheese. Pour the egg mixture over, then scatter with remaining Cheddar on top.
4. Slide the baking pan into Rack Position 1, select Convection Bake, set temperature to 350ºF (180ºC) and set time to 14 minutes.
5. When cooking is complete, the egg should be set and the quiche should be puffed.
6. Remove the quiche from the oven and top with chopped parsley, then slice to serve.

530.Keto Cheese Quiche

Servings:8
Cooking Time: 1 Hour
Ingredients:
- Crust:
- 1¼ cups blanched almond flour
- 1 large egg, beaten
- 1¼ cups grated Parmesan cheese
- ¼ teaspoon fine sea salt
- Filling:
- 4 ounces (113 g) cream cheese
- 1 cup shredded Swiss cheese
- $^1/_3$ cup minced leeks
- 4 large eggs, beaten
- ½ cup chicken broth
- ⅛ teaspoon cayenne pepper
- ¾ teaspoon fine sea salt
- 1 tablespoon unsalted butter, melted
- Chopped green onions, for garnish
- Cooking spray

Directions:
1. Spritz the baking pan with cooking spray.
2. Combine the flour, egg, Parmesan, and salt in a large bowl. Stir to mix until a satiny and firm dough forms.
3. Arrange the dough between two grease parchment papers, then roll the dough into a $^1/_{16}$-inch thick circle.
4. Make the crust: Transfer the dough into the prepared pan and press to coat the bottom.
5. Slide the baking pan into Rack Position 1, select Convection Bake, set temperature to 325ºF (163ºC) and set time to 12 minutes.
6. When cooking is complete, the edges of the crust should be lightly browned.
7. Meanwhile, combine the ingredient for the filling, except for the green onions in a large bowl.
8. Pour the filling over the cooked crust and cover the edges of the crust with aluminum foil.
9. Slide the baking pan into Rack Position 1, select Convection Bake, set time to 15 minutes.
10. When cooking is complete, reduce the heat to 300ºF (150ºC) and set time to 30 minutes.
11. When cooking is complete, a toothpick inserted in the center should come out clean.
12. Remove from the oven and allow to cool for 10 minutes before serving.

531.Banana Cake

Servings:8
Cooking Time: 20 Minutes
Ingredients:
- 1 cup plus 1 tablespoon all-purpose flour
- ¼ teaspoon baking soda

- ¾ teaspoon baking powder
- ¼ teaspoon salt
- 9½ tablespoons granulated white sugar
- 5 tablespoons butter, at room temperature
- 2½ small ripe bananas, peeled
- 2 large eggs
- 5 tablespoons buttermilk
- 1 teaspoon vanilla extract
- Cooking spray

Directions:
1. Spritz the baking pan with cooking spray.
2. Combine the flour, baking soda, baking powder, and salt in a large bowl. Stir to mix well.
3. Beat the sugar and butter in a separate bowl with a hand mixer on medium speed for 3 minutes.
4. Beat in the bananas, eggs, buttermilk, and vanilla extract into the sugar and butter mix with a hand mixer.
5. Pour in the flour mixture and whip with hand mixer until sanity and smooth.
6. Scrape the batter into the pan and level the batter with a spatula.
7. Slide the baking pan into Rack Position 1, select Convection Bake, set temperature to 325ºF (163ºC) and set time to 20 minutes.
8. After 15 minutes, remove the pan from the oven. Check the doneness. Return the pan to the oven and continue cooking.
9. When done, a toothpick inserted in the center should come out clean.
10. Invert the cake on a cooling rack and allow to cool for 15 minutes before slicing to serve.

532.Dehydrated Crackers With Oats

Servings:x
Cooking Time:x
Ingredients:
- 3 tablespoons (20g) psyllium husk powder
- 2 teaspoons fine sea salt
- 1 teaspoon freshly ground black pepper
- 2 teaspoons ground turmeric, divided
- 3 tablespoons melted coconut oil
- 1 cup (125g) sunflower seeds
- ½ cup (75g) flaxseeds
- ¾ cup (50g) pumpkin seeds
- ¼ cup (35g) sesame seeds
- 2 tablespoons (30g) chia seeds
- 1½ cups (150g) rolled oats
- 1½ cups (360ml) water
- 1 large parsnip (10 ounces/300g), finely Grated

Directions:
1. In a large bowl Blend All of the seeds, Oats, psyllium husk, pepper, salt and 1 teaspoon ground turmeric.

2. Whisk coconut water and oil together in a measuring Cup. Add to the dry ingredients and blend well until all is totally saturated and dough becomes very thick.
3. Mix grated parsnip using 1 tsp turmeric and stir to blend.
4. Shape the first half to a disc and place it with a rolling pin, firmly roll dough to a thin sheet that the size of this dehydrate basket.
5. Put dough and parchment paper at the dehydrate basket.
6. Repeat steps 4 with remaining dough.
7. Hours and allow Rotate Remind. Place dehydrate baskets in rack positions 5 and 3. Press START.
8. Dehydrate crackers until tender. When prompted By Rotate Remind, rotate the baskets leading to back and change rack amounts.
9. Eliminate baskets out of oven and let rest for 10 minutes. Split crackers into shards.
10. Container for up to two months.

533.Sweet Air Fried Pecans

Servings: 4 Cups
Cooking Time: 10 Minutes
Ingredients:
- 2 egg whites
- 1 tablespoon cumin
- 2 teaspoons smoked paprika
- ½ cup brown sugar
- 2 teaspoons kosher salt
- 1 pound (454 g) pecan halves
- Cooking spray

Directions:
1. Spritz the air fryer basket with cooking spray.
2. Combine the egg whites, cumin, paprika, sugar, and salt in a large bowl. Stir to mix well. Add the pecans to the bowl and toss to coat well.
3. Transfer the pecans to the basket.
4. Put the air fryer basket on the baking pan and slide into Rack Position 2, select Air Fry, set temperature to 300ºF (150ºC) and set time to 10 minutes.
5. Stir the pecans at least two times during the cooking.
6. When cooking is complete, the pecans should be lightly caramelized. Remove from the oven and serve immediately.

534.Cauliflower And Pumpkin Casserole

Servings:6
Cooking Time: 50 Minutes
Ingredients:
- 1 cup chicken broth
- 2 cups cauliflower florets
- 1 cup canned pumpkin purée

- ¼ cup heavy cream
- 1 teaspoon vanilla extract
- 2 large eggs, beaten
- $^1/_3$ cup unsalted butter, melted, plus more for greasing the pan
- ¼ cup sugar
- 1 teaspoon fine sea salt
- Chopped fresh parsley leaves, for garnish
- TOPPING:
- ½ cup blanched almond flour
- 1 cup chopped pecans
- $^1/_3$ cup unsalted butter, melted
- ½ cup sugar

Directions:
1. Pour the chicken broth in the baking pan, then add the cauliflower.
2. Slide the baking pan into Rack Position 1, select Convection Bake, set temperature to 350ºF (180ºC) and set time to 20 minutes.
3. When cooking is complete, the cauliflower should be soft.
4. Meanwhile, combine the ingredients for the topping in a large bowl. Stir to mix well.
5. Pat the cauliflower dry with paper towels, then place in a food processor and pulse with pumpkin purée, heavy cream, vanilla extract, eggs, butter, sugar, and salt until smooth.
6. Clean the baking pan and grease with more butter, then pour the purée mixture in the pan. Spread the topping over the mixture.
7. Put the baking pan back to the oven. Select Bake and set time to 30 minutes.
8. When baking is complete, the topping of the casserole should be lightly browned.
9. Remove the casserole from the oven and serve with fresh parsley on top.

535.Southwest Seasoning

Servings: About ¾ Cups
Cooking Time: 0 Minutes

Ingredients:
- 3 tablespoons ancho chile powder
- 3 tablespoons paprika
- 2 tablespoons dried oregano
- 2 tablespoons freshly ground black pepper
- 2 teaspoons cayenne
- 2 teaspoons cumin
- 1 tablespoon granulated onion
- 1 tablespoon granulated garlic

Directions:
1. Stir together all the ingredients in a small bowl.
2. Use immediately or place in an airtight container in the pantry.

536.Chinese Pork And Mushroom Egg Rolls

Servings: 25 Egg Rolls
Cooking Time: 33 Minutes

Ingredients:
- Egg Rolls:
- 1 tablespoon mirin
- 3 tablespoons soy sauce, divided
- 1 pound (454 g) ground pork
- 3 tablespoons vegetable oil, plus more for brushing
- 5 ounces (142 g) shiitake mushrooms, minced
- 4 cups shredded Napa cabbage
- ¼ cup sliced scallions
- 1 teaspoon grated fresh ginger
- 1 clove garlic, minced
- ¼ teaspoon cornstarch
- 1 (1-pound / 454-g) package frozen egg roll wrappers, thawed
- Dipping Sauce:
- 1 scallion, white and light green parts only, sliced
- ¼ cup rice vinegar
- ¼ cup soy sauce
- Pinch sesame seeds
- Pinch red pepper flakes
- 1 teaspoon granulated sugar

Directions:
1. Line the air fryer basket with parchment paper. Set aside.
2. Combine the mirin and 1 tablespoon of soy sauce in a large bowl. Stir to mix well.
3. Dunk the ground pork in the mixture and stir to mix well. Wrap the bowl in plastic and marinate in the refrigerator for at least 10 minutes.
4. Heat the vegetable oil in a nonstick skillet over medium-high heat until shimmering. Add the mushrooms, cabbage, and scallions and sauté for 5 minutes or until tender.
5. Add the marinated meat, ginger, garlic, and remaining 2 tablespoons of soy sauce. Sauté for 3 minutes or until the pork is lightly browned. Turn off the heat and allow to cool until ready to use.
6. Put the cornstarch in a small bowl and pour in enough water to dissolve the cornstarch. Put the bowl alongside a clean work surface.
7. Put the egg roll wrappers in the basket.
8. Put the air fryer basket on the baking pan and slide into Rack Position 2, select Air Fry, set temperature to 400ºF (205ºC) and set time to 15 minutes.
9. Flip the wrappers halfway through the cooking time.
10. When cooked, the wrappers will be golden brown. Remove the egg roll wrappers from the oven and allow to cool for 10 minutes or until you can handle them with your hands.
11. Lay out one egg roll wrapper on the work surface with a corner pointed toward you. Place 2 tablespoons of the pork mixture on the egg roll wrapper and fold corner up over the mixture. Fold left and right corners toward the center and continue to roll. Brush a bit of the dissolved cornstarch on

the last corner to help seal the egg wrapper. Repeat with remaining wrappers to make 25 egg rolls in total.

12. Arrange the rolls in the basket and brush the rolls with more vegetable oil.
13. Select Air Fry and set time to 10 minutes. Return to the oven. When done, the rolls should be well browned and crispy.
14. Meanwhile, combine the ingredients for the dipping sauce in a small bowl. Stir to mix well.
15. Serve the rolls with the dipping sauce immediately.

537. Taco Beef And Chile Casserole

Servings:4
Cooking Time: 15 Minutes
Ingredients:
- 1 pound (454 g) 85% lean ground beef
- 1 tablespoon taco seasoning
- 1 (7-ounce / 198-g) can diced mild green chiles
- ½ cup milk
- 2 large eggs
- 1 cup shredded Mexican cheese blend
- 2 tablespoons all-purpose flour
- ½ teaspoon kosher salt
- Cooking spray

Directions:
1. Spritz the baking pan with cooking spray.
2. Toss the ground beef with taco seasoning in a large bowl to mix well. Pour the seasoned ground beef in the prepared baking pan.
3. Combing the remaining ingredients in a medium bowl. Whisk to mix well, then pour the mixture over the ground beef.
4. Slide the baking pan into Rack Position 1, select Convection Bake, set temperature to 350ºF (180ºC) and set time to 15 minutes.
5. When cooking is complete, a toothpick inserted in the center should come out clean.
6. Remove the casserole from the oven and allow to cool for 5 minutes, then slice to serve.

538. Bartlett Pears With Lemony Ricotta

Servings:4
Cooking Time: 8 Minutes
Ingredients:
- 2 large Bartlett pears, peeled, cut in half, cored
- 3 tablespoons melted butter
- ½ teaspoon ground ginger
- ¼ teaspoon ground cardamom
- 3 tablespoons brown sugar
- ½ cup whole-milk ricotta cheese
- 1 teaspoon pure lemon extract
- 1 teaspoon pure almond extract
- 1 tablespoon honey, plus additional for drizzling

Directions:

1. Toss the pears with butter, ginger, cardamom, and sugar in a large bowl. Toss to coat well. Arrange the pears in the baking pan, cut side down.
2. Put the air fryer basket on the baking pan and slide into Rack Position 2, select Air Fry, set temperature to 375ºF (190ºC) and set time to 8 minutes.
3. After 5 minutes, remove the pan and flip the pears. Return to the oven and continue cooking.
4. When cooking is complete, the pears should be soft and browned. Remove from the oven.
5. In the meantime, combine the remaining ingredients in a separate bowl. Whip for 1 minute with a hand mixer until the mixture is puffed.
6. Divide the mixture into four bowls, then put the pears over the mixture and drizzle with more honey to serve.

539. Corn On The Cob With Mayonnaise

Servings:4
Cooking Time: 10 Minutes
Ingredients:
- 2 tablespoons mayonnaise
- 2 teaspoons minced garlic
- ½ teaspoon sea salt
- 1 cup panko bread crumbs
- 4 (4-inch length) ears corn on the cob, husk and silk removed
- Cooking spray

Directions:
1. Spritz the air fryer basket with cooking spray.
2. Combine the mayonnaise, garlic, and salt in a bowl. Stir to mix well. Pour the panko on a plate.
3. Brush the corn on the cob with mayonnaise mixture, then roll the cob in the bread crumbs and press to coat well.
4. Transfer the corn on the cob in the basket and spritz with cooking spray.
5. Put the air fryer basket on the baking pan and slide into Rack Position 2, select Air Fry, set temperature to 400ºF (205ºC) and set time to 10 minutes.
6. Flip the corn on the cob at least three times during the cooking.
7. When cooked, the corn kernels on the cob should be almost browned. Remove from the oven and serve immediately.

540. Chicken Sausage And Broccoli Casserole

Servings:8
Cooking Time: 20 Minutes
Ingredients:
- 10 eggs
- 1 cup Cheddar cheese, shredded and divided
- ¾ cup heavy whipping cream

- 1 (12-ounce / 340-g) package cooked chicken sausage
- 1 cup broccoli, chopped
- 2 cloves garlic, minced
- ½ tablespoon salt
- ¼ tablespoon ground black pepper
- Cooking spray

Directions:
1. Spritz the baking pan with cooking spray.
2. Whisk the eggs with Cheddar and cream in a large bowl to mix well.
3. Combine the cooked sausage, broccoli, garlic, salt, and ground black pepper in a separate bowl. Stir to mix well.
4. Pour the sausage mixture into the baking pan, then spread the egg mixture over to cover.
5. Slide the baking pan into Rack Position 1, select Convection Bake, set temperature to 400ºF (205ºC) and set time to 20 minutes.
6. When cooking is complete, the egg should be set and a toothpick inserted in the center should come out clean.
7. Serve immediately.

541.Jewish Blintzes

Servings: 8 Blintzes
Cooking Time: 10 Minutes
Ingredients:
- 2 (7½-ounce / 213-g) packages farmer cheese, mashed
- ¼ cup cream cheese
- ¼ teaspoon vanilla extract
- ¼ cup granulated white sugar
- 8 egg roll wrappers
- 4 tablespoons butter, melted

Directions:
1. Combine the farmer cheese, cream cheese, vanilla extract, and sugar in a bowl. Stir to mix well.
2. Unfold the egg roll wrappers on a clean work surface, spread ¼ cup of the filling at the edge of each wrapper and leave a ½-inch edge uncovering.
3. Wet the edges of the wrappers with water and fold the uncovered edge over the filling. Fold the left and right sides in the center, then tuck the edge under the filling and fold to wrap the filling.
4. Brush the wrappers with melted butter, then arrange the wrappers in a single layer in the air fryer basket, seam side down. Leave a little space between each two wrappers.
5. Put the air fryer basket on the baking pan and slide into Rack Position 2, select Air Fry, set temperature to 375ºF (190ºC) and set time to 10 minutes.
6. When cooking is complete, the wrappers will be golden brown.
7. Serve immediately.

542.Caesar Salad Dressing

Servings: About ²/₃ Cup
Cooking Time: 0 Minutes
Ingredients:
- ½ cup extra-virgin olive oil
- 2 tablespoons freshly squeezed lemon juice
- 1 teaspoon anchovy paste
- ¼ teaspoon kosher salt or ⅛ teaspoon fine salt
- ¼ teaspoon minced or pressed garlic
- 1 egg, beaten
- Add all the ingredients to a tall, narrow container.

Directions:
1. Purée the mixture with an immersion blender until smooth.
2. Use immediately.

543.Sweet And Sour Peanuts

Servings:9
Cooking Time: 5 Minutes
Ingredients:
- 3 cups shelled raw peanuts
- 1 tablespoon hot red pepper sauce
- 3 tablespoons granulated white sugar

Directions:
1. Put the peanuts in a large bowl, then drizzle with hot red pepper sauce and sprinkle with sugar. Toss to coat well.
2. Pour the peanuts in the air fryer basket.
3. Put the air fryer basket on the baking pan and slide into Rack Position 2, select Air Fry, set temperature to 400ºF (205ºC) and set time to 5 minutes.
4. Stir the peanuts halfway through the cooking time.
5. When cooking is complete, the peanuts will be crispy and browned. Remove from the oven and serve immediately.

544.Roasted Carrot Chips

Servings: 3 Cups
Cooking Time: 15 Minutes
Ingredients:
- 3 large carrots, peeled and sliced into long and thick chips diagonally
- 1 tablespoon granulated garlic
- 1 teaspoon salt
- ¼ teaspoon ground black pepper
- 1 tablespoon olive oil
- 1 tablespoon finely chopped fresh parsley

Directions:
1. Toss the carrots with garlic, salt, ground black pepper, and olive oil in a large bowl to coat well. Place the carrots in the air fryer basket.
2. Put the air fryer basket on the baking pan and slide into Rack Position 2, select Roast, set temperature to 360ºF (182ºC) and set time to 15 minutes.
3. Stir the carrots halfway through the cooking time.

4. When cooking is complete, the carrot chips should be soft. Remove from the oven. Serve the carrot chips with parsley on top.

545. Spicy Air Fried Old Bay Shrimp

Servings: 2 Cups
Cooking Time: 10 Minutes
Ingredients:
- ½ teaspoon Old Bay Seasoning
- 1 teaspoon ground cayenne pepper
- ½ teaspoon paprika
- 1 tablespoon olive oil
- ⅛ teaspoon salt
- ½ pound (227 g) shrimps, peeled and deveined
- Juice of half a lemon

Directions:
1. Combine the Old Bay Seasoning, cayenne pepper, paprika, olive oil, and salt in a large bowl, then add the shrimps and toss to coat well.
2. Put the shrimps in the air fryer basket.
3. Put the air fryer basket on the baking pan and slide into Rack Position 2, select Air Fry, set temperature to 390ºF (199ºC) and set time to 10 minutes.
4. Flip the shrimps halfway through the cooking time.
5. When cooking is complete, the shrimps should be opaque. Serve the shrimps with lemon juice on top.

546. Parsnip Fries With Garlic-yogurt Dip

Servings:4
Cooking Time: 10 Minutes
Ingredients:
- 3 medium parsnips, peeled, cut into sticks
- ¼ teaspoon kosher salt
- 1 teaspoon olive oil
- 1 garlic clove, unpeeled
- Cooking spray
- Dip:
- ¼ cup plain Greek yogurt
- ⅛ teaspoon garlic powder
- 1 tablespoon sour cream
- ¼ teaspoon kosher salt
- Freshly ground black pepper, to taste

Directions:
1. Spritz the air fryer basket with cooking spray.
2. Put the parsnip sticks in a large bowl, then sprinkle with salt and drizzle with olive oil.
3. Transfer the parsnip into the basket and add the garlic.
4. Put the air fryer basket on the baking pan and slide into Rack Position 2, select Air Fry, set temperature to 360ºF (182ºC) and set time to 10 minutes.
5. Stir the parsnip halfway through the cooking time.

6. Meanwhile, peel the garlic and crush it. Combine the crushed garlic with the ingredients for the dip. Stir to mix well.
7. When cooked, the parsnip sticks should be crisp. Remove the parsnip fries from the oven and serve with the dipping sauce.

547. Buttery Knots With Parsley

Servings: 8 Knots
Cooking Time: 5 Minutes
Ingredients:
- 1 teaspoon dried parsley
- ¼ cup melted butter
- 2 teaspoons garlic powder

Directions:
1. 1 (11-ounce / 312-g) tube refrigerated French bread dough, cut into 8 slices
2. Combine the parsley, butter, and garlic powder in a bowl. Stir to mix well.
3. Place the French bread dough slices on a clean work surface, then roll each slice into a 6-inch long rope. Tie the ropes into knots and arrange them on a plate.
4. Transfer the knots into the baking pan. Brush the knots with butter mixture.
5. Put the air fryer basket on the baking pan and slide into Rack Position 2, select Air Fry, set temperature to 350ºF (180ºC) and set time to 5 minutes.
6. Flip the knots halfway through the cooking time.
7. When done, the knots should be golden brown. Remove from the oven and serve immediately.

548. Classic Worcestershire Poutine

Servings:2
Cooking Time: 33 Minutes
Ingredients:
- 2 russet potatoes, scrubbed and cut into ½-inch sticks
- 2 teaspoons vegetable oil
- 2 tablespoons butter
- ¼ onion, minced
- ¼ teaspoon dried thyme
- 1 clove garlic, smashed
- 3 tablespoons all-purpose flour
- 1 teaspoon tomato paste
- 1½ cups beef stock
- 2 teaspoons Worcestershire sauce
- Salt and freshly ground black pepper, to taste
- ²/₃ cup chopped string cheese

Directions:
1. Bring a pot of water to a boil, then put in the potato sticks and blanch for 4 minutes.
2. Drain the potato sticks and rinse under running cold water, then pat dry with paper towels.
3. Transfer the sticks in a large bowl and drizzle with vegetable oil. Toss to coat well. Place the potato sticks in the air fryer basket.

4. Put the air fryer basket on the baking pan and slide into Rack Position 2, select Air Fry, set temperature to 400ºF (205ºC) and set time to 25 minutes.
5. Stir the potato sticks at least three times during cooking.
6. Meanwhile, make the gravy: Heat the butter in a saucepan over medium heat until melted.
7. Add the onion, thyme, and garlic and sauté for 5 minutes or until the onion is translucent.
8. Add the flour and sauté for an additional 2 minutes. Pour in the tomato paste and beef stock and cook for 1 more minute or until lightly thickened.
9. Drizzle the gravy with Worcestershire sauce and sprinkle with salt and ground black pepper. Reduce the heat to low to keep the gravy warm until ready to serve.
10. When done, the sticks should be golden brown. Remove from the oven. Transfer the fried potato sticks onto a plate, then sprinkle with salt and ground black pepper. Scatter with string cheese and pour the gravy over. Serve warm.

549.Chocolate Buttermilk Cake

Servings:8
Cooking Time: 20 Minutes
Ingredients:
- 1 cup all-purpose flour
- $^2/_3$ cup granulated white sugar
- ¼ cup unsweetened cocoa powder
- ¾ teaspoon baking soda
- ¼ teaspoon salt
- $^2/_3$ cup buttermilk
- 2 tablespoons plus 2 teaspoons vegetable oil
- 1 teaspoon vanilla extract
- Cooking spray

Directions:
1. Spritz the baking pan with cooking spray.
2. Combine the flour, cocoa powder, baking soda, sugar, and salt in a large bowl. Stir to mix well.
3. Mix in the buttermilk, vanilla, and vegetable oil. Keep stirring until it forms a grainy and thick dough.
4. Scrape the chocolate batter from the bowl and transfer to the pan, level the batter in an even layer with a spatula.

5. Slide the baking pan into Rack Position 1, select Convection Bake, set temperature to 325ºF (163ºC) and set time to 20 minutes.
6. After 15 minutes, remove the pan from the oven. Check the doneness. Return the pan to the oven and continue cooking.
7. When done, a toothpick inserted in the center should come out clean.
8. Invert the cake on a cooling rack and allow to cool for 15 minutes before slicing to serve.

550.Ritzy Pimento And Almond Turkey Casserole

Servings:4
Cooking Time: 32 Minutes
Ingredients:
- 1 pound (454 g) turkey breasts
- 1 tablespoon olive oil
- 2 boiled eggs, chopped
- 2 tablespoons chopped pimentos
- ¼ cup slivered almonds, chopped
- ¼ cup mayonnaise
- ½ cup diced celery
- 2 tablespoons chopped green onion
- ¼ cup cream of chicken soup
- ¼ cup bread crumbs
- Salt and ground black pepper, to taste

Directions:
1. Put the turkey breasts in a large bowl. Sprinkle with salt and ground black pepper and drizzle with olive oil. Toss to coat well.
2. Transfer the turkey to the air fryer basket.
3. Put the air fryer basket on the baking pan and slide into Rack Position 2, select Air Fry, set temperature to 390ºF (199ºC) and set time to 12 minutes.
4. Flip the turkey halfway through.
5. When cooking is complete, the turkey should be well browned.
6. Remove the turkey breasts from the oven and cut into cubes, then combine the chicken cubes with eggs, pimentos, almonds, mayo, celery, green onions, and chicken soup in a large bowl. Stir to mix.
7. Pour the mixture into the baking pan, then spread with bread crumbs.
8. Slide the baking pan into Rack Position 1, select Convection Bake, set time to 20 minutes.
9. When cooking is complete, the eggs should be set.
10. Remove from the oven and serve immediately.